The Approved Mental Health Professional's Guide to Mental Health Law

Post-qualifying Social Work Practice – titles in the series

To order, please contact our distributor: BEBC Distribution, Albion Close, Parkstone, Poole, BH12 3LL. Telephone: 0845 230 9000, email: learningmatters@bebc.co.uk. You can also find more information on each of these titles and our other learning resources at www.learningmatters.co.uk

The Approved Mental Health Professional's Guide to Mental Health Law

Second Edition

ROBERT BROWN

Series Editor: Keith Brown

First published as *The Approved Social Worker's Guide to Mental Health Law* in 2006

This edition published in 2009 by Learning Matters Ltd

British Library Cataloguing in Publication Data
A CIP record for this book is available from the British Library.

ISBN 978 1 84445 115 9

Cover design by Code 5 Design Associates Ltd
Project management by Deer Park Productions
Typeset by PDQ Typesetting Ltd
Printed and bound in Great Britain by Bell & Bain Ltd, Glasgow

Learning Matters Ltd
33 Southernhay East
Exeter EX1 1NX
Tel: 01392 215560
info@learningmatters.co.uk
www.learningmatters.co.uk

Mixed Sources
Product group from well-managed
forests and other controlled sources
www.fsc.org Cert no. TT-COC-002769
© 1996 Forest Stewardship Council

FSC

Contents

List of abbreviations

AA	Appropriate Adult
AC	Approved Clinician
AMHP	Approved Mental Health Professional
ASW	Approved Social Worker
AWOL	Absent Without Leave
BIA	Best Interests Assessor
CCfW	Care Council for Wales
CPA	Care Programme Approach
CPN	Community Psychiatric Nurse
CQC	Care Quality Commission
CTO	Community Treatment Order
DHSS	Department of Health and Social Security
DOLS	Deprivation of Liberty Safeguards
DRO	Disablement Resettlement Officer
ECHR	European Convention on Human Rights
ECT	Electro-Convulsive Therapy
ECtHR	European Court of Human Rights
GSCC	General Social Care Council
HA	Health Authority
IMCA	Independent Mental Capacity Advocate
LA	Local Authority
LPA	Lasting Power of Attorney
LSSA	Local Social Services Authority
MCA	Mental Capacity Act 2005
MHA	Mental Health Act 1983/2007
MHRT	Mental Health Review Tribunal
MHT	Mental Health Tribunal
NHS	National Health Service
NIMHE	National Institute for Mental Health in England
NR	Nearest Relative
PACE	Police and Criminal Evidence Act 1984
PCT	Primary Care Trust
RC	Responsible Clinician
RMO	Responsible Medical Officer
SCT	Supervised Community Treatment
SI	Statutory Instrument
SOAD	Second Opinion Appointed Doctor
SSD	Social Services Department

About the author

Rob Brown is Director of the Approved Mental Health Professional's course in South West England. This is a Bournemouth University course. Rob is also the Area Mental Health Act Commissioner for Dorset and Somerset, having been a member of the Mental Health Act Commission since 1992. Rob previously worked as a Mental Welfare Officer and then as an Approved Social Worker with Hampshire County Council. He has been a lecturer at Southampton University, Stirling University and Croydon College. Together with Paul Barber and Debbie Martin, he contributes to the training of section 12 approved doctors and approved clinicians in South West England and in Wales. Rob has published widely in the field of mental health and mental capacity law. He is a Director of Edge Training Limited, and also provides consultation and supervision for mental health workers in Guernsey and Jersey.

Foreword from the Series Editor

This text replaces *The ASW's Guide to Mental Health Law* and has been thoroughly amended to take into account all the changes which have flowed from the Mental Health Act 2007.

The role of the Approved Mental Health Professional (AHMP) is very similar to that of its predecessor, the Approved Social Worker (ASW), but it may now be undertaken by nurses, occupational therapists and psychologists as well as social workers. The training is still overseen by the General Social Care Council and delivered by universities. It sits within a post-qualifying framework but it is now at post-graduate level and the new text reflects this change.

I warmly commend this text to all budding AHMPs as well as others who are interested in the operation of the Mental Health Act 1983. The text sits alongside other texts in the Post Qualifying Series – *The AHMP's Guide to Psychiatry and Medication* and *The Mental Capacity Act 2005: A Guide for Mental Health Professionals*. Readers will also find it helpful to read it in conjunction with another Learning Matters text – *Mental Health Law in England and Wales* – as this contains the full text of the Mental Health Act 1983 as well as relevant Regulations.

Keith Brown
Series Editor
Centre for Post-Qualifying Social Work
Bournemouth University

Preface to the 2009 edition

Welcome to *The Approved Mental Health Professional's Guide to Mental Health Law*. This replaces the *Approved Social Worker's Guide* and has been designed primarily for mental health professionals who are on an AMHP course or for those helping to provide placement opportunities for such an AMHP trainee. The book should also be useful for practising AMHPs, other mental health professionals, service users, carers and others interested in the field of mental health law. The law covered here is that which covers England and Wales. Note that mental health law is significantly different in Scotland, Northern Ireland, the Isle of Man and the Channel Islands.

The companion volume *Mental Health Law in England and Wales* will provide readers with a copy of the Mental Health Act 1983 itself (as amended by the 2007 Act) together with relevant Regulations. The specific competences required of Approved Mental Health Professionals are set out in separate Regulations for England and for Wales. These are included in this text at Appendices 4A and 4B respectively. There are minor differences between the English and Welsh versions. This book cross refers to these competences at the beginning of each chapter (using the English numbering system). Typical assignment questions are also included at the end of each chapter, together with a number of multiple choice questions to aid learning.

The assessment examples are based on the Bournemouth University Postgraduate Diploma in Advanced Mental Health Practice, a course delivered in partnership with a number of local authorities which meets the General Social Care Council (GSCC) standards and requirements for social work in mental health services at higher specialist level. The course also meets the GSCC standards and requirements for the role of Approved Mental Health Professional (Mental Health Act 2007) and the Department of Health requirements for the role of Best Interests Assessor (Mental Capacity Act 2005). The course is at Masters level and many students will continue with their studies to complete an MA in Advanced Mental Health Practice. Not all AMHP courses in England or Wales will be linked so directly to the Best Interests Assessor (BIA) role. This role is part of the new Deprivation of Liberty Safeguards (DOLS) and even AMHPs who do not complete BIA training will need to be aware of how these safeguards operate as from April 2009. More detailed information is included in the companion volume *The Mental Capacity Act 2005: A Guide for Mental Health Professionals*.

Mental health law has been changing rapidly in recent years. Apart from the statutory changes, there have been several important developments in case law. This book is up to date as at the beginning of January 2009. Readers may wish to check that there has been no major recent case law which alters the position as stated here. Good sources for this purpose are **www.davesheppard.co.uk** and **www.imhap.org.uk**, although it should be noted that both of these sites require a fee-based membership. (It is worth checking with your local authority or Trust to see if they have corporate membership.) There is also mental health material on the Department of Health's website **www.dh.gov.uk** which covers England, and on the Welsh Assembly website at **www.wales.gov.uk** which covers the position in Wales.

Recent changes which are covered in this book include:

- the revisions to the Mental Health Act 1983 made by the Mental Health Act (MHA) 2007;
- changes to the Mental Capacity Act 2005 also made by the MHA 2007;

- revised Codes of Practice to each of these Acts;

- the impact of the *JE v DE and Surrey* case of 2006 which links with the continued importance of the *HL v UK* case (Bournewood).

The Guide should be read in conjunction with the Mental Health Act 1983, as amended, and the relevant Code of Practice for England or Wales. These are issued to most trainee AMHPs. The Code referred to in this text is the English version. Many trainees also find the *Reference Guide to the Mental Health Act* helpful as it is written in accessible English. The Welsh equivalent was not available at the time of going to print.

Inevitably, there will be changes to the law during the life of this volume but we hope it will help in keeping you reasonably well-informed on current mental health law. There is a list of legal references at the end of the guide.

I would like to thank Paul Barber, Anthony Harbour and Debbie Martin who have all read and commented on the book in its draft form. Their views, based on their experience and knowledge of how the law operates in practice, have been very helpful. However, I accept responsibility for any inaccuracies which remain within the text.

Finally I would like to thank Pamela Brown who kept me to task in producing this revised edition, and who encouraged me to persevere when I was struggling with some of the more arcane aspects of the recent law reform. Her support has been invaluable.

Robert Brown, South West England AMHP Programme Director
c/o Institute of Health & Community Studies, Post Qualifying Social Work Team, Bournemouth University, 4th Floor, Royal London House, Christchurch Road, Bournemouth BH1 3LT.

Chapter 1

Introduction and definitions of mental disorder

BECOMING AN APPROVED MENTAL HEALTH PROFESSIONAL

This chapter should help candidates to achieve the following competences:

Application of knowledge: the legal and policy framework

Applied knowledge of:

2a(i) mental health legislation, related codes of practice, national and local policy guidance.

Application of knowledge: mental disorder

Critical understanding of:

3a   a range of models of mental disorder, including the contribution of social, physical and developmental factors;

3b   the social perspective on mental disorder and mental health needs in working with patients, their relatives, carers and other professionals;

3c   the implications of mental disorder for patients, their relatives and carers.

Common law

Although the role of the approved mental health professional (AMHP) is rooted firmly in statute there are sometimes overlaps with the common law. The *Oxford Dictionary of Law* (Martin and Law, 2006, p104) gives three basic definitions of common law:

1. *The part of English law based on rules developed by the royal courts during the first three centuries after the Norman Conquest (1066) as a system applicable to the whole country, as opposed to local customs...*

2. *Rules of law developed by the courts as opposed to those created by statute.*

3. *A general system of law deriving exclusively from court decisions.*

Montgomery (2002, p7) has described common law as:

The rules which are extrapolated from the practice of the judges in deciding cases. Judges should take a consistent approach to recurring issues and are obliged to follow the decisions of earlier cases, at least when they have been given by the higher courts. Once a matter has been resolved by a judge it therefore sets a precedent which enshrines the legal rule.

Some practitioners have referred to this as 'common sense under a wig'.

An example of an area covered by common law rather than statute is intervention in an emergency for an informal patient. Even if the patient lacks capacity they may be an immediate risk to others and relying on the Mental Capacity Act may not be possible in terms of treatment or restraint. See Chapter 6 for a more detailed discussion of this area of law.

Civil liberties vs welfarism

Before considering models and definitions of mental disorder in depth it is important to think of the consequences which might flow from being seen as mentally disordered. This depends to some extent on the prevailing ideology as reflected in law and practice. One way of looking at the effects of different ideologies on mental health law is to contrast the views of those with 'civil libertarian' leanings such as Thomas Szasz with those of a more 'welfarist' persuasion represented by the Zito Trust. If one were to adopt Szasz's views (disputing the notion of 'mental illness' but, if conceding that it might exist, adopting the view that people should make their own decisions about their treatment, as with physical illness), then presumably there would be no need for mental health law at all. There might be a case to consider law relating to mental incapacity linked to brain injury, dementia, demonstrable learning disability, etc., but this would not allow for the detention of people whom psychiatrists consider to be suffering from schizophrenia, depression, etc.

A welfarist approach might make an assumption that mental illness is linked to a degree of mental incapacity (as in the term 'lack of insight') but whether or not this is the case, a welfarist view would be that it is sometimes necessary to intervene against someone's will to protect a person from themselves or for the protection of others.

The contrast between these competing ideologies is illustrated in Figure 1.1. The Mental Health Act 1983 can be seen as positioned somewhere in the middle of the upper continuum illustrated. AMHPs, doctors, tribunals and courts are left to make decisions as to when the circumstances justify intervention. With the exception of ECT treatment, however, mental capacity is not the relevant test used in the Mental Health Act. The criteria needed are a mental disorder of a nature or degree to warrant intervention plus an appropriate level of risk.

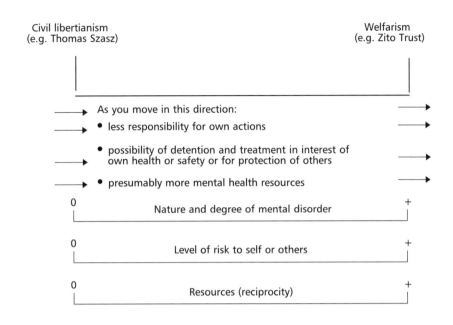

Figure 1.1. Different perspectives on mental health law

Gostin (1975) made the ethical point that, if you deprive someone of liberty, you should have a duty to provide a good quality service. One part of the Mental Health Act which addresses this issue is section 117 relating to after-care. Consistent guidance that section 117 services should not incur charges could be seen to reflect the link between the positive end of the resource continuum with the welfarist intervention point. Similarly the Richardson Committee on the Reform of the Mental Health Act considered the principle of 'reciprocity' (see Chapter 11). Free after-care services have been retained in the reformed Mental Health Act despite the controversy on this subject. The same is not true, however, for the new Deprivation of Liberty Safeguards (DOLS) or indeed where guardianship is used.

Another way of using Figure 1.1 is to imagine a point in the middle of the upper continuum where detention would be justified if there was:

- mental disorder of a nature or degree to justify this; *and*

- a level of risk to self or others which also justified detention.

Mental health terminology and the law

Common law distinguished 'idiots' from 'lunatics' before the first of the Acts. These terms correspond with the distinction between people with a learning disability and those who are mentally ill. Historically, the groups have sometimes been dealt with in separate legislation and sometimes together, as in the Mental Health Act 1983.

1713/44   Vagrancy Acts allowed detention of 'Lunaticks or mad persons'.

1774   Act for regulating private madhouses.

3

1845   Lunatics Act included 'Persons of unsound mind'.

1886   Idiots Act provided separately for idiots and imbeciles.

1890   Lunacy (Consolidation) Act ignored the distinction.

1913   Mental Deficiency Act – favoured segregation of 'mental defectives': *idiots* were unable to guard themselves against common physical dangers such as fire, water or traffic; *imbeciles* could guard against physical dangers but were incapable of managing themselves or their affairs; *feeble-minded* needed care or control for protection of self or others; *moral defectives* had vicious or criminal propensities (use of this category later included many poor women with unsupported babies).

1927   Mental Deficiency Act emphasised care outside institutions. Mental deficiency was defined as 'a condition of arrested or incomplete development of mind existing before the age of 18 years whether arising from inherent causes or induced by disease or injury'.

1930   Mental Treatment Act allowed for voluntary admissions.

1946   NHS Act – ended distinction between paying and non-paying patients.

1948   National Assistance Act – made provision for those in need.

1959   Mental Health Act. Mental disorder means: 'mental illness; arrested or incomplete development of mind, psychopathic disorder, and any other disorder or disability of mind'. Further classifications for long-term compulsion were: mental illness, severe subnormality, subnormality, psychopathic disorder, with a kind of treatability test for the last two.

1970   LA Social Services Act created Social Services Departments (SSDs).

1983   Mental Health Act. The broad definition is exactly the same as in the 1959 Act. However, the classifications were changed to:
mental illness (undefined);
severe mental impairment: 'a state of arrested or incomplete development of mind which includes severe impairment of intelligence and social functioning and is associated with abnormally aggressive or seriously irresponsible conduct on the part of the person concerned';
mental impairment: 'a state of arrested or incomplete development of mind (not amounting to severe mental impairment) which includes significant impairment of intelligence and social functioning and is associated with abnormally aggressive or seriously irresponsible conduct on the part of the person concerned';
psychopathic disorder: 'a persistent disorder or disability of mind (whether or not including significant impairment of intelligence) which results in abnormally aggressive or seriously irresponsible conduct on the part of the person concerned'.

1984	Police and Criminal Evidence Act (plus its Codes of Practice) uses the term 'mental disorder' as per the Mental Health Act and the revised PACE Codes use the concept of the mentally vulnerable adult.
2002	Draft Mental Health Bill definition: 'any disability or disorder of mind or brain which results in an impairment or disturbance of mental functioning'.
2003	Mental Capacity Bill – people unable to make a decision 'because of an impairment of, or a disturbance in the functioning of, the mind or brain'.
2004	Revised Draft Mental Health Bill definition of mental disorder was: 'an impairment of or a disturbance in the functioning of mind or brain resulting from any disability or disorder of the mind or brain'.
2005	Parliamentary Scrutiny Committee accepted the above definition but stated: 'that a broad definition of mental disorder in the draft Bill must be accompanied by explicit and specific exclusions which safeguard against the legislation being used inappropriately as a means of social control'. However, the final version as a result of reforms is . . .
2007	'Any disorder or disability of the mind'. The word 'brain' is removed which gives at least some potential space between the Mental Health Act definition and that of the functional test for incapacity in the Mental Capacity Act. However, it is still a very broad definition and the removal of most of the exclusions has potentially broadened it still further. There are no longer any separate classifications of mental disorder.

The Scottish Mental Health Act 2003 defines mental disorder as mental illness, personality disorder or learning disability. This is probably more in line with current mental health practice than the proposed definition for England and Wales.

Models of mental disorder

There are many theoretical approaches to mental disorder. In the *Journal of Mental Health* Pilgrim (2002) traces the history of the biopsychosocial model. There is also a chapter by Dallos in the Open University text, *Mental Health Matters* (Heller *et al.*). This is rather light on social explanations so the bio-social model is outlined below and a few other approaches are considered. Dallos identified three levels of analysis: societal, interpersonal and individual. He described what he saw as the most influential psychological frameworks under these headings: biological and medical, behavioural, psychodynamic, humanistic and systemic. They share important features (e.g. in terms of the importance of empathy, the therapeutic relationship and clear communication) but they can lead to different approaches to intervention.

Biological and medical frameworks

These would see problems stemming from physical causes including illness, accident and hereditary factors. Some theorists suggest that schizophrenia and depression are linked to brain defects such as neurotransmitter problems. Medical frameworks see mental health problems as similar to physical illness. This leads to classification of mental disorders and a regime of treatment which relies heavily on the use of medication. Psycho-educational approaches often have a biological view of causation but also recognise that, as with physical illness, social and environmental factors interact with the illness. Some approaches emphasise the importance of stress and lead to treatments which include work with the emotional atmosphere in families (see Leff and Vaughn, 1985).

Behavioural frameworks

These suggest psychological problems are acquired through learning experiences and are then affected by various punishments and rewards from social interaction. Treatments might include systematic desensitisation (e.g. with phobias), behaviour modification (e.g. to remove rewards which are maintaining problem behaviour) or cognitive-behavioural approaches (which would include helping people to modify immediate cognitive response to potentially upsetting situations). Cognitive-behavioural techniques have recently gained some ground within psychiatric practice in Britain.

Psychodynamic approaches

An individual's emotional experiences (especially in early childhood) are seen as the primary cause of later problems. Treatment often focuses on bringing memories of these early experiences into consciousness and thereby enabling the person to deal with them in a way that empowers them to be more autonomous. Some theorists (such as Freud) emphasised the importance of sexuality and an inability to resolve sexual feelings within a family. Treatment often focuses on the therapeutic relationship and the concept of transference (e.g. the patient transfers feelings from earlier relationships onto the therapist). Psychoanalysis is an expensive and time-intensive therapy but briefer psychodynamic techniques have also been developed.

Humanistic frameworks

These also consider unconscious processes but see people as essentially creative and motivated by a need to grow and develop. Conscious and unconscious states can be integrated leading to more autonomy and freedom. Use is made of art, music, writing, drama, etc. The emphasis is on self-direction rather than interpretation and may lead to support groups being formed or self-help groups with no therapist involvement.

Systemic frameworks

These see problems as being rooted in communications within relationships and in patterns of action rather than within the individual. Systemic family therapy focuses on communication within the family and uses feedback to look at how people's actions relate to the effects of previous actions. Repetitive relationship patterns are seen to arise partly from shared beliefs and understandings.

Social models

There are various versions of a social model of mental disorder. At one level, mental illness would be seen as a consequence of social disadvantage, the symptom of a sick society. The solution would lie in improving social and physical conditions. In 1992 David Goldberg and Peter Huxley published an influential text entitled *Common Mental Disorders: A Bio-Social Model* which sought to link some social factors in mental disorder with biological aspects. Their model looks at susceptibility to mental disorder in terms of social, psychological and biological factors. Their work is based on three key concepts:

- *vulnerability* – factors which make some people more susceptible to episodes of mental disorder: a vulnerable individual may experience symptoms after a relatively minor stress;

- *destabilisation* – the process of beginning to experience symptoms;

- *restitution* – the process of losing symptoms – factors which determine how long an episode of illness will last in a given individual.

In summarising key features of the model, Goldberg and Huxley (1992, p144) state:

> *The development of different types of symptom is seen as being determined by early childhood events, the present social circumstances and the kind of provoking event, and not at all by genetic factors. Genetic factors are seen as being very important in determining overall vulnerability towards common mental disorders and are responsible for some of the specific vulnerability to major mental disorders such as schizophrenia and bipolar illness, but they do not determine why one person will become depressed and another anxious.*

Another helpful text which gives some different perspectives on mental disorder is *Mental Health in a Multi-ethnic Society* edited by Suman Fernando (1995).

Other models

Historically and culturally there have been wide-ranging explanations for mental disorder. Some of those not included above are:

- *The moral model.* The person's behaviour is seen as bad on the basis of judgements made on their observed behaviour and that they need moral treatment.

- *The impaired model.* The person is seen as handicapped and unlikely to be restored to normality by treatment.

- *The psychedelic model.* The mad have been chosen by society to act out its problems. They can reveal themselves as particularly gifted members of society and must be allowed to develop their potential for inner exploration and to change the world through their insights.

- *The conspiratorial model.* Madness stems from the way mentally ill people are labelled. See the work of Thomas Scheff, Szasz and Laing.

Models of mental disorder and the law

People's understanding of how the mind works together with their views on mental capacity, free will, determinism and social responsibility combine to influence how they think the law should operate in this field. The MHA 1983 and proposals for legal change make assumptions and reflect some models of mental disorder more strongly than others. It helps to have a grasp of these models to consider how the law will affect service users and carers, and how it might constrain their ability to choose an approach that matches their own preferred explanations.

Definitions of mental disorder (section 1)

Introduction

Definitions of mental disorder are of central importance as the Act applies only to those believed to be mentally disordered. Section 1 states: *The provisions of this Act shall have effect with respect to the reception, care and treatment of mentally disordered patients, the management of their property and other related matters.* Judgements on mental disorder may be made by a range of people, e.g. doctors, police, magistrates, Mental Health Tribunal members. In each case, judgements must be made within the framework of the definitions given in section 1. Coming within the definition of mental disorder is not sufficient, by itself, to warrant detention in hospital. The disorder must be of a nature or degree to warrant the use of compulsion. Unless the person is seen as mentally disordered, the Act does not apply. Problems arising from including people with learning disabilities are considered below.

Broad definition of 'mental disorder'

The Mental Health Act 1983 as amended gives a broad definition of the generic term 'mental disorder' and there are no longer any specific classifications.

'Mental disorder' is described in section 1(2) as:

any disorder or disability of the mind.

This is a significant broadening of the definition that had previously been used, especially in relation to the longer-term forms of compulsion and court-related orders. A list of possible examples of mental disorder is set out in the Code of Practice (para. 3.3):

- *affective disorders, such as depression and bipolar disorder*
- *schizophrenia and delusional disorders*
- *neurotic, stress-related and somatoform disorders, such as anxiety, phobic disorders, obsessive compulsive disorders, post-traumatic stress disorder and hypochondriacal disorders*
- *organic mental disorders such as dementia and delirium (however caused)*
- *personality and behavioural changes caused by brain injury or damage (however acquired)*
- *personality disorders*
- *mental and behavioural disorders caused by psychoactive substance use…*
- *eating disorders, non-organic sleep disorders and non-organic sexual disorders*
- *learning disabilities…*
- *autistic spectrum disorders (including Asperger's syndrome)…*
- *behavioural and emotional disorders of children and adolescents.*

There is no longer a specific reference to 'mental illness' although this would clearly be included within the broader definition. In the Mental Health (Northern Ireland) Order 1986 mental illness is defined as a *state of mind which affects a person's thinking, perceiving, emotion or judgement to the extent that he requires care or medical treatment in his own interests or in the interest of other persons.* Northern Ireland is considering pursuing a more mental capacity-based form of legislation and comparisons between the countries will continue to be of interest.

Exclusions

Section 1(3) used to exclude a range of behaviours from being seen in themselves as mental disorders. These were: *promiscuity or other immoral conduct, sexual deviancy or dependence on alcohol or drugs.* The DHSS in the *Review of the Mental Health Act 1959* (1978) saw these as 'social and behavioural problems' rather than mental disorders. The revised Act has removed the exclusions (apart from dependence on alcohol or drugs) and this has led to concerns about mental health law being used to control social problems. (See the discussion in Chapter 11.) In general, Hoggett (1996) argues that the distinction in law between social or behavioural problems on the one hand and mental disorder on the other is still far from clear. The current discussions on how to deal with people who have a severe personality disorder are a good illustration of her argument.

There was some heated debate around the proposed removal of the exclusions from mental disorder as the 2007 Bill was passing through Parliament. The House of Lords wanted the addition of further exclusions while the government wished to remove all of them. As we have noted, the conclusion was that only the exclusion relating to dependence on alcohol or drugs was retained. This means that it will still not be possible to use the Act's compulsory powers on the basis of drug or alcohol dependence alone. However, as the Code of Practice notes at 3.10:

> Alcohol or drug dependence may be accompanied by, or associated with, a mental disorder which does fall within the Act's definition. If the relevant criteria are met, it is therefore possible (for example) to detain people who are suffering from mental disorder, even though they are also dependent on alcohol or drugs. This is true even if the mental disorder in question results from the person's alcohol or drug dependence.

As a result, a related or consequential mental disorder could lead to detention. The removal of the exclusions relating to promiscuity, other immoral conduct and sexual deviancy are undoubtedly controversial.

The Explanatory Notes to the Mental Health Act 2007 state at para. 24:

> Clinically, neither promiscuity nor 'other immoral conduct' by itself is regarded as a mental disorder, so the deletion of that exclusion makes no practical difference. Similarly, sexual orientation (homo-, hetero- and bi-sexuality) alone is not regarded as a mental disorder. However, there are disorders of sexual preference which are recognised clinically as mental disorders. Some of these disorders might be considered 'sexual deviance' in the terms of the current exclusion (for example paraphilias like fetishism or paedophilia). On that basis, the amendment would bring such disorders within the scope of the 1983 Act.

Barber *et al.* (2009, p23) comment:

> Clearly the government intends (so long as the other criteria are met) that paedophilia, for example, should be capable of being regarded as a mental disorder for the purposes of using the compulsory powers of the Act. If paedophilia could be considered a symptom of a personality disorder it would not have been excluded from consideration in any event under the unamended Act. The question is whether without being such a symptom, the removal of sexual deviancy as an exclusion makes it easier to argue that such conditions constitute mental disorders eligible for consideration for use of the compulsory powers. Of course all other criteria would have to be met (e.g. as to risk), but an argument can be anticipated that rather than being true mental disorders they are behaviours deviating from society's norms and therefore falling foul of the Winterwerp criteria for what constitutes lawful detention on the basis of unsoundness of mind . . . As Fennell (2007, pp49–50) points out the mere presence of such conditions in manuals such as ICD-10 or DSM IV does not establish them as mental disorders for legal purposes. Nor does the non-appearance of a condition in the manuals mean that it cannot legally be considered a mental disorder.

If an AMHP is asked to assess a person at a police station (where they have been taken following an arrest for an alleged offence or under section 136 of the Mental Health

Act) and the person is an alleged paedophile, any decision would need to be especially well recorded in terms of any judgement on the nature or degree of any possible mental disorder. Fortunately even the section 2 medical recommendations now require the doctors to give a clinical description of the mental disorder. This is an area where there may be some legal challenge.

Learning disability

There is a school of thought which believes that people with learning disabilities should be excluded from mental health legislation. Some groups consider that such people should either be dealt with under separate legislation (e.g. based on mental incapacity) or should not be subject to any form of compulsion. The counter view is that people with learning disabilities should be included for all aspects of the Mental Health Act. The compromise position adopted in 1982 has been preserved in the recently revised Act. This means that at least a minority of people with learning disabilities are covered by the Mental Health Act in general, and that an even smaller group, who are abnormally aggressive or seriously irresponsible, are liable to longer-term compulsion in some circumstances. There was some confusion generated by this compromise. Even after publication in 1983 of the consolidated Mental Health Act, some people believed that the Act stated that people with learning disabilities could be detained only if they were also abnormally aggressive or seriously irresponsible. In fact, this restriction applies only to some longer-term sections (e.g. sections 3, 7 and 37). A look at the Parliamentary Scrutiny Committee report (p33) shows that confusion continued to exist after 2000, as their explanation of the 1983 Act contained errors, e.g. stating that arrested or incomplete development of mind must be associated with abnormally aggressive or seriously irresponsible conduct before someone can be detained under section 2.

One by-product of the compromise in the 1983 Act was the exclusion of some people from the provisions of guardianship where they might have benefited from it. These are people who have arrested or incomplete development of mind, who are subject to exploitation or neglect, but would not be seen as abnormally aggressive or seriously irresponsible, thereby excluding them from the definition of mental impairment. Apart from a change in behaviour, the only way such individuals could be received into guardianship was where the relevant professionals took a liberal interpretation of the definition. However, some doctors and others, understandably, were not willing to see someone who was exploited or neglected as 'seriously irresponsible' just because they have failed to rectify the position for themselves. The death of Beverley Lewis drew this problem to people's attention. In a Court of Appeal case (*Re F a child* (Care order: Sexual abuse (1999)) the court overturned a county court judge's decision (when displacing her father as nearest relative) that a 17-year-old with learning disability who wished to return home where she would be at risk of abuse was acting in a 'seriously irresponsible' manner. The Appeal Court preferred a more restrictive interpretation of this phrase. Subsequent court decisions have followed this line.

The position from November 2008 is that learning disability can be seen as a mental disorder and needs specific consideration only when looking at long-term compulsion. At this point the definition of learning disability is defined in section 1(4) as:

> *a state of arrested or incomplete development of the mind which includes significant impairment of intelligence and social functioning.*

For longer-term compulsion learning disability will not constitute a mental disorder unless 'associated with abnormally aggressive or seriously irresponsible conduct' on the part of the patient. It follows that, for example, neither section 3 nor section 7 can be invoked without this qualification being met. This in effect recreates the previous position when the term 'mental impairment' was used to cover such patients.

Particular care will need to be taken by AMHPs and doctors when completing the relevant forms as those used for applications and medical recommendations do not make this behavioural requirement explicit. AMHPs should be alert so that as soon as they see a reference to learning disability in a recommendation for section 3 they check to see that the behavioural issue is included in the doctor's description. The additional behavioural test will not be an issue where the patient also has another form of mental disorder. It may be of some interest to note that the Code of Practice suggests that autistic spectrum disorders should be seen as mental disorders in their own right.

> **3.16** *The learning disability qualification does not apply to autistic spectrum disorders (including Asperger's syndrome). It is possible for someone with an autistic spectrum disorder to meet the criteria for compulsory measures under the Act without having any other form of mental disorder, even if their autistic spectrum disorder is not associated with abnormally aggressive or seriously irresponsible behaviour. While experience suggests that this is likely to be necessary only very rarely, the possibility should never automatically be discounted.*

In conclusion we are left with a situation where some very vulnerable patients with learning disabilities could be detained under section 2 but, at the end of the 28 days, unless there was evidence of abnormally aggressive or seriously irresponsible conduct, the Mental Health Act could no longer be used. The Mental Capacity Act might provide some protection but whether the safeguards are as robust as with the Mental Health Act is open to question.

The 'appropriate medical treatment' test

The government was determined to remove the 'treatability' test contained in the unamended Act. It was seen as a bar to admitting certain patients (especially those with personality disorders who posed a risk to others) whom the government did not wish to see excluded from compulsory admission. There was a counter-argument that some therapeutic purpose should be required before a person could be admitted and treated compulsorily. A compromise was reached whereby for section 3 there is a requirement that 'appropriate medical treatment' is available. Of some significance is that the medical recommendations now require the doctors to specify the hospital where a bed is available offering the appropriate treatment. The AMHP could apply to a hospital listed only on the medical recommendations. This, combined with changes in the Code's guidance on the use of section 2 and section 3, may lead to a decline in the number of section 3 admissions from the community and a corresponding increase for section 2 where there is no such appropriate treatment test.

'Medical treatment' itself is defined in section 145 of the Mental Health Act 1983:

> *Any reference in this Act to medical treatment in relation to mental disorder shall be construed as a reference to medical treatment the purpose of which is to alleviate, or prevent a worsening of, the disorder or one or more of its symptoms or manifestations.*

This introduces a therapeutic purpose test but no requirement that treatment is 'likely' to achieve its aims as was the case with the old 'treatability test'. The definition of medical treatment is very broad. Section 145(1) states:

> *'Medical treatment' includes nursing, psychological intervention and specialist mental health habilitation, rehabilitation and care.*

The Code of Practice states at para. 6.18:

> *An indication of unwillingness to co-operate with treatment generally, or with a specific aspect of treatment, does not make such treatment inappropriate.*

The test will require some consideration by the professionals involved with assessments for section 3 detention but it is unlikely to act as a barrier to admission in many cases. The key for staff will be to look at the nature and degree of the mental disorder and consider how the proposed treatment relates to these aspects. Given the broad definition of mental disorder and of medical treatment the availability of a hospital bed is likely to be a far more crucial factor and the revisions to the Act have done nothing to pressurise health authorities into ensuring that beds are available for patients where professionals consider admission is necessary.

Summary of 'mental disorder' as defined in section 1 of the MHA 1983

For all detentions up to 28 days (e.g. sections 2, 4, 136):

- 'any disorder or disability of the mind' – but a person should not be seen as suffering from a mental disorder by reason only of dependence on alcohol or drugs.

For compulsion under longer-terms sections (e.g. sections 3, 7 or 37):

As above with two additional restrictions:

- appropriate medical treatment must be available, and the doctors must identify on their recommendations where this would be located;

- where the patient is identified as having a learning disability (defined in section 1(4) as: *a state of arrested or incomplete development of the mind which includes significant impairment of intelligence and social functioning*) then this must also be *associated with abnormally aggressive or seriously irresponsible conduct.*

ACTIVITY **1.1**

Sample questions on definitions

(Questions are typical AMHP examination questions and are usually in three parts.)

1a *What is the relevant definition of 'mental disorder' as per section 1 of the Mental Health Act 1983 when considering a possible compulsory admission under section 2?*

1b *List anything which, by itself, would be excluded from being a mental disorder under section 1.*

1c *Using one of these as an example, identify why the exclusion might be a problem for those considering the use of section 2.*

2a *What are the essential elements of the definition of 'learning disability' as given in section 1 of the Mental Health Act 1983? When does the definition become relevant?*

2b *What relevance does this issue have to the protection of a vulnerable adult with a learning disability?*

2c *What alternatives to the Mental Health Act might be considered for such a patient, and what are some of the advantages and disadvantages of these?*

Multiple choice questions *(Answers in Appendix 9)*

1 *For the purposes of an admission under section 3 which of the following could, by themselves, be considered as a form of 'mental disorder'?*
   (a) Learning disability ☐
   (b) Dependence on alcohol ☐
   (c) Disorder of mind ☐
   (d) Dependence on drugs ☐
   (e) Disability of mind ☐
   (f) Learning disability associated with abnormally aggressive or seriously irresponsible conduct ☐

2. *Psychopathic disorder does not appear in the Mental Health Act 1983 as amended.*
   (a) True ☐
   (b) False ☐

3. *Learning disability is defined in the Act as 'a state of arrested or incomplete development of mind which includes significant impairment of intelligence and social functioning'.*
   (a) True ☐
   (b) False ☐

Chapter 2

Civil admissions, guardianship and community treatment orders

Periods of compulsion for Part 2 patients (including access to Mental Health Tribunals and whether Part 4 consent to treatment rules apply)

Section number and purpose	Maximum duration	Can patient apply to the Tribunal?	Can nearest relative apply to the Tribunal?	Automatic tribunal hearing?	Consent to treatment rules?*
2 Admission for assessment	**28 days** Not renewable	Yes. Within first 14 days	No – s23 gives discharge power but see s25	No	Yes
3 Admission for treatment	**6 months** Renewed for 6 months and then yearly	Yes. Within first 6 months and then in each period	No – s23 gives discharge power but see s25	Yes. At 6 months and then every 3 years (yearly if under 18)	Yes
4 Admission for assessment in an emergency	**72 hours** Not renewable but second doctor can change to s2	Yes. Only relevant if s4 converted to a s2	No	No	No

5(2) Doctor or AC's holding power	**72 hours** Not renewable	No	No	No	No
5(4) Nurse's holding power	**6 hours –** not renewable but doctor or AC can change to 5(2)	No	No	No	No
7 Reception into guardianship	**6 months** Renewable for 6 months and then yearly	Yes. Within first 6 months and then in each period	No – s23 gives them power to discharge	No	No
17A Community Treatment Order (**CTO**)	**6 months** Extendable by 6 months and then yearly	Yes. Within first 6 months and then in each period	No – s23 gives them power to discharge but see s25	Only if CTO is revoked	Yes Part 4A
19 Transfer between guardianship and hospital	**6 months** Renewable for 6 months and then yearly	Yes. In first 6 months and then in each period	No – s23 gives them power to discharge, but see s25	Yes – at 6 months and every 3 years; yearly if under 18	Yes
25 Restriction by RC of discharge by NR	Variable	No	Yes. Within 28 days of being informed. (No appeal if s2)	No	N/A
29 Appointment of acting NR by court	Variable	No	Yes. Within one year and then yearly	No	N/A
135 Warrant to search for and remove patient	**72 hours** Not renewable	No	No	No	No
136 Police power in public places	**72 hours** Not renewable	No	No	No	No

* Where consent to treatment rules do not apply, a patient is in the same position as an informal patient and should not be treated without their consent except where covered by the Mental Capacity Act or in an emergency under common law. Chapter 6 has fuller information on consent to treatment.

Compulsory admission to hospital and detention under sections 2, 3, 4, 5 or 135 of the MHA 1983

Introduction

This chapter concentrates on civil admissions (as opposed to those involving the courts – see Chapter 5). There are variations in the criteria for admissions to hospital between the different sections and these are set out below. Before looking at each of the sections in turn, however, it should be stressed that the need for the AMHP to seek the 'least restrictive alternative' is common to all of them (see Chapter 4). Careful attention should be paid to the grounds for detention. In practice, the expression 'a danger to himself or others' is often used erroneously for section 2 in place of the actual grounds, i.e. that detention is necessary for the patient *in the interests of his own health or safety or with a view to the protection of other persons*. The 'danger' grounds come into play only where the nearest relative intends to discharge the patient (see the last paragraph on section 2 beginning 'Section 11(3)').

Similarly, mistakes are made by people not concentrating on whether it is an 'or' or an 'and' in the text. Note, for example, that it could be either the nature *or* degree of mental disorder which makes an admission appropriate. Again, an admission may be necessary for the health *or* safety of the patient *or* with a view to the protection of others. All three conditions do not need to be met, so health grounds alone could suffice. In contrast, note the importance of the *and* between section 2(2)(a) and (b) below. The requirements of (a) *and* (b) must be met before detention is possible.

Section 131 promotes the use of informal admission wherever possible. The philosophy of the Act is to seek the least restrictive alternative and this should be borne in mind when considering the use of any of the following sections. However, note the potential effect of the European Court's decision in *HL* v *UK* (The Bournewood case) described after the discussion on section 5 later in this chapter.

Admission for assessment – section 2

Section 2 allows for a patient who meets certain criteria to be compulsorily admitted to hospital and to be detained there for up to 28 days. The admission is for assessment (or for assessment followed by medical treatment) rather than for observation as was the case with the 1959 Act because, in the words of the 1981 White Paper: *it implies more active intervention to form a diagnosis and to plan treatment* (Cmnd 8405).

Two doctors need to sign recommendations (singly or jointly) based on their examinations of the patient. Section 12 requires at least one doctor to have special experience in the diagnosis or treatment of mental disorder and one should preferably have previous acquaintance with the patient. What amounts to 'previous acquaintance' was dealt with in *Reed (Trainer)* v *Bronglais Hospital* (2001).

In this case the doctor in question:

- attended a case conference which gave much background information on the patient and included the minutes of two previous case conferences;
- following the case conference, saw the patient for about five minutes;
- 'scanned' the medical records received from the Family Health Authority;
- then saw the patient again to make his recommendation.

The court held the words should be given their ordinary meaning and that the reference in the Code to 'personal' knowledge did not import any greater requirement. The doctor had sufficient 'previous acquaintance', and any doctor would have who had some previous knowledge of the patient and was not coming to him or her 'cold'.

The recommendations will state as per section 2(2):

(a) *he is suffering from mental disorder of a nature or degree which warrants the detention of the patient in a hospital for assessment (or for assessment followed by medical treatment) for at least a limited period; and*

(b) *he ought to be so detained in the interests of his own health or safety or with a view to the protection of other persons.*

An application to hospital must be based on these two medical recommendations and may be made by either an AMHP or the patient's nearest relative (NR). The Code of Practice states at para. 4.28:

An AMHP is usually a more appropriate applicant than a patient's nearest relative, given an AMHP's professional training and knowledge of the legislation and local resources, together with the potential adverse effect that an application by the nearest relative might have on their relationship with the patient.

Then at para. 4.30 the Code states:

Doctors who are approached directly by a nearest relative about making an application should advise the nearest relative that it is preferable for an AMHP to consider the need for a patient to be admitted under the Act and for the AMHP to make any consequent application. Doctors should also advise the nearest relative of their right to require a local social services authority (LSSA) to arrange for an AMHP to consider the patient's case. Doctors should never advise a nearest relative to make an application themselves in order to avoid involving an AMHP in an assessment.

If the nearest relative makes an application for detention, section 14 requires an AMHP to provide a social circumstances report to the hospital. If an AMHP had been bypassed or had earlier refused to make an application, their report should include an account of the reasons for this. The Code recommends that AMHPs provide assistance with conveyance where the nearest relative has made an application but it does so in much more guarded tones than the previous edition. At para. 11.15 it states:

If the nearest relative is the applicant, any AMHP and other professionals involved in the assessment of the patient should give advice and assistance. But they should not assist in a patient's detention unless they believe it is justified and lawful.

Section 11(3) requires the AMHP, when applying for a section 2 detention, to inform the nearest relative of their rights to discharge the patient under section 23. This, together with section 25, allows the nearest relative to discharge the patient if they have given 72 hours' written notice to the hospital managers of their intention to discharge the patient. The responsible clinician (RC) may block this only if they are able to produce within the 72 hours *a report certifying that, in the opinion of that clinician, the patient, if discharged, would be likely to act in a manner dangerous to other persons or to himself.*

The next section illustrates the various risk levels set out in the Mental Health Act.

Risk levels and the Mental Health Act

Two-stage approach to a Mental Health Act assessment

1   The first important step in any intervention is to assess a person's mental health. If they have a mental disorder of a nature or degree which warrants compulsory intervention one can then move to the chart below.

2   Check the chart to note significance of different risk criteria for detention and guardianship.

(The illustration is of an imagined scale from no risk at the bottom to extremely high at the top.)

100%	**(For example, certain death if person not detained)**
	In any case where a person was seen by the RC to be above this line, the RC would bar any attempt by the NR to discharge the patient
V. high	**Patient, if discharged, would be likely to act in a manner dangerous to others or self**
	In any case where a person was seen to be above this line they could be detained under section 2 or 3 but could be discharged by the nearest relative giving 72 hours' notice unless RC blocks as above
High	**Detention necessary for health or safety of patient or for the protection of other persons**
	In any case where a person was seen to be above this line they could be received into guardianship under s7 but could be discharged by NR at any time
Less	**Guardianship necessary in interest of welfare of patient or the protection of others**
	On this scale, there can be no compulsory intervention until at least the grounds for guardianship are met.
0%	**No perceived risk**

There is particular significance where a person is seen to be within the lightly shaded area between 'high' and 'very high' risk levels. The nearest relative would be able to order the patient's discharge (giving 72 hours' notice) but the RC would be unable to block this as they do not perceive the patient as dangerous. If the RC and the AMHP nevertheless consider that the patient should still be detained (i.e. the nearest relative's intervention has not altered the situation to drop the risk level below the middle heavily-shaded line marked 'high'), the AMHP should consider making an application to the county court for the displacement of the nearest relative under section 29.

Admission for treatment – section 3

This allows a patient to be compulsorily admitted to hospital and detained there for up to six months in the first instance. If the grounds are still met, detention may be renewed for six months and after that for a year at a time. The renewal process involves the RC examining the patient within the last two months of the period of detention, consulting with another professional and obtaining the agreement of another professional who has been professionally concerned with the patient that the grounds for section 3 are met, and submitting a report to the hospital managers. If the patient has not had an MHT hearing during the first six months, there will be an automatic one if detention is renewed.

An admission under section 3 is for treatment and two doctors sign recommendations (singly or jointly) based on their examinations of the patient. As with section 2, at least one doctor must be approved under section 12 and one should preferably have previous acquaintance with the patient. The recommendations will state that:

- *he is suffering from mental disorder of a nature or degree which makes it appropriate for him to receive medical treatment in a hospital; and*
- *it is necessary for the health or safety of the patient or for the protection of other persons that he should receive such treatment and it cannot be provided unless he is detained under this section; and*
- *appropriate medical treatment is available for him.*

An application to a hospital must be based on these two medical recommendations and may be made by either an AMHP or the patient's nearest relative. If the AMHP intends to apply, they must contact the nearest relative unless this is not reasonably practicable or would involve unreasonable delay. If the nearest relative objects to the application, it may not be made. If the AMHP thinks the nearest relative is acting unreasonably they may make an application to the county court under section 29 for the displacement of the nearest relative. It would be unusual not to be able to contact the nearest relative for section 3 unless the AMHP was unable to trace where they were.

Paragraph 4.59 of the Code states that circumstances in which the nearest relative need not be informed or consulted would include situations where:

- *it is not practicable for the AMHP to obtain sufficient information to establish the identity or location of the nearest relative, or where to do so would require an excessive amount of investigation involving*

unreasonable delay; and
- *consultation is not possible because of the nearest relative's own health or mental incapacity.*

The Code also refers to the case of *R (on the application of E)* v *Bristol City Council* (2005) which is explored in more detail in Chapter 3 on relatives. The effect of the *Bristol* case on the Code is the statement at para. 4.60 that:

There may also be cases where, although physically possible, it would not be reasonably practicable to inform or consult the nearest relative because there would be a detrimental impact on the patient which would result in infringement of the patient's right to respect for their privacy and family life under article 8 of the European Convention on Human Rights and which could not be justified by the benefit of the involvement of the nearest relative. Detrimental impact may include cases where patients are likely to suffer emotional distress, deterioration in their mental health, physical harm, or financial or other exploitation as a result of the consultation.

However, there is an appropriate warning at para. 4.61 that:

Consulting and notifying the nearest relative is a significant safeguard for patients. Therefore decisions not to do so on these grounds should not be taken lightly. AMHPs should consider all the circumstances of the case, including:

- *the benefit to the patient of the involvement of their nearest relative;*
- *the patient's wishes (taking into account whether they have the capacity to decide whether they would want their nearest relative involved and any statement of their wishes they have made in advance);*
- *any detrimental effect that involving the nearest relative would have on the patient's health and wellbeing; and*
- *whether there is any good reason to think that the patient's objection may be intended to prevent information relevant to the assessment being discovered.*

There is further useful guidance for AMHPs in the Code at para. 4.63:

If they do not consult or inform the nearest relative, AMHPs should record their reasons. Consultation must not be avoided purely because it is thought that the nearest relative might object to the application.

At para. 4.64 advice is given that when they are consulting nearest relatives AMHPs should, where possible:

- *ascertain the nearest relative's views about both the patient's needs and the nearest relative's own needs in relation to the patient;*
- *inform the nearest relative of the reasons for considering an application for detention and what the effects of such an application would be; and*
- *inform the nearest relative of their role and rights under the Act.*

Chapter 3 of this book includes further discussion on nearest relative issues.

The choice between section 2 and section 3

This is a matter for professional judgment of the criteria involved. The guidance in the new Code is significantly different from the previous edition. Combined with the effects of the 'appropriate medical treatment' test and the requirement to name the relevant hospital in the medical recommendation for a section 3 detention it would seem likely that the number of section 3 applications from the community will fall whereas the numbers of section 2 applications will rise.

The Code now states at para. 4.26 that section 2 should be used in circumstances where:

- *the full extent of the nature and degree of a patient's condition is unclear;*
- *there is a need to carry out an initial in-patient assessment in order to formulate a treatment plan, or to reach a judgement about whether the patient will accept treatment on a voluntary basis following admission; or*
- *there is a need to carry out a new in-patient assessment in order to re-formulate a treatment plan, or to reach a judgement about whether the patient will accept treatment on a voluntary basis.*

Section 3 should be used where the following criteria are met:

- *the patient is already detained under section 2 (detention under section 2 cannot be renewed by a new section 2 application); or*
- *the nature and current degree of the patient's mental disorder, the essential elements of the treatment plan to be followed and the likelihood of the patient accepting treatment on a voluntary basis are already established.*

There are no longer any other warnings against using section 2 as was the case with the previous Code. Staff who were ASWs will recall, as an example, being advised by the Code not to use section 2 because an objection to a section 3 was anticipated as being likely. This advice has disappeared. Jones (2008) is a strong advocate of using section 2 before going on to look at section 3 later. Certainly many well know that patients would still come under the list where factors indicate a section 2 application.

AMHPs would be well advised, except where a patient is already detained under section 2, not to accept referrals 'for a section 3' just because the patient is known. They should agree to assess but with an open mind as to the outcome, including the possibility, even where detention is indicated, of a section 2 or section 3. If they accept from the outset that there is no need for assessment in hospital and that it is appro-priate just to look at section 3 the implications of *R v Wilson ex p. Williamson* (1996) may prove problematic. The case has been widely quoted to support the view that using a section 2 as a stopgap measure because a section 3 has been blocked would be unlawful. Thus an AMHP who agrees that a section 3 is appropriate and who is then prevented by a nearest relative objection from making such an application would need to apply to the county court for a displacement of the nearest relative and would not be able to fall back on a section 2 as an interim measure. This problem has not disappeared but it may be less frequent if the changes in the Act and Code lead to a decline in the number of patients going straight on to a section 3 before they are in hospital.

Short-term detentions and holding powers – sections 4, 135 and 5

These are second-best solutions compared with detention under sections 2 or 3. They are temporary responses to crises where circumstances do not allow a full assessment before invoking compulsory powers. Section 5 should not be used just to demonstrate to patients that they cannot leave hospital when they wish to. Each use of the section should be followed as soon as possible by an assessment of the need for further detention. The sections last for a maximum of 72 hours (for sections 4 and 135 this is timed from the moment when the patient is admitted to hospital or arrives at the place of safety) or until the assessment is completed, whichever is the sooner. They are not renewable, although a section 4 can be converted to a section 2 by the addition of a second medical recommendation and section 5(4) can be changed to a section 5(2) if the doctor or approved clinician in charge of the patient's treatment deems this appropriate. None of the sections allows for an appeal to the MHT (because of the short time period involved) and patients are not covered by consent to treatment procedures set out in Part 4 of the Act. Therefore these patients have the same right to refuse treatment as any informal patient.

Admission for assessment in cases of emergency – section 4

Where only one doctor is available and waiting for a second doctor would involve 'undesirable delay', it is possible to effect an admission under section 4. An application may be made by either an AMHP or the nearest relative. Paragraph 5.6 of the Code states:

An emergency may arise where the patient's mental state or behaviour presents problems which those involved cannot reasonably be expected to manage while waiting for a second doctor. To be satisfied that an emergency has arisen, the person making the application and the doctor making the supporting recommendation should have evidence of:

- *an immediate and significant risk of mental or physical harm to the patient or to others;*
- *danger of serious harm to property; or*
- *a need for physical restraint of the patient.*

Apart from the urgent necessity for admission, grounds are basically the same as for section 2. The doctor providing the recommendation does not need to be section 12 approved and may not have previous acquaintance with the patient. This significantly reduces the safeguards for the patient and should be avoided if possible. It is important to remind the hospital to let the AMHP know if the section is converted to a section 2 so that the AMHP can inform the nearest relative as required by section 11(3).

AMHP reports for applications under sections 2, 3 or 4

Paragraph 4.94 of the Code states that the AMHP should:

provide an outline report for the hospital at the time the patient is first admitted or detained, giving reasons for the application and details of any practical matters about the patient's circumstances which the hospital should know. Where possible, the report should include the name and telephone number of the AMHP or a care co-ordinator who can give further information. LSSAs should consider the use of a standard form on which AMHPs can make this outline report.

Local authority circular LAC(99)32 contains a suggested approach at para. 9.1:

(a) *In those instances where a compulsory admission is being considered, the needs of and arrangements for children involved with the patient should be considered by the [AMHP] as an integral element within the assessment. This information should be recorded by the [AMHP] and communicated to the hospital in the event of admission. The [AMHP] should alert their colleagues in children's services if they have any concerns about child care arrangements for dependent children of the patient. It would assist this process if documents were designed to incorporate information from this element of the assessment.*

(b) *Similarly, the [AMHP] should provide the hospital with information about the views of other person(s) with parental responsibility for the children of the patient, where it is appropriate to do so and if these can be ascertained. [AMHPs] should be sensitive to situations where the relationship between parents has broken down so that any decision about child visiting is not used inappropriately in residence or contact disputes.*

(c) *In the vast majority of cases where no concerns are identified, arrangements should be made to support the patient and child and to facilitate contact.*

Warrant to search for and remove patients – section 135

This section covers two main sets of circumstances where an AMHP, constable or other person might need to enter premises and remove a patient. Section 135 (1) states:

> *If it appears to a justice of the peace, on information on oath laid by an Approved Mental Health Professional, that there is reasonable cause to suspect that a person believed to be suffering from mental disorder-*
>
> *(a) has been, or is being, ill-treated, neglected or kept otherwise than under proper control, in any place within the jurisdiction of the justice, or*
>
> *(b) being unable to care for himself, is living alone in any such place,*
>
> *the justice may issue a warrant authorising any constable [. . .] to enter, if need be by force, any premises specified in the warrant in which that person is believed to be, and, if thought fit, to remove him to a place of safety with a view to the making of an application in respect of him under Part II of this Act, or of other arrangements for his treatment or care.*

In using the warrant, the constable needs to be accompanied by an AMHP and by a doctor. As a result of a House of Lords decision in *Ward* v *Commissioner of Police* (2005), magistrates may not apply additional requirements, e.g. naming the AMHP, doctor or police officer who would have to then attend. Any AMHP, doctor or police officer may attend.

The 'place of safety' to which the patient is taken could be a hospital, a police station, social services premises or any suitable place where the occupier is willing to receive the patient. The patient may be kept there for up to 72 hours or until the assessment is completed, whichever is the sooner.

Paragraph 10.21 of the Code states:

> *A police station should be used as a place of safety only on an exceptional basis. It may be necessary to do so because the person's behaviour would pose an unmanageably high risk to other patients, staff or users of a healthcare setting. It is preferable for a person thought to be suffering from a mental disorder to be detained in a hospital or other healthcare setting where mental health services are provided (subject, of course, to any urgent physical healthcare needs they may have).*

The Code continues at para. 10.22:

> *A police station should not be assumed to be the automatic second choice if the first choice place of safety is not immediately available. Other available options, such as a residential care home or the home of a relative or friend of the person who is willing to accept them temporarily, should also be considered.*

Despite this advice there are parts of the country where a police station is still the usual place of safety.

Section 135(2) covers circumstances where a patient liable to be taken to hospital or elsewhere under the Act appears to be on premises where entry has been refused or is likely to be refused. A constable (or other authorised person) may apply for a warrant which will authorise a constable to enter the premises and remove the patient. This might be used for a patient who has refused to return to hospital after a period of leave or who has absconded from hospital or from the place in which they are required to reside when subject to guardianship, or a community patient who is refusing to go to a hospital despite having been recalled.

Application in respect of patient already in hospital – section 5

Section 5 allows for detention of a person under section 2 or 3 even if they are already an in-patient. It also contains provisions for preventing in-patients from leaving hospital where an assessment for detention under one of these sections is incomplete.

Under section 5(2) the doctor or approved clinician in charge of a patient's treatment (or, if they are absent, one nominee) may sign Form H1 (or HO12 in Wales) stating that the patient should be detained under Part 2 of the Act. They pass the form to the hospital managers who may detain the patient for up to 72 hours to enable a full assessment of the need for a section 2 or 3 to take place. The patient could at this point be in any hospital, not necessarily a psychiatric unit. The power cannot be used to extend a section 2 or 3 which is about to expire.

For patients already receiving psychiatric treatment, there is provision under section 5(4) for specified nurses to detain them for up to six hours if they sign Form H2 (or HO13 in Wales) indicating that:

(a) *this patient, who is receiving treatment for mental disorder as an in-patient of this hospital, is suffering from mental disorder to such a degree that it is necessary for the patient's health or safety or protection of others for this patient to be immediately restrained from leaving the hospital; and*

(b) *it is not practicable to secure the immediate attendance of a registered medical practitioner or an approved clinician (who is not a registered practitioner) for the purposes of furnishing a report under section 5(2) of the Mental Health Act 1983.*

Informal or 'voluntary'?

With its advice relating to section 5 of the Act the 1993 version of the Code of Practice led to an interesting debate concerning the definition of an informal patient. There is still a lack of understanding about the distinction between informal and voluntary. For example, the current Code makes a fairly common mistake when in its Annex A it states on p361 that an informal patient is also sometimes known as a voluntary patient. In current law all voluntary patients should be informal but not all informal patients will be voluntary as some will lack the capacity to have agreed to admission.

From the Percy Commission, which led to the 1959 Act, there was a presumption that a 'non-objecting' patient should be grouped with those consenting rather than those dissenting. This meant that professionals involved in the admission procedure tended not to use compulsion where there was an absence of dissent. The definition of an informal patient, however, given in para. 8.4 of the 1993 Code for the purposes of a section 5, suggested that there should have been active consent:

> *An informal in-patient, for the purposes of this Section, is one who has understood and accepted the offer of a bed, who has freely appeared on the ward and who has co-operated in the admission procedure. The Section, for example, cannot be used for an out-patient attending a hospital's accident and emergency department.*

The last sentence may give an indication of the area this advice was supposed to clarify. This issue was addressed in the *R v Bournewood Community and Mental Health Trust ex p. L* (1993) case. In December 1997, the Appeal Court ruled that where a hospital had the intention and the ability to prevent a patient from leaving, then the patient was, in effect, detained and should therefore be so detained by the Mental Health Act if they were to be kept in hospital and treated. This ruling gave such patients the protection offered by the Act (e.g. consent to treatment rules and the role of the Mental Health Act Commission). In June 1998, however, the House of Lords ruled that a compliant mentally incapacitated patient could effectively be detained and treated in hospital. If the patient subsequently showed signs of being unwilling to remain in hospital, they should be assessed with a view to possible detention.

The revised form of words which were used in para. 8.4 of the third edition of the Code of Practice were as follows:

> *For the purposes of s.5(2), informal patients are usually voluntary patients, that is, those who have the capacity to consent and who consent to enter hospital for in-patient treatment. Patients who lack the capacity to consent but do not object to admission for treatment may also be informal patients (see para. 2.8). The section cannot be used for an out-patient attending a hospital's accident and emergency department. Admission procedures should not be implemented with the sole intention of then using the power in section 5(2).*

Paragraph 2.8 referred to here stated:

> *If at the time of admission, the patient is mentally incapable of consent, but does not object to entering hospital and receiving care or treatment, admission should be informal . . . The decision to admit a mentally incapacitated patient informally should be made by the doctor in charge of the patient's treatment in accordance with what is in the patient's best*

interest and is justifiable on the basis of the common law doctrine of necessity...If a patient lacks capacity at the time of an assessment or review, it is particularly important that both clinical and social care requirements are considered, and that account is taken of the patient's ascertainable wishes and feelings and the views of their immediate relatives and carers on what would be in the patient's best interests.

HL v *UK*: the European Court judgment of 2004

This final court stage of the Bournewood saga has had profound implications for English mental health law. Extracts from the judgment are reproduced below.

The applicant was born in 1949 and lives in Surrey. He has suffered from autism since birth. He is unable to speak and his level of understanding is limited. He is frequently agitated and has a history of self-harming behaviour. He lacks the capacity to consent or object to medical treatment. For over 30 years he was cared for in Bournewood Hospital...He was an in-patient at the Intensive Behavioural Unit (IBU) from 1987. The applicant's responsible medical officer (who had cared for him since 1977) was Dr M...In March 1994 he was discharged on a trial basis to paid carers, Mr and Mrs E, with whom he successfully resided until 22 July 1997 [when] he was at the day centre when he became particularly agitated, hitting himself on the head with his fists and banging his head against the wall. Staff could not contact Mr and Mrs E and got in touch with a local doctor who administered a sedative.

HL remained agitated and on the recommendation of the local authority care services manager (AF) with overall responsibility for the applicant, he was taken to the A & E unit at the hospital. He was seen by a psychiatrist (Dr P) and transferred to the IBU. It was recorded that he made no attempt to leave. 'Dr P and Dr M considered that the best interests of the applicant required his admission for in-patient treatment.' Dr M considered detention under the 1983 Act but concluded it 'was not necessary as the applicant was compliant and did not resist admission'. Dr M later confirmed that she would have recommended HL's detention if he had resisted admission. The carers were discouraged from visiting at this point. In a report on August 18th Dr M concluded that HL suffered from a mood disorder as well as autism and that his discharge would be against medical opinion.

On 29 October 1997 the Court of Appeal indicated it would decide the appeal in the applicant's favour. HL was then held on section 5(2) and on 31 October an application for section 3 was made. On 2 November he was seen by his carers for the first time since July.

Application was made to the MHRT in November and independent psychiatric reports were obtained recommending HL's discharge. Before an MHRT hearing application was also made for a Managers' Hearing. On 5 December HL was allowed home on section 17 leave and on 12 December the managers discharged him from the section 3.

The European Court noted that the following safeguards were available to those detained under the Mental Health Act 1983:

1   statutory criteria need to be met and applied by two doctors and an applicant;

2   Part 4 consent to treatment procedures;

3   applications and automatic referrals to Mental Health Review Tribunals;

4   nearest relative powers (including discharge powers);

5   section 117 after-care;

6   the Code of Practice and the Mental Health Act Commission;

7   section 132 rights to information.

The key to the decision of the European Court is Article 5 of the European Convention on Human Rights, i.e. the right to liberty and security of person:

> *No one shall be deprived of their liberty except for specific cases and in accordance with procedure prescribed by law, e.g. after conviction, lawful arrest on suspicion of having committed an offence, lawful detention of person of unsound mind, to prevent spread of infectious diseases. Everyone deprived of liberty by arrest or detention shall be entitled to take proceedings by which the lawfulness of the detention shall be decided speedily by a Court and release ordered if the detention is not lawful.*

The court concluded that HL was 'deprived of his liberty' within the meaning of Article 5.1 of the European Convention on Human Rights. It was not crucial that the door was locked or lockable.

> *The Court considers the key factor in the present case to be that the health care professionals treating and managing the applicant exercised complete and effective control over his care and movements from the moment he presented acute behavioural problems on 22 July 1997 to the date he was compulsorily detained on 29 October 1997.*

It was clear that *the applicant would only be released from the hospital to the care of Mr and Mrs E as and when those professionals considered it appropriate.* HL *was under continuous supervision and control and was not free to leave.*

The court accepted that HL was suffering from a mental disorder of a kind or degree warranting compulsory confinement. However, the court found that there had been a breach of Article 5.1 in that there was an absence of procedural safeguards to protect against arbitrary deprivation of liberty in the reliance on the common law doctrine of necessity. Article 5.4 was also breached in that the applicant had no right to have the lawfulness of his detention reviewed speedily by a court. Judicial review and habeas corpus proceedings were not adequate. The court did not find there had been a breach of Article 14 which covers discrimination.

Implications

Each case will need to be looked at on its own merits but in a situation similar to that of HL it would not be safe to rely on the common law or the Mental Capacity Act (prior to the introduction of the new Deprivation of Liberty Safeguards) where the criteria for detention under the Mental Health Act appear to be met.

The Department of Health initial guidance was published in December 2004 and stated:

32. *Until these safeguards are established in law, the effect of the judgement is that it would be unlawful for an NHS body or a local authority (without the prior authorisation of the High Court) to arrange or provide care or treatment for an incapacitated patient in a way that amounted to deprivation of liberty within the meaning of article 5 of the Convention, unless the patient were detained under the Mental Health Act 1983.*

33. *Nonetheless, the NHS and local authorities will need to continue to provide care and treatment for incapacitated patients, and it is important that neither the safety of those patients nor the quality of the care they receive is jeopardised during the interim period.*

34. *Pending the development of new safeguards described above, NHS bodies and local authorities will want to consider what steps they can take in the short term to protect incapacitated people against the risk of arbitrary deprivation of liberty and minimise the risk of further successful legal challenges.*

The Deprivation of Liberty Safeguards are covered separately in Chapter 11.

Guardianship – section 7

Guardianship is a form of community compulsion which is used in a limited way and in comparatively small numbers in England and Wales. It has received some attention recently for three main reasons: the introduction of the Community Treatment Order has focused attention on the issue of compulsion in the community; it has a new power to convey to a place in the first instance; the introduction of DOLS has raised the question of whether guardianship is an alternative approach.

The Code of Practice (at Para. 26.4) states that guardianship:

> *provides an authoritative framework for working with a patient, with a minimum of constraint, to achieve as independent a life as possible within the community. Where it is used, it should be part of the person's overall care plan*

Guardianship may be applied through a civil route (s7) or, very infrequently, via the courts (s37). For civil admissions, the applicant may be an Approved Mental Health Professional or the nearest relative as defined in section 26. The application is based on two medical recommendations and is made to the local authority. Social services departments vary in their procedures for making decisions on guardianship applications and some are negative in their attitude to this piece of legislation. The relevant local authority is the one where the patient lives unless the guardian is a private individual when their address determines the relevant authority. Guardianship lasts up to six months, is renewable for a further six months and then yearly.

The guardian may be the local authority or a private individual approved by the local authority. However, private individuals hardly ever act as guardians. For example, in 2008 there were 410 new cases where the local authority was the guardian and only four where the guardian was a private individual or other organisation.

The grounds for using guardianship

No one under the age of 16 can be received into guardianship. For a mentally disordered child under 16 who requires some supervision in the community, childcare law (including the rights of parents and the local authority) is available.

The grounds for guardianship under section 7 or section 37 are similar. Section 7(2) states:

A guardianship application may be made in respect of a patient on the grounds that –

(a) *he is suffering from mental disorder of a nature or degree which warrants his reception into guardianship under this section; and*

(b) *it is necessary in the interests of the welfare of the patient or for the protection of other persons that the patient should be so received.*

Note that if the mental disorder is learning disability this must be associated with abnormally aggressive or seriously irresponsible conduct. The forms do not raise this point so AMHPs need to be alert to the issue. This was discussed in Chapter 1 and readers may recall the significance of the *Re F* (1999) case which significantly reduces the occasions where guardianship can be used to protect vulnerable adults with learning disabilities. The Mental Capacity Act may need to be relied on for this group of patients and many would consider that this lacks the robust safeguards of the Mental Health Act.

There is no such problem in using guardianship for other vulnerable patients such as those with dementia as there is no secondary behavioural test. This is an unhappy situation.

The guardian's powers are set out in section 8(1) and give the guardian:

1 the power to require the patient to reside at a place specified by the authority or person named as guardian;

2 the power to require the patient to attend at places and times so specified for the purpose of medical treatment, occupation, education or training;

3 the power to require access to the patient to be given, at any place where the patient is residing, to any medical practitioner, approval social worker or other person so specified.

The changes to the Mental Health Act resulting from the 2007 Act include the new power to convey except in the first instance (as well as retaining the old power to return the person when they have absconded from the place of residence). Note that Parts 4 and 4A of the Act on consent to treatment do not apply to guardianship. Thus there is no statutory route to make a patient accept treatment, such as medication, against their will. If the patient lacks capacity the Mental Capacity Act may provide some limited ability to treat without the valid consent of the patient.

Guardianship does not give any powers in relation to property and affairs. For these reasons there may sometimes be occasions where the powers of a deputy or the donee of a financial Lasting Power of Attorney (LPA) become relevant. Equally an LPA may have granted powers to an attorney to make certain health or welfare decisions on behalf of the patient. The donee would not, however, be able to override decisions made by the guardian which fell within their powers, such as where the patient should live. The relationship between the role of attorney and the nearest relative could clearly be important.

There is a myth that guardianship cannot be used to place people into residential care. The Code of Practice (at para. 26.11) starts by stating:

> *where an adult is assessed as requiring residential care but lacks the capacity to make a decision about whether they wish to be placed there, guardianship is unlikely to be necessary where the move can properly, quickly and efficiently be carried out on the basis of:*

> - *section 5 of the MCA or the decision of an attorney or deputy; or*
> - *(where relevant) the MCA's deprivation of liberty safeguards.*

But the Code then continues at para. 26.12 to state:

> *But guardianship may still be appropriate in such cases if:*

> - *there are other reasons – unconnected to the move to residential care – to think that the patient might benefit from the attention and authority of a guardian;*
> - *there is a particular need to have explicit statutory authority for the patient to be returned to the place where the patient is to live should they go absent; or*
> - *it is thought to be important that decisions about where the patient is to live are placed in the hands of a single person or authority – for example, where there have been long-running or particularly difficult disputes about where the person should live.*

The third situation is far from uncommon and the identification of a clear decision-maker will often be important.

The Code of Practice at para. 26.15 introduces a list of responsibilities that fall to local authorities and this provides a useful checklist. It states that each local authority should have a policy setting out the arrangements for:

- *receiving, scrutinising and accepting or refusing applications for guardianship. Such arrangements should ensure that applications are properly but quickly dealt with;*
- *monitoring the progress of each patient's guardianship, including steps to be taken to fulfil the authority's statutory obligations in relation to private guardians and to arrange visits to the patient;*
- *ensuring the suitability of any proposed private guardian, and that they are able to understand and carry out their duties under the Act;*
- *ensuring that patients under guardianship receive, both orally and in writing, information in accordance with regulations under the Act;*
- *ensuring that patients are aware of their right to apply to the Tribunal and that they are given the name of someone who will give them the necessary assistance, on behalf of the LSSA, in making such an application;*
- *authorising an approved clinician to be the patient's responsible clinician;*
- *maintaining detailed records relating to guardianship patients;*
- *ensuring that the need to continue guardianship is reviewed in the last two months of each period of guardianship in accordance with the Act; and*
- *discharging patients from guardianship as soon as it is no longer required.*

AMHPs may wish to check that their approving authority has covered all of these areas in their policy documents.

Frequency of the use of guardianship

The use of guardianship varies considerably in different areas. Overall its use has declined since 2000 after significant increases in the 1990s. From a very low base of 60 new guardianships in England in 1983–4, the numbers increased to 672 new cases in 1999–2000. The number of new cases then declined to 414 new cases in 2007–8.

It is also possible to look at guardianship in terms of continuing cases on a given date. Here the numbers are more stable. On 31 March 2005, there were 966 people in guardianship compared with 161 in 1984. Table 2.1 illustrates the significant variations around the country.

Supervised after-care was introduced in 1996. It provided similar powers to guardianship but was available only to patients who had been detained on long-term sections. The publicity around its introduction may have contributed to increased use of guardianship in the late 1990s. The Community Treatment Order which replaces Supervised After-care has different implications and the relationship with guardianship is considered later in the chapter.

Table 2.1. Continuing guardianships at 31 March 2008 for 31 English local authorities

Local authority	Total	Population	Per 100,000
Halton (Widnes)	12	118,208	10.15
Barnsley	22	218,000	10.09
Liverpool	39	450,000	8.70
Middlesbrough	12	143,000	8.39
Bolton	15	260,000	5.77
Southampton	12	217,445	5.51
Isle of Wight	5	132,731	3.77
Kent	45	1,329,728	3.38
Plymouth	8	240,720	3.32
Swindon	6	180,051	3.32
Gloucestershire	18	564,559	3.19
Devon	21	704,493	2.98
Bath	5	169,040	2.96
Islington	5	175,797	2.84
Portsmouth	5	186,701	2.68
North Somerset	5	188,564	2.65
Hertfordshire	25	1,004,600	2.49
Bournemouth	3	163,444	1.84
Bristol	7	380,615	1.84
Wiltshire	7	432,973	1.62
Cornwall	8	501,267	1.60
Manchester	7	439,540	1.59
Bexley	3	217,200	1.38
Dorset	5	390,980	1.28
South Gloucestershire	3	245,641	1.22
Lewisham	3	247,000	1.21
Hampshire	14	1,248,800	1.12
Somerset	4	498,093	0.80
Poole	1	138,288	0.72
Surrey	5	1,059,015	0.47
Lambeth	0	261,150	0.00
Totals from sample	**330**	**12,507,643**	**2.64**
Total England	**919**	**49,138,831**	**1.87**

Sources: www.statistics.gov.uk and Government Statistical Service.

The use of guardianship varies considerably between local authorities as Table 2.1 shows. There appears to be no satisfactory explanation for these differences apart from the preferences of staff and the willingness of local authority managers to support the use of guardianship.

Leave of absence and absence without leave
Section 17 leave under the MHA 1983

This provision was amended in 1996 at the same time as supervised after-care was introduced. The amendment effectively increased the length of time for which a patient can be on leave. The main features of section 17 leave are as follows:

- The RC may grant leave to any patient liable to be detained under Part 2 of the Act to enable them to be absent from the hospital.
- Hospital Order (section 37 – see Chapter 5) patients may be granted leave by the RC but restricted patients may be granted leave only with the permission of the Secretary of State for Justice.
- The Code (para. 21.3) states that patients subject to section 35, 36 or 38 may not be granted leave by the RC.
- Leave may be subject to any conditions the RC thinks necessary in the interests of the patient or for the protection of others. It may be granted indefinitely, on specified occasions or for a specific period. It may not go beyond the renewal date for the section.
- A patient could be granted leave to another hospital (e.g. nearer home or where physical treatment is needed) and could later be transferred under section 19.
- The RC may direct the patient should remain in custody when on leave.
- The RC may revoke leave in writing and recall the patient to hospital if they consider it necessary in the interest of the patient's health or safety or for the protection of others.
- A patient may not be recalled to hospital for the sole purpose of renewing the detention.
- A patient on leave is still liable to be detained and therefore is still subject to the consent to treatment provisions of Part 4 of the Act.
- The duty to provide section 117 after-care applies when a patient is on leave (Code para. 27.2).
- A Community Treatment Order could be made while a patient is on section 17 leave.

In terms of recording there is no statutory form but para. 21.21 of the Code states:

Hospital managers should establish a standardised system by which responsible clinicians can record the leave they authorise and specify the conditions attached to it. Copies of the authorisation should be given to the patient and to any carers, professionals and other people in the community who need to know. A copy should also be kept in the patient's notes. In case they fail to return from leave, an up-to-date description of the patient should be available in their notes.

The Code of Practice includes two important statements:

21.6 *Only the patient's responsible clinician can grant leave of absence to a patient detained under the Act. Responsible clinicians cannot delegate the decision to grant leave of absence to anyone else. In the absence of the usual responsible clinician (e.g. if they are on leave), permission can be granted only by the approved clinician who is for the time being acting as the patient's responsible clinician.*

21.7 *Responsible clinicians may grant leave for specific occasions or for specific or indefinite periods of time. They may make leave subject to any conditions which they consider necessary in the interests of the patient or for the protection of other people.*

A patient liable to be detained under section 3 may have this renewed, even if on leave, if there is a significant hospital element to the treatment plan: *B* v *Barking, Havering and Brentwood Community Healthcare NHS Trust* (1999), together with *R (on the application of DR)* v. *Mersey Care NHS Trust* (2002) and *R (CS)* v *MHRT* (2004).

The last case involved a patient who had been on section 17 leave for three months. Hospital attendance was limited to a four-weekly ward round and weekly sessions with a ward psychologist. The judge noted that it was:

. . . clear to me the RMO was engaged in a delicate balancing exercise by which she was, with as light a touch as she could, encouraging progress to discharge. Her purpose was to break the persistent historical cycle of admission, serious relapse and readmission. It may be that in the closing stages of the treatment in hospital her grasp on the claimant was gossamer thin, but to view that grasp as insignificant is, in my view, to misunderstand the evidence.

With a broad definition of what amounts to a hospital, section 17 leave in some cases is virtually a community treatment order (CTO). As the new requirement is just for the RC to consider the use of section 17A when granting leave for more than seven consecutive days, it may be that many RCs continue to rely on section 17 to maintain patients in the community. However, early indications are that CTOs are more numerous than expected.

Absence without leave (section 18)

When a detained patient is absent without leave he or she may be taken into custody and returned to hospital. Changes in 1996 extended the period during which patients on long-term sections may be so taken. This is six months or the end of the period of detention, whichever is longer. If the detention section has lapsed, the patient may be detained for a week for the RC to examine the patient and consider a possible renewal of detention.

For any patient who is returned having been absent without leave for more than 28 days, the RC must consult an AMHP and one or more other professionals who have been concerned with the patient's medical treatment.

If the power of entry is needed but refused, consideration should be given to the use of section 135(2) (see p 25) or the police powers under section 17(1)(d) of the Police and Criminal Evidence Act 1984. When a patient in guardianship absents themselves without permission from any place where they are required to reside, they may be taken into custody and returned to that place.

Community treatment orders – section 17A

Community treatment orders were introduced as an essential part of the Mental Health Act 2007 reforms. They provide a new framework for ensuring that certain patients receive compulsory care and treatment within the community. The Code of Practice refers to the treatment regime as supervised community treatment (SCT) (although it should be noted that this term does not exist anywhere in the 1983 Act as revised).

The government's main aim in replacing Supervised After-care with the Community Treatment Order was to ensure that patients would not be left untreated in the community. However, they had to make a number of compromises as the Bill went through Parliament. In particular, the House of Lords obtained a number of concessions on the issue of compulsory treatment. It will be interesting to see how frequently the measure is used or whether RCs will rely more on long-term section 17 leave and possibly even guardianship where accommodation and social treatments are the key issues.

Section 17(2A) requires the RC to consider the use of a CTO in any case where he is granting section 17 leave that will exceed seven consecutive days.

A CTO can be made only when a patient is liable to be detained in a hospital for treatment. Patients of any age who are liable to be detained under sections 3, 37, 45A, 47 and 48 can be made subject to a CTO by their RC, if they obtain the agreement of an AMHP and if the criteria set out in section 17A(5) are met:

(a) *the patient is suffering from mental disorder of a nature or degree which makes it appropriate for him to receive medical treatment;*
(b) *it is necessary for his health or safety or for the protection of other persons that he should receive such treatment;*
(c) *subject to his being liable to be recalled as mentioned in paragraph (d) below, such treatment can be provided without his continuing to be detained in a hospital;*
(d) *it is necessary that the responsible clinician should be able to exercise the power under section 17E(1) below to recall the patient to hospital;*
(e) *appropriate medical treatment is available for him.*

The relevant form (CTO1 in England) requires that the RC and the AMHP both state that these criteria are met. The AMHP also needs to state that it is appropriate to make the CTO, and where discretionary conditions are set, that they agree that they are necessary or appropriate.

A patient who is made subject to a CTO will have two conditions attached to the order and these are set out on the form itself. Section 17B(3) states:

> *The order shall specify –*
>
> (a) *a condition that the patient make himself available for examination under section 20A below; and*
> (b) *a condition that, if it is proposed to give a certificate under Part 4A of this Act in his case, he make himself available for examination so as to enable the certificate to be given.*

Section 17B(2) states that the RC may also specify discretionary conditions if they obtain the agreement of the AMHP. Any discretionary conditions must be considered:

> *… necessary or appropriate for one or more of the following purposes –*
>
> (a) *ensuring that the patient receives medical treatment;*
> (b) *preventing risk of harm to the patient's health or safety;*
> (c) *protecting other persons.*

Although the RC needs the agreement of the AMHP before making these conditions, they can subsequently be varied or suspended by the RC at any time without the agreement of an AMHP. The Code notes this at para. 25.31 but states:

> *The responsible clinician has the power to vary the conditions of the patient's CTO, or to suspend any of them. The responsible clinician does not need to agree any variation or suspension with the AMHP. However, it would not be good practice to vary conditions which had recently been agreed with an AMHP without discussion with that AMHP.*

This is an area that may need to be monitored.

Failure by the patient to comply with a mandatory condition provides grounds to recall a patient but this is not true of failure to comply with a discretionary condition. In this case the RC would need to believe that the patient required treatment in hospital and that there would be a risk of harm to the health or safety of the patient or to others if they were not recalled to hospital for treatment of their mental disorder

The Code of Practice at para. 25.34 gives some guidance about the sorts of conditions that might be attached to a patient's CTO.

> *They might cover matters such as where and when the patient is to receive treatment in the community; where the patient is to live; and avoidance of known risk factors or high-risk situations relevant to the patient's mental disorder.*

It is generally accepted that the cumulative effect of the conditions imposed on a patient should not amount to a deprivation of liberty. The Code (paras 28.7–8) states that an incapacitated patient whose care and treatment amounts to a deprivation of liberty may be subject to DOLS which could co-exist with a CTO. The community order would have certain conditions but the deprivation of liberty would need to be covered by the DOLS procedure being followed.

A patient who is subject to a CTO may be recalled to hospital by the RC. Notice of recall must be in writing and can take place only if either the patient has failed to comply with a mandatory condition or they require medical treatment in hospital for their mental disorder and there would be a risk of harm to the health or safety of the patient or to others if they were not recalled to hospital for treatment of their mental disorder. In deciding whether to recall a patient to hospital the RC may take into account any failure to comply with a discretionary condition.

The Code gives some guidance on recall (para. 25.51):

> The responsible clinician should consider in each case whether recalling the patient to hospital is justified in all the circumstances. For example, it might be sufficient to monitor a patient who has failed to comply with a condition to attend for treatment, before deciding whether the lack of treatment means that recall is necessary.

If a patient is served with a notice of recall but does not comply with this then they can be returned under the authority of section 18 of the Act. This may require obtaining a warrant under section 135(2).

A patient who has been recalled can be detained in hospital for up to 72 hours, during which time the RC may do one of the following:

1 treat the patient and then allow them to return home within 72 hours from the time of recall (this course of action may be quite common after recall because the patient is subject to Part 4 on recall instead of Part 4A and this makes it much easier to compel the patient to have medication), or

2 revoke the CTO (which has the effect of making the patient subject to section 3 again), with the agreement of an AMHP, if the grounds for detention are met, or

3 discharge the CTO completely.

Revocation

The RC together with an AMHP may revoke a CTO in writing if the criteria for detention under section 3 are met, i.e.:

- the patient is suffering from a mental disorder of a nature or degree which makes it appropriate for him to receive medical treatment in a hospital; and

- it is necessary for the health or safety of the patient or for the protection of other persons that he should receive such treatment and it cannot be provided unless he is detained under this section; and

- appropriate medical treatment is available for him.

The effect of revocation is that the patient remains in hospital under their original detention section but the patient will start a new detention period of six months from the time of revocation. However, for consent to treatment purposes, the protection of Part 4 is preserved (e.g. the patient does not have to restart a period of three months before being eligible for a second opinion appointed doctor (SOAD).

Revocation triggers an automatic Mental Health Tribunal reference by the managers.

Extending a CTO

Section 20A of the Act sets out the provisions and criteria for the extension of CTOs. A CTO lasts for six months in the first instance but can be extended for a further six months and then yearly. The RC, with the agreement of an AMHP, needs to be satisfied that the criteria for a CTO are still met.

Discharging a CTO

The patient can apply for a Mental Health Tribunal hearing once in each period. The tribunal can discharge the CTO but it does not have the power to vary the conditions. The hospital managers also have the power of discharge so the patient may request a hearing. Finally the nearest relative can discharge the patient (giving 72 hours' written notice) unless the patient had formerly been on a Part 3 section (e.g. s37) rather than subject to section 3. The RC can block the NR discharge if they believe the patient might behave in a manner dangerous to themselves or others. Discharge from a CTO has the effect of discharging the initial liability for detention.

CTO, section 17 leave or guardianship?

The Code of Practice offers some guidance regarding which might be the most appropriate community provision in situations where any of the three would be possible (i.e. where the patient is detained in hospital for treatment). Paragraph 28.3 states that guardianship:

> . . . is social care-led and is primarily focused on patients with welfare needs.
> Its purpose is to enable patients to receive care in the community where it
> cannot be provided without the use of compulsory powers.

Paragraph 28.4 continues by stating that section 17 leave:

> . . . is primarily intended to allow a patient detained under the Act to be
> temporarily absent from hospital where further in-patient treatment as a
> detained patient is still thought to be necessary. It is clearly suitable for short-
> term absences, to allow visits to family and so on. It may also be useful in the

longer term, where the clinical team wish to see how the patient manages outside hospital before making the decision to discharge.

The limitations on longer-term section 17 leave really arise from the case law requirement that there be some hospital element as a significant part of the care plan. Where patients are required to attend clinics in buildings that are designated as hospitals this is unlikely to be much of an obstacle. Finally, para. 28.5 states that the CTO:

. . . is principally aimed at preventing the 'revolving door' scenario and the prevention of harm which could arise from relapse. It is a more structured system than leave of absence and has more safeguards for patients. A key feature of SCT is that it is suitable only where there is no reason to think that the patient will need further treatment as a detained in-patient for the time being, but the responsible clinician needs to be able to recall the patient to hospital.

One aspect of the CTO which differs from supervised after-care may actually lead to an increase in the use of guardianship. This is the lack of any legal sanction whereby a patient who is required to live somewhere can be returned there if they abscond. The CTO looks as though it may be most effective for the patient who is 'on the edge of compliance' with medical treatment but would not voluntarily accept it.

Discharge and after-care of patients under section 117

The purpose of after-care is stated in para 27.5 of the Code of Practice as follows:

After-care is a vital component in patients' overall treatment and care. As well as meeting their immediate needs for health and social care, after-care should aim to support them in regaining or enhancing their skills, or learning new skills, in order to cope with life outside hospital.

Section 117 places a specific duty on health and social services authorities (in co-operation with relevant voluntary agencies) to provide after-care to a patient who has been detained under sections 3, 37, 45A, 47 or 48 and is discharged and leaves hospital.

- The requirement still applies even if there is a gap between the date when the section is lifted and the date when the patient leaves hospital.

- There is a need to assess the needs of each individual to whom this section applies.

- The services should continue to be provided until both the health and social services authorities are satisfied that the person concerned no longer needs the services.

- Supervised after-care first introduced the possibility of requiring the patient to accept the services and this is now possible with a Community Treatment Order.

- Services provided under section 117 are community care services for the purposes of the NHS and Community Care Act 1990.

- If a need is then identified it must be provided but there is probably discretion as to the level and precise nature of the service (*R* v *Gloucestershire CC ex p. Barry* [1997]).

Proper implementation of the Care Programme Approach (CPA) should ensure that the legal requirements of section 117 are met. Authorities should be able to identify clearly which patients are covered by section 117.

Charging for services

This has been a contentious area for some years. Essentially section 117 services should be free to the service user. The *Bournewood* case also drew attention to the fact that there are some benefits of being detained on section 3 in that residential and domiciliary services can be very expensive and may become free for someone who has been detained. This point is picked up in the preface to the eleventh edition of Jones's Manual (2008) where he includes it as one of the reasons for using the Mental Health Act to detain a patient in hospital rather than the new DOLS procedure.

In *R* v *Manchester City Council, ex p. Stennett* (2002) the House of Lords ruled that section 117 imposes a freestanding duty to provide after-care services rather than being a passport to services provided under other legislation. There is no power to charge people for section 117 services and therefore they must be provided free. This would include any medication which was part of the patient's psychiatric treatment. A number of authorities have had to reimburse people as a result of the *Stennett* judgment.

General services

See National Assistance Act 1948 and NHS Act 1977. Note that DoH Circular LAC(93)10 sets out arrangements for the provision of social services which apply to mentally disordered persons: accommodation; social work service; social rehabilitation; occupational, social and recreational facilities. These are considered in more detail in Chapter 9.

When planning for a patient's after-care it is important that health and social services staff are aware that section 133 of the Mental Health Act requires hospital managers to give the nearest relative notice of intention to discharge a detained patient (except if the patient or nearest relative has requested otherwise). If practicable, this notice should be given at least seven days before the intended date of discharge. This provision applies to all discharges from detention and not just to section 3. Carers have suggested that this provision is frequently ignored by hospitals (see Chapter 3). Hospital managers must take reasonable steps to identify the patient's nearest relative.

ACTIVITY **2.1**

Sample questions on Part 2 of the Mental Health Act 1983

1a What are the main grounds which need to exist before a doctor can recommend that a person should be detained in hospital for assessment under section 2 of the Act?

1b How does the expression 'dangerous to other persons or himself' compare with these grounds and what is its significance?

1c If the dangerousness test was considered to apply, how might an AMHP then become involved?

2a Who can apply to a magistrate for a warrant to be issued under section 135(1) so that a person believed to be suffering from mental disorder can be searched for and removed to a place of safety?

2b Who is required to be involved in the execution of a section 135(1) warrant and what issues might this raise in practice?

2c Identify any human rights issues associated with the use of section 135(1).

3a Who may grant leave to a patient detained on section 3?

3b What should this person do in granting leave and what conditions can be imposed?

3c When do you think it might be seen as justifiable for a patient to be kept subject to section 17 leave for a long period rather than being made subject to a community treatment order?

Multiple choice questions
(Answers in Appendix 9)

1 Which of the following criteria are necessary before a doctor can recommend compulsory admission on section 3?
   (a) The patient is suffering from a mental disorder of a nature or degree which makes it appropriate for him to receive medical treatment in a hospital. ☐
   (b) The patient is a danger to himself or others. ☐
   (c) Appropriate medical treatment is available to him. ☐
   (d) Treatment is likely to alleviate or prevent a deterioration of his condition. ☐
   (e) Treatment cannot be provided unless the patient is detained. ☐
   (f) Admission is necessary for the health or safety of the patient or for the protection of other persons. ☐

2 Sections 135 and 136 allow people to be moved from one place of safety to another.
   (a) True ☐
   (b) False ☐

3 A duly completed application form combined with the necessary medical recommendations provides sufficient authority for the applicant to force their way into the patient's home.
   (a) True ☐
   (b) False ☐

Chapter 3

Relatives and carers

The nearest relative under the MHA 1983

Introduction

The nearest relative has a number of important rights and functions under the Act. These are discussed later and include the right to:

- insist on an AMHP's assessment of the need for a person's detention in hospital;

- be consulted where practicable* before a section 3 is applied for (and in effect block it);

- apply for a person's detention in hospital;

- order the patient's discharge.

  * 'Where practicable' has been defined in *R (E) v Bristol* (2005) in a way which gives the AMHP a fair degree of flexibility.

The first problem is to identify who exactly is the nearest relative. It will not necessarily be the person identified by the patient as their next of kin and, indeed, the patient has little control over who will be seen in law as the nearest relative. It is worth noting that in *Re D* (mental patient: habeas corpus) (Court of Appeal, 2000) the judge stated:

The question the court had to consider in deciding whether the application for detention had been validly made was not whether the social worker consulted with the legally correct nearest relative, but whether the patient's daughter appeared to him to be the correct relative.

Section 26 provides a list of people considered to be relatives under the Act. Being a relative is of itself important as AMHPs should have regard to any wishes they express (see s13(1)); it may enable them to apply to the county court for a ruling on a nearest relative issue (see later in the chapter) and being such a relative is a prerequisite to being nearest relative (apart from where the court intervenes or where powers are transferred under Regulation 24).

Complications concerning children and 'the five-year rule' (whereby people in some settings find another resident may become their nearest relative) are discussed later. What follows here is a quick guide to enable an AMHP to make a reasonable decision in identifying the nearest relative.

Disagreements or mistakes in identifying a nearest relative

There have been some problems where the AMHP or the hospital managers decide after an admission that the wrong person has been identified as the nearest relative. There are different views as to the correct way to respond to this situation and in such a case staff would be well advised to seek legal advice.

Another important point before actually identifying the nearest relative is that in a judicial review (*R v MHRT for West Midlands and North West ex parte H*, 2000) it was held that restricted patients do not have a nearest relative. This is because there is no legal function for a nearest relative for such a patient. When compiling reports for Mental Health Tribunals it is important, therefore, not to refer to anyone as the nearest relative.

How to identify the nearest relative

To identify a person's nearest relative go through the following four stages:

1 *Make a list* of any of the following who are ordinarily resident in the UK, the Channel Islands or the Isle of Man (*this assumes the patient is ordinarily so resident; if not, then the nearest relative may be someone who is, similarly, not so resident), i.e. list the patient's:

- husband, wife or civil partner
  (a) unless permanently separated from the patient by agreement or by a court order, or where one partner has deserted the other;
  (b) may be someone who has lived as husband, wife or civil partner for the last six months or more if patient not legally married, or patient is married or has civil partner but (a) applies;
- son or daughter

- father or mother
- brother or sister
- grandparent
- grandchild
- uncle or aunt
- nephew or niece
- any other person with whom the patient has ordinarily resided for five years or more.

In compiling the list, include half-blood relationships, treat illegitimate children as the legitimate children of their mothers and do not include in-law relationships.

2 *Cross out* anyone under the age of 18 unless they are the patient's spouse or parent.

3 *Highlight* (with a highlighter pen) anyone on the list who ordinarily resides with *or* cares for the patient (or did so before the patient was admitted to hospital).

'Caring for' ** is a matter of judgment and could include shopping, cooking or providing other care. If only one person is highlighted they are the nearest relative. If more than one person is highlighted (or no one) then go to:

4 *Rank* in order of priority. If more than one person was highlighted above under (3) then rank only those who were highlighted. If no one was highlighted the ranking applies to everyone on the list. The person highest in the list under (1) is the nearest relative. If there is more than one person in the same category, then whole-blood relatives are preferred to half-blood and elder is preferred to younger.

* *Patients not ordinarily resident in the UK.* Some parts of the country with airports and seaports are used to contacting people in various parts of the world if the person is identified as having a mental disorder at the point of entry. The same situation applies whenever the patient is not ordinarily resident in the UK or listed areas. This may include students, holidaymakers, etc.

** In *re D* (mental patient: Habeas corpus) (2000) the judge stated *the words 'cared for' were not defined in the Act but they were clear everyday words set in the context where a social worker had to act in a common-sense manner.* The word 'ordinarily' in section 4 applied to 'residing with' and not to 'caring', so a person may only recently have started providing the care.

Discussion points

1 *Listing relatives.* 'Illegitimate' is an old-fashioned word that has somehow survived in this legislation. Given the number of parents who are not married it immediately poses a problem in identifying relatives. AMHPs are often the first people who have to identify the nearest relative and it is a difficult area to approach.

2 Another strange question that has been identified is:

'When aren't aunts aunts?' It would seem that only blood relationships would count here, so that your mother's brother is your uncle, but this uncle's wife is not your aunt for the purposes of the MHA 1983. This is a recipe for confusion. (Barber et al. 2009, p105)

3 *The Children Act 1989*. It is unusual for children under 18 to be detained under the Mental Health Act. There is a lower age limit of 16 for guardianship but there is no lower age limit for detention. In cases where admission is considered, the nearest relative will usually be the older parent. If a child is living with a person under a residence order within the meaning of the Children Act, then that person will be the nearest relative. If there are two people then they will share the role. If a local authority has parental responsibility under a care order, then it will be the nearest relative. In those rare cases where the child is a ward of court, no application for detention may be made without the court's leave. Chapter 36 of the Code of Practice to the Mental Health Act 1983 gives some specific advice on children and young people under the age of 18.

4 *'The five-year rule'*. The Act introduced a new category of persons to be treated as if they are relatives. These are defined in section 26(7) as persons with whom the patient has been 'ordinarily residing for a period of not less than five years'. Together with the preference in section 26(4) for making the nearest relative the person whom 'the patient ordinarily resides with or is cared for by', this has created some strange situations in practice. Consider the situation of a patient who has lived in an old people's home with the same group of people for more than five years. If they eat together and share common facilities, they could be included within the meaning of 'the patient ordinarily resides with'. Assuming none of the other residents is a blood relative, the eldest of them will probably be nearest relative. This will apply even if the patient has blood relatives elsewhere, unless one is 'caring for' the patient. Eldergill (1998) takes a different view and argues that this would apply only if the person had voluntarily chosen to live with a specific person. *There must be some element of choice before a person may be said to ordinarily reside with another* (Eldergill 1998, p103). Each case would need to be determined on its own facts and the degree and kind of contact with other residents would clearly be significant.

5 *Patient objects to nearest relative – European Convention on Human Rights*. The Act requires an AMHP to consult with the nearest relative where practicable but this poses a problem where the patient objects to contact (e.g. where there has been abuse) on the grounds that it violates their human rights. Article 8 states everyone has a right to respect for their private and family life, their home and correspondence.

In the case of *JT* v *UK* (2000) JT was detained under section 3. She was moved to a secure unit in November 1984 and to a special hospital in 1987. Her detention was subject to periodic review by MHRTs and she was discharged in January 1996. JT complained to the Commission that she had been unable to change her nearest relative in violation of Article 8. Her nearest relative was her mother with whom she had had a difficult relationship. JT had wanted to nominate another person so personal information, mainly in relation to MHRTs, was not released to her mother or to her stepfather (against whom the applicant had made allegations of sexual abuse). The Commission declared admissible the complaint under Article 8, para. 1 concerning her inability to change her nearest relative during her period of detention. The case was struck out by the European Court of Human Rights after a friendly settlement was reached: the UK government agreed to amend the law to allow a detainee to apply to the county court to have a nearest relative replaced if the patient reasonably objected to that person acting in that capacity (Times Law Report 0504-2000 – see Chapter 11). There was a long delay before this was addressed in the Mental Health Act 2007, and in the meantime the High Court provided some relief in the *R* v *Bristol* case (2005). The judge ruled that the ASW (now AMHP) had discretion to decide not to consult the nearest relative of a competent patient who objected and whose psychiatrist said such consultation would be detrimental to the patient's health.

The Code reflects this new position:

4.60 There may also be cases where, although physically possible, it would not be reasonably practicable to inform or consult the nearest relative because there would be a detrimental impact on the patient which would result in infringement of the patient's right to respect for their privacy and family life under Article 8 of the European Convention on Human Rights and which could not be justified by the benefit of the involvement of the nearest relative. Detrimental impact may include cases where patients are likely to suffer emotional distress, deterioration in their mental health, physical harm, or financial or other exploitation as a result of the consultation.

4.61 Consulting and notifying the nearest relative is a significant safeguard for patients. Therefore decisions not to do so on these grounds should not be taken lightly. AMHPs should consider all the circumstances of the case, including:

- *the benefit to the patient of the involvement of their nearest relative;*
- *the patient's wishes (taking into account whether they have the capacity to decide whether they would want their nearest relative involved and any statement of their wishes they have made in advance);*
- *any detrimental effect that involving the nearest relative would have on the patient's health and wellbeing; and*
- *whether there is any good reason to think that the patient's objection may be intended to prevent information relevant to the assessment being discovered.*

Another option, covered below, would be for the patient or the AMHP to apply to the county court to displace an 'unsuitable' nearest relative.

Changing or displacing the nearest relative

If mentally competent, a nearest relative may authorise someone else to perform their functions under Regulation 24 of the Mental Health (Hospital, Guardianship and Treatment) (England) Regulations 2008. (In Wales the equivalent is Regulation 33.) This other person need not be a relative as defined by the Act but they must not be in one of the categories (such as persons under the age of 18) excluded under section 26(5). The authorisation needs to be in writing (or can be in electronic form if the recipient agrees) and copies lodged with the person authorised and with the hospital managers (for detained or community patients) or the local authority (for guardianship). The donor should also notify the patient. The authorisation begins when it is received by the person authorised and cannot be relied on until that point. This procedure may be useful in the circumstances outlined above concerning the five-year rule (where the eldest resident could authorise a suitable relative) or in any other cases where both parties are agreeable. This might be where those involved do not feel that the legal nearest relative is the right person to carry out that function. There is no requirement to obtain the patient's agreement but see the note below on 'suitability'. (Also see below for a sample form – the Regulation number would need to be changed to 33 for Wales but the content could be the same.) The nearest relative can revoke this at any time in writing (or electronically if the recipient agrees).

There will be some circumstances (e.g. where the nearest relative of the patient is not capable of acting as such by reason of mental disorder) where use of the Regulations would not be the appropriate action and where an application to the county court is needed. The court may direct someone to carry out nearest relative's functions on application from (s29(2)):

> *(za) the patient;*
> *(a) any relative of the patient;*
> *(b) any other person with whom the patient is residing (or if the patient is then an in-patient in a hospital, was last residing before he was admitted);*
> *(c) an Approved Mental Health Professional.*

The grounds for an application are set out in section 29(3):

> *(a) that the patient has no nearest relative within the meaning of this Act, or that it is not reasonably practicable to ascertain whether he has such a relative, or who that relative is;*
> *(b) that the nearest relative of the patient is incapable of acting as such by reason of mental disorder or other illness;*
> *(c) that the nearest relative of the patient unreasonably objects to the making of an application for admission for treatment or a guardianship application in respect of the patient;*
> *(d) that the nearest relative of the patient has exercised without due regard to the welfare of the patient or the interests of the public his power to discharge the patient from hospital or guardianship under this Part of this Act, or is likely to do so; or*
> *(e) that the nearest relative of the patient is otherwise not a suitable person to act as such.*

Where (c) or (d) apply, and the patient is already detained under section 2, the detention will last until the court reaches a decision. If the court's decision is to make an order giving someone else the functions of the nearest relative, there is a further seven-day period which would allow a section 3 assessment form to be completed. Where (a), (b) or (e) are the grounds the court can specify a time limit for the order. If (c) or (d) obtain, or where no time limit is set under (a) or (b), the order lasts until the patient is no longer liable to detention or subject to guardianship or a CTO.

The important changes brought about by the Mental Health Act 2007 reforms are that the patient can now make an application and that the ground of 'unsuitability' is introduced. The ability for the patient to apply to the court was not as radical a response as had been considered at one stage. There were proposals to introduce a 'nominated person' to be chosen by the patient but these were dropped before the final version of the Bill went to parliament.

Where the patient or the AMHP makes application to displace on the new ground that *the nearest relative of the patient is otherwise not a suitable person to act as such* the question will arise as to what would amount to unsuitability. It will be for the court to decide in the final analysis. Even if the AMHP does not make the application it may be that the court will ask their opinion. The Code (at para. 8.13) gives advice on factors that might lead an AMHP to consider that a nearest relative is unsuitable to act as such:

> . . . *any reason to think that the patient has suffered, or is suspected to have suffered, abuse at the hands of the nearest relative (or someone with whom the nearest relative is in a relationship), or is at risk of suffering such abuse;*

> *any evidence that the patient is afraid of the nearest relative or seriously distressed by the possibility of the nearest relative being involved in their life or their care; and*

> *a situation where the patient and nearest relative are unknown to each other, there is only a distant relationship between them, or their relationship has broken down irretrievably.*

Whatever the grounds might be for applying to the county court for the appointment of a nearest relative an AMHP needs to plan ahead with regard to who might take the role on. Paragraph 8.18 of the Code states:

> *When applying to displace a nearest relative, AMHPs should nominate someone to become the acting nearest relative in the event that the application is successful. Wherever practicable, they should first consult the patient about the patient's own preferences and any concerns they have about the person the AMHP proposes to nominate. AMHPs should also seek the agreement of the proposed nominee prior to an application being made, although this is not a legal requirement.*

The AMHP's local authority should provide help and guidance on the issue of who should be nominated. It will rarely make sense for this person to be the AMHP because of the potential conflict in roles. The court will need evidence that the nominated person is willing to take on the function.

Rights and functions of the nearest relative

The nearest relative is able to be the applicant

The nearest relative is able to be the applicant for detentions in hospital under sections 2, 3, and 4 and for guardianship under section 7. Paragraph 4.28 of the Code of Practice states:

> *An application for detention may be made by an AMHP or the patient's nearest relative. An AMHP is usually a more appropriate applicant than a patient's nearest relative, given an AMHP's professional training and knowledge of the legislation and local resources, together with the potential adverse effect that an application by the nearest relative might have on their relationship with the patient.*

Then at para 4.30 there is a further statement:

> *Doctors who are approached directly by a nearest relative about making an application should advise the nearest relative that it is preferable for an AMHP to consider the need for a patient to be admitted under the Act and for the AMHP to make any consequent application. Doctors should also advise the nearest relative of their right to require a local social services authority (LSSA) to arrange for an AMHP to consider the patient's case. Doctors should never advise a nearest relative to make an application themselves in order to avoid involving an AMHP in an assessment.*

The number of nearest relative applications has fallen to such a low figure that statistics are no longer kept by the Department of Health.

Where the nearest relative is the applicant

Where the nearest relative makes an application for detention section 14 requires an AMHP to provide a social circumstances report to the hospital. Like the previous Code of Practice the revised version still recommends that AMHPs provide assistance with conveyance where the nearest relative is the applicant but the advice is given in a more guarded way. Paragraph 11.15 states:

> *If the nearest relative is the applicant, any AMHP and other professionals involved in the assessment of the patient should give advice and assistance. But they should not assist in a patient's detention unless they believe it is justified and lawful*

If the AMHP had earlier refused to make an application, their report would no doubt include an account of the reasons for this. Experience suggests that in most circumstances hospitals would not wish to admit a patient where an AMHP had made a decision not to apply, unless the circumstances had changed. The Code, however, still gives the following advice at para. 4.79:

An AMHP should, when informing the nearest relative that they do not intend to make an application, advise the nearest relative of their right to do so instead. If the nearest relative wishes to pursue this, the AMHP should suggest that they consult with the doctors involved in the assessment to see if they would be prepared to provide recommendations anyway.

Depending on the reasons for the AMHP declining to make an application this advice might be seen as rather contentious and in some circumstances, e.g. based on human rights reasons, the AMHP may consider that they have cogent reasons for departing from the Code of Practice.

Section 11(3) requires the AMHP to 'take such steps as are practicable' to inform the nearest relative

Section 11(3) requires the AMHP to *take such steps as are practicable* to inform the nearest relative *before or within a reasonable time after an application for the admission of a patient for assessment* that an application is being, or has been, made and of their rights to discharge a patient under section 23. If they choose to exercise this power, the nearest relative must give the hospital managers 72 hours' written notice of their intention. It would be advisable for the AMHP to explain that the responsible clinician (RC) may block this discharge if able to produce within the 72 hours *a report certifying that in the opinion of that officer, the patient, if discharged, would be likely to act in a manner dangerous to other persons or to himself.* (See Table 2.2 in Chapter 2 which illustrates these risk criteria.)

Where an AMHP is unable to meet the above requirement

Where an AMHP is unable to meet the above requirement to notify the nearest relative before an admission for assessment (under section 2) they should ensure that they persist with efforts to contact the nearest relative after an admission because the Act is worded as follows at section 11(3):

Before or within a reasonable time after an application for the admission of a patient for assessment is made by an approved mental health professional, that professional shall take such steps as are practicable to inform the person (if any) appearing to be the nearest relative of the patient that the application is to be or has been made and of the power of the nearest relative under section 23(2)(a) below.

Strangely there is no statutory duty to follow up a section 3 application in the same way and there is no longer a reference in the Code of Practice to this issue. It would therefore be left to the judgment of the AMHP whether to pursue this issue, especially in cases where, after admission, the patient has asked the hospital not to contact the nearest relative.

The right to object

The AMHP must not make an application for the detention of a patient under section 3 or for guardianship under section 7 if the nearest relative objects. Under the provisions of section 11(4) the AMHP must consult with the nearest relative before making such an application unless it appears to them that in the circumstances such consultation is not reasonably practicable or would involve unreasonable delay. 'Not reasonably practicable' would include cases where the nearest relative was not capable of acting as such because of mental disorder or other illness (see also the discussion on Article 8 above).

Where a nearest relative is consulted para. 4.64 of the Code states that the AMHP should, where possible:

- *ascertain the nearest relative's views about both the patient's needs and the nearest relative's own needs in relation to the patient;*
- *inform the nearest relative of the reasons for considering an application for detention and what the effects of such an application would be; and*
- *inform the nearest relative of their role and rights under the Act.*

The right to discharge the patient

The power of the nearest relative to discharge a patient from detention by way of section 23 is an intriguing piece of law which Bartlett and Sandland (2007, p21) use as an example of history's impact on current law. They state that it:

> . . . originates in the nineteenth-century statutes. If the confinement was in the private sector, the relative was responsible for paying the patient's upkeep, and therefore was perceived to have the right to demand the release of the patient, to limit their own financial exposure. If instead the patient was confined in a county asylum, the right to order release was conditional on an undertaking by the person ordering the release that the individual would no longer be chargeable on the poor law. The right to release was thus a way to enforce public economy in care provision, and to limit the shame of the family at receiving poor relief.

Perhaps a more thorough review of the Act might have led to a more logical overhaul of the role of the nearest relative under the Mental Health Act.

The power of discharge from guardianship is immediate (i.e. no 72-hour notice is required) and the RC has no barring powers. The new power for the nearest relative to discharge a patient from a community treatment order requires 72 hours' notice and, as with discharge from detention, the RC can bar this if they think the patient is likely to be dangerous to themselves or others.

Where the nearest relative chooses to exercise their power of discharge from hospital there is no longer a statutory form which can be used. Instead para. 29.23 of the Code states:

Hospital managers should offer nearest relatives any help they require, such as providing them with a standard letter to complete. [Figure 3.1] illustrates what a standard letter might look like.

To the managers of
[INSERT NAME AND ADDRESS OF HOSPITAL IN WHICH THE PATIENT IS DETAINED, OR (FOR A SUPERVISED COMMUNITY TREATMENT PATIENT) THE RESPONSIBLE HOSPITAL.]

Order for discharge under section 23 of the Mental Health Act 1983
My name is [GIVE YOUR NAME]

and my address is [GIVE YOUR ADDRESS]

[Complete A, B or C below]

A. To the best of my knowledge and belief, I am the nearest relative (within the meaning of the Mental Health Act 1983) of [NAME OF PATIENT].

OR
B. I have been authorised to exercise the functions of the nearest relative of [NAME OF PATIENT]

by the county court.

OR
C. I have been authorised to exercise the functions of the nearest relative of [NAME OF PATIENT]

by that person's nearest relative.

I give you notice of my intention to discharge the person named above, and I order their discharge from [SAY WHEN YOU WANT THE PATIENT DISCHARGED FROM DETENTION OR SUPERVISED COMMUNITY TREATMENT].

[Please note: you must leave at least 72 hours between when the hospital managers get this letter and when you want the patient discharged.]

Signed

Date

Figure 3.1 Illustrative standard letter for nearest relatives to use to discharge patients

The right to an assessment

Under section 13(4) it is:

> ... the duty of a local social services authority, if so required by the nearest relative of a patient residing in their area, to make arrangements under subsection (1) above for an approved mental health professional to consider the patient's case with a view to making an application for his admission to hospital; and if in any such case that professional decides not to make an application he shall inform the nearest relative of his reasons in writing.

The phrase 'as soon as practicable' was removed from the previous version of this section in terms of requiring the local authority to direct an AMHP to consider the case but it is hard to see this effectively reducing the pressure to make an assessment. It would be sensible for each case to be passed to an AMHP immediately and they would then consider how best to respond. Jones (2008, p102) states that this duty:

> ... does not necessarily mean that the AMHP undertakes an assessment of the patient or even interviews the patient. The extent and nature of the inquiries made by the AMHP would depend upon the knowledge that the local mental health service has about the patient. If the patient has been the subject of a recent mental health assessment, the AMHP's obligation would be confined to identifying whether there has been a change in the patient's situation that would justify a reassessment.

In other cases further inquiries would be needed such as contacting the patient's GP and, if at any stage a decision is made not to proceed with an application, the AMHP would need to write to the nearest relative. As the Code states at para. 4.80:

> Such a letter should contain, as far as possible, sufficient details to enable the nearest relative to understand the decision while at the same time preserving the patient's right to confidentiality.

The Code no longer indicates that authorities should issue AMHPs with guidance on what would constitute such a request from a nearest relative and whether they should include referrals routed via GPs or other professionals. This is an unfortunate omission and such guidance would certainly be helpful as referrals from nearest relatives will rarely make an explicit reference to section 13(4). Jones (2008, p101) submits the view that:

> If a nearest relative indicates concern about the patient by saying, for example, that the patient 'ought to be in hospital' or that 'something ought to be done' about the patient, the nearest relative should be informed of his power under this subsection and asked whether he or she wishes to exercise it.

Yeates (2005) has argued from a nearest relative perspective that she is very much in favour of the section 13(4) right and would use it in preference to seeking to be the applicant. In the lead up to the law reform Yeates also argued for the retention of the nearest relative function rather than the proposed 'nominated person' as she was concerned about close blood relatives being excluded from Mental Health Act matters. The late change in the government's plans met her preference while giving the patient the right to seek to displace a NR if they can show that they are 'unsuitable'.

Information from hospital managers

Unless the patient objects, or the nearest relative requests otherwise, the hospital managers have a duty under section 132 to give information to the nearest relative of a detained patient. This will cover information on the relevant section, tribunal rights, consent to treatment information etc. Section 132A requires similar information to be given regarding community patients.

Notice of discharge

Section 133 requires hospitals to give the nearest relative seven days' notice of the intended discharge of a patient from detention unless the patient or nearest relative has asked for this information not to be given, or unless it was the nearest relative who ordered the discharge. This duty would include information on those patients being discharged onto section 17A.

This requirement appears to be a much-ignored part of the Act which adds fuel to the fire of some relatives' arguments that they are not kept properly informed.

Patients on CTOs are also covered in that this section has been extended to include a duty on the responsible hospital to give seven days' notice where there is an intention to discharge a patient from the order.

Responsible clinicians in particular need to be made aware of this duty.

Quick route to the nearest relative

(Table 3.1 is for use with any complicated cases. This could be expanded or included within other documentation.)

1 *Insert brief details* of any of the following who are ordinarily resident in the UK, Channel Islands or Isle of Man (assuming the patient is ordinarily so resident; if not, the nearest relative may be someone who is, similarly, not so resident). *Ensure that anyone who qualifies for the list below, and who is living with or caring for the patient, is included.* In compiling the list, include half-blood relationships, treat illegitimate children as the legitimate children of their mothers, and do not include in-law relationships.

Table 3.1. Quick route to the nearest relative

Relationship (where there is more than one person in a category underline the eldest	Name and contact address or telephone number where this might be useful	One tick for each person in category	Tick if 18 or over. Insert age if under 18	Tick if living with or caring** for patient at point of assessment or at time of admission to hospital/ guardianship
Husband, wife or civil partner* Include anyone who has lived as if husband, wife or civil partner for last six months or more				
Son or daughter				
Father or mother				
Brother or sister				
Grandparent				
Grandchild				
Uncle or aunt				
Nephew or niece				
Five-year rule Anyone with whom patient has ordinarily resided for five years or more				

* Unless permanently separated by agreement or court order or where a partner has deserted the other.
** 'Caring for' is a matter of AMHP judgment but should usually be substantial and sustained.

2   If only one person is ticked in both of the final two columns they are the nearest relative.

3   Rank in order of priority. If more than one person is ticked under (2) above, the nearest relative is the highest of those listed. If no one was so ticked, the ranking applies to everyone on the list. If there is more than one person in a category, whole-blood relatives are preferred to half-blood, and elder is preferred to younger.

Suggested documentation for Regulation 24

To use this form you need to be sure (a) that the first person named is indeed the nearest relative, and (b) that they are not incapable of acting as such through reasons of mental disorder or other illness. (See page 59 for the form).

Carers' legislation (Carers (Recognition and Services) Act 1995)

Introduction

This legislation began as a Private Member's Bill. It received government support at its second reading but was significantly amended at Committee stage. Its sponsor, Mr Malcolm Wicks MP, described its purpose as follows:

> It is crucial to ensure that local authorities take proper account of carers' circumstances when carrying out an assessment of the need for community care services of the person being cared for. (Hansard, 1995, HC Vol 258, col 430)

Based on the general household survey, Wicks considered that there were something in the region of 6.8 million carers in Britain. An estimated 1.5 million carers provide care for 20 hours a week or more.

The Act was amended by the Carers and Disabled Children Act 2000 and the Carers (Equal Opportunities) Act 2004.

The main provisions of the Act

Section 1 is the key provision for England and Wales and the first part is set out below.

> ***Assessment of ability of carers to provide care: England and Wales.***
>
> 1.   *(1) Subject to subsection (3) below, in any case where –*
>   - (a) *a local authority carries out an assessment under section 47(1)(a) of the National Health Service and Community Care Act 1990 of the needs of a person ('the relevant person') for community care services, and*
>   - (b) *an individual ('the carer') provides or intends to provide a substantial amount of care on a regular basis for the relevant person,*
>   *the carer may request the local authority, before they make their decision as to whether the needs of the relevant person call for the provision of any services, to carry out an assessment of his ability to provide and to continue to provide care for the relevant person, and if he makes such a request, the local authority shall carry out such an assessment and shall take into account the results of that assessment in making that decision.*

Letter from the Nearest Relative under the Mental Health Act 1983 delegating the functions to another person under Regulation 24 of the Mental Health (Hospital, Guardianship and Treatment) (England) Regulations 2008.

I (full name) ....

of (address) ....

....

(telephone no.)

being the nearest relative of..

as (state relationship to patient)..

within the meaning of the Mental Health Act 1983, hereby authorise

(full name) ....

of (address) ....

(telephone no.)

(state relationship to patient) ....

to perform in respect of the patient the functions conferred upon the nearest relative by Part 2 and section 66 of the Mental Health Act 1983.

This authorisation is to last: ☐ until further notice, or

(please tick one box) ☐ until.......... (specify date), or

☐ until the end of the current detention/ guardianship/CTO

I understand that I may revoke this authority at any time (despite whichever box I have ticked above) by giving notice in writing to the person authorised and

(a) in the case of hospital detention or Community Treatment Order, the hospital managers, or

(b) in the case of guardianship, the local authority and private guardian (if any).

I agree to a copy of this letter being passed to the person authorised, the hospital managers and, in the case of guardianship, the local authority and private guardian, to act as a notice of my delegation of nearest relative functions under the Mental Health Act 1983 and associated Regulations.

(To be signed by donor):

Signed .... Date................................

I acknowledge receipt of this authorisation to exercise the functions of nearest relative.

I understand that this authorisation takes effect on my receipt of this document.

(to be signed and dated by recipient):

Signed .... Date................................

Figure 3.2 Suggested documentation for Regulation 24

(2) Subject to subsection (3) below, in any case where –

    (a) a local authority assess the needs of a disabled child for the purposes of Part III of the Children Act 1989 or section 2 of the Chronically Sick and Disabled Persons Act 1970, and

    (b) an individual ('the carer') provides or intends to provide a substantial amount of care on a regular basis for the disabled child,

the carer may request the local authority, before they make their decision as to whether the needs of the disabled child call for the provision of any services, to carry out an assessment of his ability to provide and to continue to provide care for the disabled child, and if he makes such a request, the local authority shall carry out such an assessment and shall take into account the results of that assessment in writing that decision . . .

Notes on the Act

- 'Assessment' would include reassessment.

- The phrase 'intends to provide' may have particular relevance when assessing the situation before someone is discharged from hospital.

- 'Substantial amount of care on a regular basis' can be seen as linking with section 26(4) of the Mental Health Act 1983 in some circumstances (e.g. the issue of a carer taking priority over other relatives when trying to determine who is the nearest relative). In *Re D* (mental patient: habeas corpus) (Court of Appeal, 9 May 2000) the judge stated:

  The words 'cared for' were not defined in the Act but they were clear everyday words set in the context where a social worker had to act in a common-sense manner in a very difficult situation. The [original] judge had been correct in declining to supplement the language of the section. The amount of care provided was more than minimal even though it fell short of long-term care of the kind envisaged in s1(b) of the Carers (Recognition and Services) Act 1995.

- Paid carers or those acting for voluntary organisations are excluded from these provisions.

- Children are included and may need to be encouraged to make requests so assessments of their ability to provide care are formally made.

Carers and Disabled Children Act 2000

This legislation allows local authorities to provide services and support directly to carers. This can include direct payments. A carer's own needs can now be directly assessed. The Act also introduced a short-term break voucher scheme designed to provide flexibility in the timing of carers' breaks. Any services to carers may be subject to a charge.

Section 2 of the Act requires a local authority to carry out an assessment of a person aged 16 or over who informally provides or intends to provide a substantial amount of care on a regular basis for someone aged 18 or over if that person asks the authority to assess their ability to do so.

Other relevant legislation

Chapter 9 looks at a range of other legislation which might be relevant. For example, section 8 of the Disabled Persons (Services, Consultation and Representation) Act 1986 requires the local authority to have regard to the ability of a carer to continue providing care for a disabled person ('disabled person' includes people with a mental disorder).

Schedule 8 of the NHS Act 1977 and section 111 of the Local Government Act 1972 enables social services departments to provide facilities such as information and carers' support groups without having to be asked for an assessment.

ACTIVITY 3.1

Sample questions on relatives and carers

1a *You are an AMHP and have determined the identity of a patient's nearest relative. You have decided an application under section 2 is appropriate. According to the Mental Health Act and the Code what should you do with regard to the nearest relative?*

1b *From an early stage the patient makes it clear that they object to you speaking to the nearest relative and that, if detained, they will block the hospital from making contact with the nearest relative. Why is the Human Rights Act 1998 relevant here?*

2a *Who can apply to the County Court for the appointment of a nearest relative?*

2b *What aspects of this area of law have been amended to be compliant with the European Convention on Human Rights?*

2c *What arguments might be put for or against seeking a nearest relative for someone who does not seem to have one at the point of assessing for a section 3 admission?*

3a *You are trying to determine who is a patient's nearest relative.*

Having made a list of relatives, what would be the significance of one or more of them living with the patient at the time of the admission to hospital?

3b *Give two examples of when this issue might cause a problem and how the AMHP could possibly help to resolve this?*

Multiple choice questions
(Answers in Appendix 9)

1 *Which of the following can make a written order to discharge a patient detained in hospital under Part 2 of the Act?*

ACTIVITY **3.1** *continued*

    (a) *The hospital managers* ☐
    (b) *The nearest relative* ☐
    (c) *Any relative* ☐
    (d) *An approved mental health professional* ☐
    (e) *The responsible clinician* ☐

2 *Which of these may apply to the County Court for the appointment of someone to act as nearest relative?*
    (a) *Any relative of the patient* ☐
    (b) *The hospital managers* ☐
    (c) *Any other person with whom the patient is residing* ☐
    (d) *The patient* ☐
    (e) *An approved clinician* ☐
    (f) *An approved mental health professional* ☐
    (g) *The responsible clinician* ☐

Chapter 4

The role of the Approved Mental Health Professional

AMHP functions under the MHA

The following list summarises the main functions of the AMHP as laid down the Mental Health Act 1983. This chapter will look at some of these functions in detail:

- deciding whether to make an application for compulsory admission to hospital for assessment or for treatment under Part 2 of the Act (s13);

- deciding whether to make an application for guardianship under section 7 of the Act (s13);

- informing or consulting with the nearest relative (NR) about an application (s11);

- conveying a patient to hospital (or a place of residence) on the basis of an application as above (s6);

- responding to a referral from an NR for an MHA assessment, and, if an application is not made, giving the reasons for this in writing to the NR (s13);

- providing a social circumstance report for the hospital for any patient detained on the basis of an application made by the NR (s14);

- confirming that a CTO should be made and agreeing to any conditions (s17A);

- agreeing to the extension of a CTO (s20A);

- agreeing to the revocation of a CTO (s17F);

- applying to the county court for the displacement of an existing nearest relative and/or the appointment of an acting nearest relative (s29);

- having the right to enter and inspect premises where a mentally disordered patient is living (s115);

- applying for a warrant to enter premises under section 135 to search for and remove a patient to a place of safety (s135);

- having the power to take a patient into custody and take them to the place they ought to be when they have gone absent without leave (AWOL) (s138);

- interviewing a patient arrested by the police on section 136;

- making a decision on whether a patient subject to section 136 should be moved from one place of safety to another.

Guiding principles

Section 118 requires a number of principles to be covered in the Code of Practice and these should govern the practice of AMHPs. Note that the principles are set out with different emphases in the Welsh Code. The mental health strategy document *Adult Mental Health Services for Wales* (Welsh Assembly 2001) established four underpinning principles to guide those involved in planning, commissioning, managing, working in, or using mental health services. They are: empowerment, equity, effectiveness and efficiency. The Welsh principles are grouped under these headings.

In the English Code the following headings are used to group the topics given in section 118 of the Act: purpose, least restriction, respect, participation and finally, effectiveness, efficiency and equity. The English Code then states:

Purpose principle
1.2 *Decisions under the Act must be taken with a view to minimising the undesirable effects of mental disorder, by maximising the safety and wellbeing (mental and physical) of patients, promoting their recovery and protecting other people from harm.*

Least restriction principle
1.3 *People taking action without a patient's consent must attempt to keep*

to a minimum the restrictions they impose on the patient's liberty, having regard to the purpose for which the restrictions are imposed.

Respect principle

1.4 *People taking decisions under the Act must recognise and respect the diverse needs, values and circumstances of each patient, including their race, religion, culture, gender, age, sexual orientation and any disability. They must consider the patient's views, wishes and feelings (whether expressed at the time or in advance), so far as they are reasonably ascertainable, and follow those wishes wherever practicable and consistent with the purpose of the decision. There must be no unlawful discrimination.*

Participation principle

1.5 *Patients must be given the opportunity to be involved, as far as is practicable in the circumstances, in planning, developing and reviewing their own treatment and care to help ensure that it is delivered in a way that is as appropriate and effective for them as possible. The involvement of carers, family members and other people who have an interest in the patient's welfare should be encouraged (unless there are particular reasons to the contrary) and their views taken seriously.*

Effectiveness, efficiency and equity principle

1.6 *People taking decisions under the Act must seek to use the resources available to them and to patients in the most effective, efficient and equitable way, to meet the needs of patients and achieve the purpose for which the decision was taken.*

In its advice on using the principles the Code states that all decisions should be lawful which would require compliance with the Human Rights Act 1998. This is of great importance (and was a statement notably missing from the first draft of the Code). AMHPs could depart from the Code if they had cogent reasons for doing so (see later discussion on the *von Brandenburg* case in Chapters 4 and 7 and the reference to the *Munjaz* case in Chapter 10). The European Convention on Human Rights would be of critical importance if this were to happen (see Appendix 2).

Assessment for possible compulsory admission or guardianship

The key professionals in assessing a person's need for possible compulsory admission to hospital, or for guardianship, are two doctors and an Approved Mental Health Professional. Although the nearest relative may apply for detention, the Code of Practice states at para. 4.28:

An AMHP is usually a more appropriate applicant than a patient's nearest relative, given an AMHP's professional training and knowledge of the legislation and local resources, together with the potential adverse effect that an application by the nearest relative might have on their relationship with the patient.

In practice, nearest relative applications are very rare.

The Mental Health Act 1983 sets out the criteria which must be satisfied before a person can be detained. These have already been considered in Chapter 2 of this guide. This chapter will consider the process of assessment and the guidance contained in the Code of Practice. Chapter 4 of the Code of Practice covers applications for detention. There are separate chapters on guardianship and community treatment orders.

Interpreters

There are a number of places where the Code refers to interpreters. Those occasions where this relates to the work of an AMHP are grouped together here for convenience. The first is a general statement from Chapter 2 of the Code (para. 2.5):

> *Where an interpreter is needed, every effort should be made to identify who is appropriate to the patient, given the patient's gender, religion, language, dialect, cultural background and age. The patient's relatives and friends should only exceptionally be used as intermediaries or interpreters. Interpreters (both professional and non-professional) must respect the confidentiality of any personal information they learn about the patient through their involvement.*

A Mental Health Act assessment provides a thorough test of a worker's skills even in their first language. It would be wise for all AMHPs to be sure that they have developed skills for working with interpreters. Paragraph 4.41 states:

> *Given the importance of good communication, it is essential that those professionals who assess patients are able to communicate with the patient effectively and reliably to prevent potential misunderstandings. AMHPs should establish, as far as possible, whether patients have particular communication needs or difficulties and take steps to meet them, for example by arranging a signer or a professional interpreter. AMHPs should also be in a position, where appropriate, to supply suitable equipment to make communication easier with patients who have impaired hearing, but who do not have their own hearing aid.*

In the paragraphs on working with people who are deaf the Code indicates that the AMHP would normally be expected to be the one to book the interpreters. At para. 4.107:

> *Unless different arrangements have been agreed locally, the AMHP involved in the assessment should be responsible for booking and using registered qualified interpreters with expertise in mental health interpreting, bearing in mind that the interpretation of thought-disordered language requires particular expertise. Relay interpreters (interpreters who relay British Sign Language (BSL) to hands-on BSL or visual frame signing or close signing) may be necessary, such as when the deaf person has a visual impairment, does not use BSL to sign or has minimal language skills or a learning disability.*

In para. 4.108 the point made in Chapter 2 is developed:

Reliance on unqualified interpreters or health professionals with only limited signing skills should be avoided. Family members may (subject to the normal considerations about patient confidentiality) occasionally be able to assist a professional interpreter in understanding a patient's idiosyncratic use of language. However, family members should not be relied upon in place of a professional interpreter, even if the patient is willing for them to be involved.

One final piece of information which might be helpful for AMHPs to know is given in para. 32.36 of the Code, in the chapter on Mental Health Tribunals:

Where necessary, the Tribunal will provide, free of charge, interpretation services for patients and their representatives. Where patients or their representatives are hard of hearing or have speech difficulties (or both), the Tribunal will provide such services of sign language interpreters, lip speakers or palantypists as may be necessary. Hospital managers and LSSAs should inform the Tribunal well in advance if they think any such services might be necessary.

Informing or consulting the nearest relative

The AMHP's responsibilities towards the nearest relative are dealt with in some detail in Chapter 3. Parapraphs 4.57–4.59 of the Code summarise the main requirements:

When AMHPs make an application for detention under section 2, they must take such steps as are practicable to inform the nearest relative that the application is to be (or has been) made and of the nearest relative's power to discharge the patient.

Before making an application for detention under section 3, AMHPs must consult the nearest relative, unless it is not reasonably practicable or would involve unreasonable delay.

Circumstances in which the nearest relative need not be informed or consulted include those where:
- *it is not practicable for the AMHP to obtain sufficient information to establish the identity or location of the nearest relative, or where to do so would require an excessive amount of investigation involving unreasonable delay; and*
- *consultation is not possible because of the nearest relative's own health or mental incapacity.*

The consultation with the nearest relative can take place before the two medical recommendations are obtained (*Re Whitbread*, 1997).

AMHPs should not assume that the person listed as nearest relative on a previous detention is still necessarily in that role. The Code of Practice has never covered this issue but the Reference Guide gives an opinion when it states at para. 33.19:

> *The identity of the nearest relative will change if the current nearest relative dies or if (for example) the nearest relative is a spouse or civil partner and the marriage or civil partnership ends.*

And then at para. 33.20:

> *It may also change for some other reason not directly involving the existing nearest relative, e.g. the patient marries, or another relative reaches the age of 18, or comes to live in the UK, and therefore becomes eligible to be the nearest relative.*

The appendices to this Guide provide AMHPs with checklists for assessments under sections 2, 3, 4 and 7 to ensure that all necessary actions have been taken. These should be read in conjunction with any local procedures.

AMHP responsibility for actions and section 139

There are a number of myths concerning the AMHP's position in terms of responsibility for actions that they take under the Mental Health Act. For example, some people seem to consider that AMHPs are acting as free agents and that their approving authorities have no responsibility for their actions. While it would be true to say that the AMHP has a personal duty to make the decision on whether to apply for detention, the local authority still carries some responsibility and, of course, decides whether an AMHP is currently competent to perform as such.

Section 139 of the Mental Health Act is of importance when considering the liability of an AMHP for actions taken in relation to the Act. It states at section 139(1):

> *No person shall be liable, whether on the grounds of want of jurisdiction or any other ground, to any civil or criminal proceedings to which he would have been liable apart from this section in respect of any act purporting to be done in pursuance of this Act or any regulations or rules made under this Act unless the act was done in bad faith or without reasonable care.*

It then sets out the procedure which must be followed before proceedings can be taken. Section 139(2):

> *No civil proceedings shall be brought against any person in any court in respect of any such act without the leave of the High Court; and no criminal proceedings shall be brought against any person in any court in respect of any such act except by or with the consent of the Director of Public Prosecutions.*

This does not prevent the patient from applying to the High Court for a writ of habeas corpus so that the lawfulness of the detention can be tested.

Whether a person has acted in bad faith or without reasonable care is a question of fact with the burden of proof lying with the applicant. The relevance of the Code of

Practice to any action against an AMHP can be seen in paragraph v of the introduction that states:

> While the Act does not impose a legal duty to comply with the Code, the people listed above to whom the Code is addressed must have regard to the Code. The reasons for any departure should be recorded. Departures from the Code could give rise to legal challenge, and a court, in reviewing any departure from the Code, will scrutinise the reasons for the departure to ensure that there is sufficiently convincing justification in the circumstances.

The ability of the AMHP to make an independent decision was seen as important by parliament. Jones (2008, p97) comments on this when he considers the AMHP's position when deciding whether or not to make an application as per section 13 of the Act:

> The responsibilities under this provision are placed on the Approved Mental Health Professional and not on the employing authority (Nottingham City Council v Unison [2004] EWHC893, para 18). An AMHP is therefore personally liable for his or her actions when deciding whether to make an application in respect of the patient. He or she should exercise his or her own judgement, based upon social and medical evidence, and not act at the behest of his or her employer, medical practitioners or other persons who might be involved with the patient's care ... The judgement to be exercised applies not only to the decision on whether an application should be made in respect of the patient; it also applies to the question of what section of this Act to invoke.

Hoggett (1996, p250) took a critical stance on section 139 when she stated that:

> There is no necessary connection between vexatiousness and the use of compulsion under the Mental Health Act. There is no evidence that the floodgates would open if section 139 were entirely repealed. There is more evidence, from a series of reports and investigations, that mental patients are in a peculiarly powerless position which merits, if anything, extra safeguards rather than the removal of those available to everyone else.

In terms of good practice which would be consistent with acting in good faith and reasonable care, it could be suggested that an AMHP needs to be 'angst-ridden but strangely decisive', i.e. concerned to respect a person's right to freedom, but prepared to intervene decisively where the level of mental disorder and risk requires it. They need to show an awareness of relevant law and procedures and, in particular, as public authorities, a good grasp of, and commitment to, the European Convention on Human Rights.

The importance of the AMHP role was emphasised by Lord Bingham in the House of Lords judgment on the *von Brandenburg* case when he said:

> I would, secondly, resist the lumping together of the ASW and the recommending doctor or doctors as 'the mental health professionals'. It is the ASW who makes the application, not the doctors.

The question being raised was:

> When a mental health review tribunal has ordered the discharge of a patient, is it lawful to readmit him under section 2 or section 3 of the [Mental Health Act 1983] where it cannot be demonstrated that there has been a relevant change of circumstances?

The outcome was essentially that an AMHP must not fly in the face of a tribunal decision of which they are aware:

> An ASW may not lawfully apply for the admission of a patient whose discharge has been ordered by the decision of a mental health review tribunal of which the ASW is aware unless the ASW has formed the reasonable and bona fide opinion that he has information not known to the tribunal which puts a significantly different complexion on the case as compared with that which was before the tribunal. (R v East London and the City Mental Health NHS Trust and another (Respondents) ex parte von Brandenburg (2003))

Management and supervision of AMHPs

This part of the chapter gives details of some key issues involved in the management and supervision of AMHPs. It places the role of the approved mental health professional in context and clarifies which tasks can be performed only by an AMHP. It also lists tasks that they are likely to be involved in, but which can also be performed by other staff.

Statutory basis for employing AMHPs

Section 114 of the Mental Health Act 1983 states the following:

> (1) A local social services authority may approve a person to act as an approved mental health professional for the purposes of this Act.
> (2) But a local social services authority may not approve a registered medical practitioner to act as an approved mental health professional.
> (3) Before approving a person under subsection (1) above, a local social service authority shall be satisfied that he has appropriate competence in dealing with persons who are suffering from mental disorder.

AMHPs replace ASWs (approved social workers) who came into existence in 1984. The functions of the AMHP remain essentially unchanged from those of the ASW other than the new roles in relation to community treatment orders. ASWs were social workers who had undertaken additional training to equip them to perform specific tasks under the Act. In addition to social workers registered with the General Social Care Council (GSCC) or Care Council for Wales (CCfW) the following professional groups are able to train to become AMHPs:

- nurses (who need to be first-level mental health or learning disability nurses);
- registered occupational therapists; and

- chartered psychologists (who need to hold a relevant practising certificate issued by the British Psychological Society).

AMHPs need to be approved by an LSSA even if they are employed by an NHS Trust or other body. As we noted earlier the LSSA cannot direct the decisions of an AMHP, who must reach their own independent judgment.

Although approved by one LSSA, an AMHP may act on behalf of a number of English local authorities. However, note that to act as an AMHP on behalf of a Welsh LSSA an AMHP must be separately approved in Wales.

Training courses for AMHPs are delivered by accredited universities (approved by the GSCC or the CCfW). Successful candidates may then be approved by a local authority for a period of five years before they are required to go through a re-approval process.

ASWs automatically became AMHPs in November 2008. Most completed short courses to learn the implications of the changes brought about by the MHA 2007.

If an AMHP exercises their power under section 115 to enter and inspect premises where a mentally disordered patient is living they are required to have some form of identification. Ideally, this should be a sealed ID card and include: photograph, name, approving local authority details and contact number, date of appointment as AMHP and/or expiry date, signature of relevant senior officer. Some authorities find it helpful to quote section 115 rights of access on the reverse.

Management, consultation and supervision

Apart from legal advice, which should be available from the approving local authority, AMHPs need management, consultation and supervision which is specific to their role.

As far as legal advice is concerned, the National Institute for Mental Health in England (NIMHE 2008, p14) has suggested that local authorities

> *review the legal advice service that is available to AMHPs (and other professionals) and how it can be organised across organisations. A clear pathway should be agreed locally, ensuring that the AMHP can access impartial advice in situations where there are conflicting views or opinions between different professionals and organisations.*

The issue of management, consultation and supervision which is specific to the role of the AMHP is dealt with in the same document (NIMHE 2008, p13):

> *All organisations employing AMHPs (and the LSSAs on whose behalf they act, if different) will wish to consider the following issues in supporting them in their role – that the AMHP has access to:*
> - *professional supervision from an approved and experienced AMHP;*
> - *information about AMHP practice in general;*
> - *advice on any problems the AMHP might encounter (for example regarding access to beds, the police, or ambulance services); and*

- advice and support on how to work to resolve problems with partner organisations.

Employers should also act in circumstances where an AMHP may require further training, mentoring or support, for example after an unusual or controversial situation.

The importance of maintaining the AMHP's independence became clearer to the government in the latter stages of the mental health reform process. Guidance which has now been issued places considerable emphasis on this as, for example, in the passage below from NIMHE (2008, p14).

Even before the changes brought about by the Act, with the formation of partnership arrangements in mental health services, some LSSAs do not currently employ any senior managers with responsibility for, or experience and knowledge of, the ASW (now AMHP) role.

To support the independence of the AMHP role, and to ensure that AMHPs are appropriately supported in undertaking their duties, LSSAs may wish to consider having at least one directly employed senior manager or lead officer who has direct knowledge and experience of the AMHP role or service. This would be one way of helping to ensure that AMHPs have:
- *access to advice and support independent of the hospital to which the patient may be admitted or from which they may receive treatment;*
- *a senior level 'champion' to highlight any problems identified by the AMHP, and to protect the role's independence.*

The recent integration of health and social services in the mental health field has led to the need for some guidance on joint working NIMHE (2008, p14):

LSSAs and NHS Trusts who co-operate to provide an AMHP service will need to consider and agree the following issues so that they are explicitly covered by their s75 and other agreements:
- *details of how the daytime service will be configured, for example central AMHP service versus team-based AMHP service;*
- *details of supervision and support arrangements, including access to senior support from the LSSA where serious issues arise, such as those related to conflicts of interest;*
- *agreement to release staff for initial and refresher AMHP training;*
- *agreement on governance issues ... including:*
  - *the collection of statistics on AMHP activity (whose responsibility it is to collect each set of information, and when and how this data will be reported, used and reviewed)*
  - *regular reporting to management, and how and in what circumstances to share feedback on issues of concern regarding services as a whole or on poor performance by an individual AMHP.*

AMHPs and their employers and supervisors should watch the Department of Health website for news of any further advice or guidance on this area.

Policy requirements from the Code of Practice

There are a number of points in the Code of Practice where local authorities are required to have a policy. Those managing AMHPs may find the following exercise helpful. Table 4.1 identifies the topic and paragraph number of references in the Code to the need for some sort of policy. *Tick if there is already a policy and note the date it was last amended* (if available).

Table 4.1. Policy requirements form the code of practice

Para.	Topic	Policy? tick/ date	Comments on existing policy or key points if new policy required
4.46	**Police assistance.** For people undertaking MHA assessments		
8.16	**Displacement of nearest relatives.** Advice to AMHPs on whether to make an application to county court.		
8.19	**Displacement of nearest relatives.** Advice to AMHPs on who to nominate when applying to court.		
8.1	**Section 135 warrants.** Guidance on how and when to apply.		
10.16	**Sections 135 and 136.** Agreed local policy needed covering all aspects.		
11.9–12	**Conveyance of patients.** Joint policy and procedure with ambulance and police.		
13.15	**Receipt of guardianship applications.** Checklist for responsible staff.		
22.12	**Guardianship patients who go AWOL.** Policy needed on action to take.		
26.15	**Guardianship** Policy needed on all aspects.		

Tasks for an AMHP involved in an MHA assessment

The following task can form the basis of an exercise near the beginning of an AMHP course.

Task: *Identify the legal basis of the requirements listed in Table 4.2 and discuss their meaning. Note section numbers (from Act) or paragraphs (Code of Practice or Reference Guide).*

Table 4.2. Tasks for an AMHP involved in an MHA assessment

No.	AMHP task – identify words within quotation marks	Source (Act, Code or Guide)
1	To interview the patient in a 'suitable manner'.	
2	To have 'regard to any wishes expressed by relatives'.	
3	Consider all the circumstances of the case including: 'the past history of the patient's mental disorder, the patient's present condition and the social, familial and personal factors bearing on it, as well as the other options available for supporting the patient, the wishes of the patient and the patient's relatives and carers, and the opinion of other professionals involved in caring for the patient'.	
4	'Because a proper assessment cannot be carried out without considering alternative means of providing care and treatment, AMHPs and doctors should, as far as possible in the circumstances, identify and liaise with services which may potentially be able to provide alternatives to admission to hospital. That could include crisis and home treatment teams.'	
5	Decide whether 'detention in a hospital is in all the circumstances of the case the most appropriate way of providing the care and medical treatment of which the patient stands in need'.	
6	Ensure that it is 'necessary or proper for the application to be made by' the AMHP.	
7	'Take such steps as are practicable' to inform the nearest relative that an application for section 2 has been, or is about to be, made and inform them of their powers of discharge under section 23.	
8	If considering section 3 consult NR to ensure that they do not object to the application being made unless 'such consultation is not reasonably practicable or would involve unreasonable delay'.	
9	'Take the patient and convey him to hospital' if an application is made by the AMHP.	
10	'If they do not consult or inform the nearest relative, AMHPs should record their reasons. Consultation must not be avoided purely because it is thought that the nearest relative might object to the application.'	
11	If the patient is admitted, the AMHP should make sure that any 'moveable property' of the patient is protected.	
12	If the nearest relative applies for section 2 or 3, an AMHP must 'interview the patient and provide the [hospital] managers with a report on his social circumstances'.	
13	If required to do so by the nearest relative, the SSD must direct an AMHP 'to consider the case with a view to making an application for his admission to hospital'. If AMHP does not apply he must give his reasons in writing to NR.	
14	'… provide an outline report for the hospital at the time the patient is first admitted or detained, giving reasons for the application and details of any practical matters about the patient's circumstances which the hospital should know.'	

ACTIVITY 4.1

Sample questions on the role of the AMHP

1a What are the main aspects of law concerned with the appointment of AMHPs?

1b What legal protection does an AMHP have in carrying out duties under the Mental Health Act 1983?

1c Identify a couple of possible dilemmas for an AMHP working in a Home Treatment Team?

2a What are the main responsibilities of an AMHP, in terms of interviewing and assessing a patient in their area with a view to a possible section 3 admission?

2b Take any one of these responsibilities and identify potential difficulties for an AMHP

Multiple choice questions
(Answers in Appendix 9)

1 Which of the following may apply to admit a patient to hospital in an emergency under section 4?
(a) Any relative ☐
(b) The nearest relative ☐
(c) An approved mental health professional ☐

2 An applicant who conveys a patient to hospital has all the powers that police officers have when they take someone into custody.
(a) True ☐
(b) False ☐

Chapter 5

Patients concerned in criminal proceedings

BECOMING AN APPROVED MENTAL HEALTH PROFESSIONAL

This chapter should help candidates to achieve the following competences:
Application of knowledge: the legal and policy framework
Applied knowledge of:

2a(i) *mental health legislation, related codes of practice, national and local policy guidance;*

2a(ii) *relevant parts of other legislation, codes of practice, national and local policy and guidance, in particular the Children Acts 1989 and 2004, the Human Rights Act and the Mental Capacity Act.*

Patients involved with the police and the courts

Introduction

Some patients are detained in hospital or received into guardianship as a result of a court order. Part 3 of the Mental Health Act 1983 covers these situations as well as those where the Secretary of State can direct people to be transferred from prisons into hospital. There were minimal amendments made by the 2007 Act reforms. This contrasted with the major changes which occurred under the 1983 Act. This contained significant changes from the position under the 1959 Act. Several of these gave effect to recommendations which were made in the Butler Report of 1975 (DHSS 1975b). One of the report's main conclusions was that too many mentally abnormal offenders were being inappropriately placed in prison. Sections 35, 36 and 38 of the 1983 Act were all new attempts to tackle this problem. There was a delay in their implementation until 1984 when it was believed resources would be in place to cope with these new patients.

Table 5.1 provides a summary of the main sections noting their purpose, duration, whether there is access to Mental Health Tribunals and whether consent to treatment provisions apply. Section 136 is included at the end of the chapter because it involves the police and is sometimes used with offenders. There is further legislation, apart from the Mental Health Act, which affects patients who offend. This is included here in a brief summary of relevant law. AMHPs are not directly involved with Part 3 of the Act so this chapter just provides a brief overview.

Table 5.1. Part 3 patients: periods of detention and further information (consent to treatment, access to MH Tribunals)

Section number and purpose	Maximum duration	Can patient apply to MHT?	Can nearest relative apply to MHT?	Will there be an automatic MHT hearing?	*Do consent to treatment rules apply?
35 Remand to hospital for psychiatric report	**28 days** May be renewed by court for further 28 days to max. 12 weeks	No	There is no nearest relative	No	No
36 Remand to hospital for psychiatric treatment	**28 days** May be renewed by court for further 28 days to max. 12 weeks	No	There is no nearest relative	No	Yes
37 Guardian-ship order by court	**6 months** May be renewed for six months and then yearly	Within first six months and then in each period	Within first year and then yearly	No	No
37 Hospital order by court	**6 months** May be renewed for six months and then yearly	In second six months and then in each period	In second six months and then in each period	If one has not been held, the hospital managers refer to MHT every three years	Yes
37/41 Restriction order by court	**Variable**	In second six months and then yearly	There is no nearest relative	If one has not been held, Justice Secretary refers every three years	Yes
38 Interim hospital order by court	**12 weeks** May be renewed by 28 days at a time to max. one year	No	There is no nearest relative	No	Yes
45A Hospital and limited directions	**Without limit of time**	In second six months and then yearly	No	If one has not been held, the Justice Secretary refers to MHT every three years	Yes
47 Transfer to a hospital of a person serving prison sentence	**6 months** May be renewed for six months and then yearly	Within first six months and then in each period	No	If one has not been held, the hospital managers refer to MHT every three years	Yes
47/49 Transfer from prison plus restrictions	Restriction order expires on earliest prison release date	In second six months period after transfer and then yearly	There is no nearest relative	If one has not been held, the Home Secretary refers to MHT every three years	Yes
48 Transfer to hospital of other prisoners	**Variable**	Within first six months and then in each period	No	If one not has been held, the Justice Secretary refers to MHT every three years	Yes
48/49 Transfer from prison and restrictions	Restriction order expires on the earliest date of release from prison	In second six months period after transfer and then yearly	There is no nearest relative	If one has not been held, the Justice Secretary refers to MHT every three years	Yes
136 Police power in public places	**72 hours** Not renewable	No	No	No	No

* Where consent to treatment rules do not apply, a patient is in the same position as an informal patient and should not be treated without their consent except in an emergency under common law or where it is possible to rely on the Mental Capacity Act. Chapter 6 has fuller information on consent to treatment.
– under section 67 the Secretary of State for Health (or Welsh Minister) can refer section 37 patients to the MHT at any time;
– under section 71 the Justice Secretary can refer restricted patients to the MHT at any time;
Note also:
– conditionally discharged restricted patients may apply to the MHT after one year and then every two years but if the patient is recalled to hospital the Justice Secretary must refer to the MHT within one month.

There is a presumption in favour of remanding a person on bail rather than in custody. This could even include a condition of residence at a hospital while, for example, reports are prepared. In these circumstances, however, the patient would be informal and not subject to detention. Where a person might otherwise be remanded to prison, the Mental Health Act 1983 introduced two new powers (see next section).

Section 35: Remand to hospital for report on accused's mental condition

Subsection (3) allows an order to be made if:

(a) *the court is satisfied, on the written or oral evidence of a registered medical practitioner, that there is reason to suspect that the accused person is suffering from mental disorder; and*

(b) *the court is of the opinion that it would be impracticable for a report on his mental condition to be made if he were remanded on bail...*

There must also be evidence that a hospital bed would be available within seven days, beginning with the date of the remand. While waiting for a bed, the accused must be kept in a 'place of safety' which for the purposes of this section could be any police station, prison or remand centre, or any hospital willing to receive the patient.

The remand is for a maximum 20 days although the court may renew this for further periods of 28 days to a maximum of 12 weeks. Part 4 provisions on consent to treatment do not apply so the person should not be treated without their consent except in an emergency under common law or in situations where the MCA can be relied on. To overcome this, some psychiatrists have sought a section 3 detention to run alongside the section 35. Section 5 does not specifically rule this out and the Code of Practice at para. 33.30 states that it might be considered if there is a delay in getting to court. The use of section 36 might be more appropriate in most such cases.

Section 36: Remand of accused person to hospital for treatment

This may be used only by the Crown Court and is restricted to those cases where it would be an alternative to a remand in custody. It applies to people waiting for trial or sentence and requires the written or oral evidence of two doctors that the person is suffering from mental disorder of a nature or degree which makes it appropriate for him to be detained in a hospital for treatment. There also needs to be appropriate medical treatment available. The remand is for a maximum of 28 days although the court may renew this for further periods of 28 days to a maximum of 12 weeks. Part 4 provisions on consent to treatment apply. Again there must be evidence that a hospital bed would be available within seven days, beginning with the date of the remand. While waiting for a bed, the accused must be kept in a place of safety as defined above. It is possible that someone may have to wait for more than three months to appear in the Crown Court. In these circumstances, the general powers of the Secretary of State to transfer prisoners may apply.

Section 37: Hospital or guardianship order

Where an offender is convicted a hospital or guardianship order may be made by the Crown Court. A magistrates' court may also make an order, even if there has not been a conviction, if they are satisfied that the offender committed the act or made the omission in question. In either case the court needs to be satisfied on the evidence of two doctors that the patient is suffering from a mental disorder and that either:

(i) *the mental disorder from which the offender is suffering is of a nature or degree which makes it appropriate for him to be detained in a hospital for medical treatment and, appropriate medical treatment is available to him; or*

(ii) *in the case of an offender who has attained the age of 16 years, the mental disorder is of a nature or degree which warrants his reception into guardianship under this Act; and*

(iii) *the Court is of the opinion, having regard to all the circumstances including the nature of the offence and the character and antecedents of the offender, and to the other available methods of dealing with him, that the most suitable method of disposing of the case is by means of an order under this section.*

The order lasts for up to six months in the first instance. It may be renewed for a further six months and then for a year at a time. The effect of a hospital order is very similar to the person being subject to section 3. Part 4 applies for consent to treatment purposes. There must be evidence that a hospital bed would be available within 28 days, beginning with the date of the order. Guardianship orders are not made very often. An order can be made only if the proposed guardian agrees to it. If the patient absconds from the place they are required to live, they may be recaptured and returned there.

Section 37/41: Hospital order with restrictions

To make a restricted hospital order the court needs the same evidence as is required for a hospital order, and in addition one of the doctors must attend court to give evidence in person. Only the Crown Court can impose restrictions and they must now be without limit of time (it used to be possible to set a specific time limit). The grounds are that it appears to the court

> *having regard to the nature of the offence, the antecedents of the offender and the risk of his committing further offences if set at large, that it is necessary for the protection of the public from serious harm.*

This means that the patient can be discharged, given leave of absence or transferred to another hospital only with the approval of the Justice Secretary. The Secretary of State may discharge the patient absolutely or conditionally. If conditionally discharged the patient will be subject to compulsory after-care from a responsible clinician. In practice a social supervisor is appointed (often an AMHP). The Mental Health Tribunal can also discharge restricted patients but the hospital managers cannot discharge and there is no nearest relative in law.

Section 38: Interim hospital order

Where a court is trying to decide whether a full hospital order is needed they can check this by making an interim hospital order. The order can be made for up to 12 weeks in the first instance and can be renewed by the court for periods of up to 28 days at a time, to a maximum of one year. Two doctors must give written or oral evidence. The court will then receive reports on how the patient reacts to treatment. Part 4 of the MHA 1983 applies so treatment may be given as with section 37.

Section 45A: Hospital and limitation directions

This is a prison sentence combined with a requirement for hospital treatment with limitation directions. Until the recent reforms its use was limited to patients with psychopathic disorder. Now that classifications have been abolished by the 2007 Act the measure is open to people with any kind of mental disorder and it remains to be seen if its use increases. The order is available only to the Crown Court. The grounds set out in subsection (2) are:

(a) *that the offender is suffering from mental disorder; and*
(b) *that the mental disorder from which the offender is suffering is of a nature or degree which makes it appropriate for him to be detained in a hospital for medical treatment; and*
(c) *that appropriate medical treatment is available for him.*

The written or oral evidence from two doctors is required.

Section 47: Transfers of sentenced prisoners

It is still possible for a prisoner to be transferred to a psychiatric hospital even after sentencing. The Home Secretary can order their transfer under section 47 if satisfied by reports from at least two doctors:

(a) *that the said person is suffering from mental illness, psychopathic disorder, severe mental impairment or mental impairment; and*
(b) *that the mental disorder from which that person is suffering is of a nature or degree which makes it appropriate for him to be detained in a hospital for medical treatment and, in the case of psychopathic disorder or mental impairment, that such treatment is likely to alleviate or prevent a deterioration of his condition.*

The transfer direction has the same effect as a section 37 hospital order made without restrictions and the patient is subject to consent to treatment provisions. Commonly, a restriction direction is also made under section 49. This has the same effect as a restriction order under section 41 described above. If the offender was sentenced to a fixed term of imprisonment the restriction lifts on the expiry of the sentence (allowing for remission).

Section 48: Removal to hospital of other prisoners

This section gives the Secretary of State for Justice powers to direct the transfer to hospital of a person who is waiting for trial or sentence and who has been remanded in custody. Two medical reports are needed stating that:

(a) the person is suffering from mental disorder of a nature or degree which makes it appropriate for him to be detained in hospital for medical treatment; and
(b) he is in urgent need of such treatment; and
(c) appropriate medical treatment is available for him.

Part 4 provisions on consent to treatment apply to this group of patients.

Other relevant law apart from the Mental Health Act

Unfit to plead (Criminal Procedure (Insanity and Unfitness to Plead) Act 1991)

If an accused person is found to be unfit to be tried, there is provision for a 'trial of the facts' to determine whether the jury is satisfied beyond reasonable doubt that the accused did the act or made the omission charged against him. The Ministry of Justice provides guidance on aspects of the trial of the facts and a circular summarises the disposal options for the court which include a guardianship order, a supervision and treatment order, a hospital admission order or absolute discharge.

The insanity defence

This applies to murder where the sentence is fixed by law and is phrased as the accused was 'labouring under such defect of reason from disease of the mind as to not know the nature and quality of the act he was doing, or, if he did know it, that he did not know it was wrong' (the M'Naghten Rules). If the defence is successful the judge must make the equivalent of a hospital order with restrictions on discharge. This measure is used infrequently.

Diminished responsibility

This is set out in section 2 of the Homicide Act 1957. The accused was suffering from such abnormality of mind as to substantially impair mental responsibility for the killing. If this argument is successful, the judge has discretion in sentencing. Any conviction will be for manslaughter rather than murder so there is no mandatory life sentence.

The Infanticide Act 1938

This can apply where the mind of a woman who kills a child under 1 'is disturbed by reason of not having fully recovered from the effect of giving birth to the child or by reason of the effect of lactation consequent on the birth'. The court may impose any appropriate sentence.

Community rehabilitation orders supervised by probation

These orders can be made in any court and for any offence other than one with a fixed penalty but they do require a conviction. The offender is then supervised by a probation officer for a specified period between six months and three years. The court must have evidence from a doctor approved under the Mental Health Act 1983. The doctor must state that the person's mental condition requires, and may be susceptible to, treatment but that the person does not need to be subject to a hospital order. The court may then specify where treatment should take place: this could be as an in-patient in a hospital or mental nursing home; as an out-patient at a specified hospital or place; by or under the direction of a named doctor. The court must explain all the requirements of the order to the offender and obtain their consent to the order. If, subsequently, the person refuses to co-operate with one of the conditions, the doctor can report this only to the supervising officer who may take proceedings for breach of probation.

Police powers under section 136

The wording of this section is straightforward:

(1) *If a constable finds in a place to which the public have access a person who appears to him to be suffering from mental disorder and to be in immediate need of care or control, the constable may, if he thinks it necessary to do so in the interests of that person or for the protection of other persons, remove that person to a place of safety within the meaning of section 135 above.*

(2) *A person removed to a place of safety under this section may be detained there for a period not exceeding 72 hours for the purpose of enabling him to be examined by a registered medical practitioner and to be interviewed by an approved mental health professional and of making any necessary arrangements for his treatment or care.*

(3) *A constable, an approved mental health professional or a person authorised by either of them for the purposes of this subsection may, before the end of the period of 72 hours mentioned in subsection (2) above, take a person detained in a place of safety under that subsection to one or more other places of safety.*

(4) *A person taken to a place of a safety under subsection (3) above may be detained there for a purpose mentioned in subsection (2) above for a period ending no later than the end of the period of 72 hours mentioned in that subsection.*

The officer does not have to suspect that any criminal offence has been committed.

For many years there have been concerns that this (and other controlling powers of the MHA) is used disproportionately with black and ethnic minority individuals. The Code of Practice (para. 10.42) states that its use with people from ethnic minorities should be monitored.

The Code has been strengthened in its advice that police stations should be used as places of safety in only a minority of cases. Paragraph 10.21 of the Code states:

> A police station should be used as a place of safety only on an exceptional basis. It may be necessary to do so because the person's behaviour would pose an unmanageably high risk to other patients, staff or users of a healthcare setting. It is preferable for a person thought to be suffering from a mental disorder to be detained in a hospital or other healthcare setting where mental health services are provided (subject, of course, to any urgent physical healthcare needs they may have).

A number of police forces have recently been very unwilling to continue using police stations. Another addition to the Code supports their approach, para. 10.22:

> A police station should not be assumed to be the automatic second choice if the first choice place of safety is not immediately available. Other available options, such as a residential care home or the home of a relative or friend of the person who is willing to accept them temporarily, should also be considered.

Paragraph 10.23 then refers to the new power to transfer patients from one place of safety to another (as a result of section 136(3) above):

> If a police station is used, health and social care agencies should work with the police in arranging, where appropriate, the transfer of the person to a more suitable place of safety. In defining responsibility for providing a prompt assessment, the locally agreed policy should set out the time within which it would be reasonable to expect the appropriate health and social care professionals to attend the police station to assess the person or to assist in arranging to transfer them.

Finally, paragraph 10.24 states:

> In identifying the most appropriate place of safety for an individual, consideration should be given to the impact that the proposed place of safety (and the journey to it) may have on the person and on their examination and interview. It should always be borne in mind that the use of a police station can give the impression that the person detained is suspected of having committed a crime. This may cause distress and anxiety to the person concerned and may affect their co-operation with, and therefore the effectiveness of, the assessment process.

Patients arrested under section 136 have the right to have another person of their choice informed of the arrest and of their whereabouts. If a police station is used as the place of safety, they have a right of access to legal advice. If a hospital is used, the Code (para. 10.46) recommends giving access to legal advice if it is requested.

Section 136(2) makes it clear that an assessment should be carried out by both an AMHP and a doctor. If the doctor arrives first and concludes admission to hospital is unnecessary or the person agrees to informal admission, the individual should still be seen by an AMHP. Only if the doctor concludes that the person is not mentally disordered at all should they be released before the arrival of the AMHP (Code para. 10.31).

If it is discovered that a patient who has been arrested on section 136 is currently subject to a CTO or is on section 17 leave, the Code (para. 10.54) advises that the RC be contacted. Out of hours there will normally be a senior clinician on duty who will be designated by the responsible hospital as the patient's RC. In relation to CTO patients the Code then states at para. 10.55:

> *Where the person is known to be on SCT and compulsory admission is indicated, the recall power should be used. An application for detention cannot be made in respect of a person who is known to be on SCT.*

Diversion, interrogation and prosecution

Apart from section 136 the police have a number of options to choose from when they are dealing with a possible offender whom they think might be mentally disordered: check if the person is an absconding detained patient and then return them to the hospital under section 18 or section 138; persuade the person to co-operate while they set up an informal or compulsory admission; use their statutory powers of arrest. Under the Police and Criminal Evidence Act 1984 (PACE) there is a Code of Practice which covers the detention, treatment and questioning of persons by police officers. This will apply where the officer suspects, or is told in good faith, that a person may be mentally ill or have significant learning difficulties or be unable to understand the significance of questions or, indeed, the significance of their own answers. If the person is detained, an 'appropriate adult' (AA) must be informed and asked to come to the police station. A person who is trained or experienced in dealing with mentally disordered people may often be seen as more appropriate than an unqualified relative. The appropriate adult should be present when the individual is told of their rights or can have them read again. They can also require the presence of a lawyer. Unless delay would involve serious risk to person or property, a mentally disordered person should not be interviewed or asked to sign a statement until the appropriate adult is present. The appropriate adult is not just an observer. They have a role in advising the person being interviewed, observing the fairness of the interview and facilitating communication with the interviewee. If a decision is taken to prosecute, the case is passed to the Crown Prosecution Service. Among other factors, they will consider the likely effect of prosecution on people who are young, old, infirm or mentally ill. In the case of mental illness, the Crown Prosecutor will require independent evidence of the illness and the likely adverse effects of prosecution.

Other relevant police powers

Section 17 of the PACE Act 1984 allows a constable to enter and search any premises for the following purposes: to execute a warrant; to arrest a person for an offence; to recapture someone who is unlawfully at large whom is he pursuing; or, finally, to save life or limb or to prevent serious damage to property.

There are also limited circumstances in which a common-law power of arrest may be made. In *Bibby* v *Chief Constable of Essex Police* (Court of Appeal, 2000) these circumstances were summarised: a sufficiently real and present threat to the peace; the threat coming from the person to be arrested; conduct clearly interfering with the rights of others with its natural consequence being 'not wholly unreasonable violence' from a third party; and, finally, unreasonable conduct from the person to be arrested.

The role of the appropriate adult

This role does not sit very comfortably with that of the AMHP but the two functions often coincide and AMHPs need to be familiar with the work of the appropriate adult (AA). Some staff will perform this task on some occasions but rarely with the same patient that they have dealt with under the Mental Health Act. A brief outline of the function was given above noting that the appropriate adult is not just an observer. They advise the person being interviewed, observe the fairness of the interview and facilitate communication with the interviewee. What follows is a selection of key elements of the recently revised PACE Codes of Practice (as implemented from February 2008).

Under Code C1.7(b), in the case of a person who is mentally disordered or mentally vulnerable, 'the appropriate adult' means:

- *a relative, guardian or other person responsible for their care or custody;*
- *someone experienced in dealing with mentally disordered or mentally vulnerable people but who is not a police officer or employed by the police;*
- *failing these, some other responsible adult aged 18 or over who is not a police officer or employed by the police.*

Note 1D to this part of the Code states:

In the case of people who are mentally disordered or otherwise mentally vulnerable, it may be more satisfactory if the appropriate adult is someone experienced or trained in their care rather than a relative lacking such qualifications. But if the detainee prefers a relative to a better qualified stranger or objects to a particular person, their wishes should, if practicable, be respected.

Under Code C11.17 if an appropriate adult is present at an interview, they should be informed that:

- *they are not expected to act simply as an observer; and*
- *the purpose of their presence is, to:*
- *advise the person being interviewed;*
- *observe whether the interview is being conducted properly and fairly;*
- *facilitate communication with the person being interviewed.*

C1.4 of the Code states:

If an Officer has any suspicion, or is told in good faith, that a person of any age may be mentally disordered or otherwise mentally vulnerable, in the absence of clear evidence to dispel that suspicion, the person shall be treated as such for the purposes of this Code.

'Mentally vulnerable' applies to any detainee who, because of their mental state or capacity, may not understand the significance of what is said, of questions, or of their replies. The Code links the term 'mental disorder' to section 1 of the Mental Health Act but also states that if the Custody Officer has any doubts about the mental state/ capacity of a person an AA should be called.

A person should always be given an opportunity to consult a solicitor privately without the AA being present.

Summary of main provisions

The flowchart in Figure 5.1 summarises the main provisions covered in this chapter. It shows a number of options from the moment a person is arrested for an offence or under section 136 of the Mental Health Act onwards. The possible outcomes are traced by the arrows and the relevant section numbers should match up with information given earlier in the chapter.

ACTIVITY 5.1

Sample questions on patients involved in criminal proceedings

1a What grounds need to exist before a person can be placed on a section 37 Hospital Order under the Mental Health Act 1983?

1b In what circumstances might restrictions be put on such an order and what are the main likely effects of such restrictions?

1c What aspects of the Mental Health Act might lead an AMHP to become involved with such a patient?

2a A woman is arrested by the police and is brought to the police station. The police suspect that she may be suffering from a mental disorder. Give two reasons why an AMHP might be called to the station.

2b List some of the issues about using a police station to hold someone who might be mentally ill. How could an AMHP ameliorate any problems?

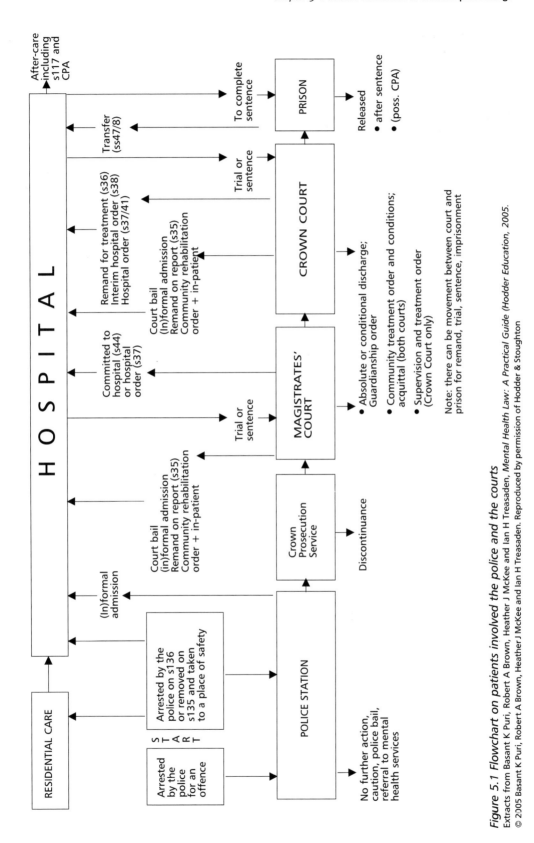

Figure 5.1 Flowchart on patients involved the police and the courts

Extracts from Basant K Puri, Robert A Brown, Heather J McKee and Ian H Treasaden, *Mental Health Law: A Practical Guide (Hodder Education, 2005.*
© 2005 Basant K Puri, Robert A Brown, Heather J McKee and Ian H Treasaden. Reproduced by permission of Hodder & Stoughton

ACTIVITY 5.1 *continued*

Multiple choice questions
(Answers in Appendix 9)

1 A patient remanded to a hospital on an interim hospital order under section
   38 may be detained after renewals for a maximum of:
   (a) 28 days ☐
   (b) 12 weeks ☐
   (c) six months ☐
   (d) a year ☐

2 A patient who is subject to a hospital order made by the court under section
   37 is first entitled to apply to the Mental Health Review Tribunal:
   (a) after six months ☐
   (b) within six months ☐
   (c) after one year ☐

Chapter 6

Consent to treatment and mental capacity

Consent to treatment under the MHA 1983

Introduction

The purpose of Parts 4 and 4A of the Act is to clarify the circumstances in which treatment for mental disorder may be given without the consent of a patient subject to compulsion. This was often a contentious issue under the 1959 Mental Health Act which gave no specific guidance on treatment. Although the 1983 Act introduced a fairly clear set of rules to follow, these have, in turn, become somewhat contentious and there are a number of complications which have arisen from case law.

The main principle adopted by the Act is that there are some patients who are liable to be detained who may need to be given treatment without their consent. Further, this may be seen as reasonable given the fact of their detention. Certain procedures, however, should be followed to offer safeguards. These essentially involve a second medical opinion from outside the hospital for more serious forms of treatment in those cases where valid consent cannot be obtained from the patient. This absence of consent could either be the result of the patient objecting to the treatment or of their being unable to give valid consent (e.g. because of mental incapacity). For the most serious treatments (such as psychosurgery), a second opinion *and* the consent of the patient are required. Because of the invasive nature of these treatments, the safeguards are also extended to informal patients. The community treatment orders have brought with them a new set of rules which are set out in Part 4A.

The Mental Health Act Commission has a general duty to oversee the operation of these parts of the Act.

Detained patients who are not covered by Part 4 of the Act are in the same position as any other patients in a general hospital and cannot be treated without their consent except where the Mental Capacity Act applies or where common law would allow it (e.g. in an emergency). It is particularly important to understand not just what the procedures are, but which patients are covered by them, as not all detained patients are included. Generally, those patients liable to detention for periods of more than 72 hours are covered, with the exception of people remanded for reports by the courts under section 35. Details of which sections are covered by the rules are included in full in the flowchart and checklist later in this chapter. The grids which can be found in this guide for patients detained under Parts 2 or 3 also provide a quick visual guide as to which patients are covered by the Part 4 or 4A rules and which are not.

A definition of medical treatment

Section 145 provides a definition of medical treatment as

> *nursing, psychological intervention and specialist mental health habilitation, rehabilitation and care . . . the purpose of which is to alleviate, or prevent a worsening of, the disorder or one or more of its symptoms or manifestations.*

Part 4 – Consent to treatment for patients liable to be detained

Sections 57, 58 and 58A set out which types of medical treatment attract specific rules. Some treatments require the approval of a second-opinion appointed doctor (SOAD) who has been appointed by the Secretary of State or the Welsh Ministers for this purpose. The categories of treatment which are specified in the Act are:

- Section 57:
  - any surgical operation for destroying brain tissue or for destroying the functioning of brain tissue (generally known as neurosurgery);
  - surgical implantation of hormones to reduce male sex drive.
- Section 58:
  - medicine after three months of treatment while detained.
- Section 58A:
  - electro-convulsive therapy (ECT) and related medicine.

These sections are considered in more detail below. Other forms of treatment could be added to this list in future by regulations.

Approved Clinicians

There are some situations when the person in charge of the treatment must be registered as an approved clinician (AC). For a detained patient this will be:

- where treatment is given without the patient's consent;

- where the patient has consented under section 58 or 58A and the certificate has been completed by an AC rather than a SOAD;

- where:
  - a CTO patient has been recalled or the CTO revoked, and
  - where the section 58 requirements have not yet been met, *but*
  - there is consent and the treatment is necessary to prevent serious suffering to the patient.

Where a CTO patient is in the community there needs to be an AC in charge of the treatment being given if the patient lacks capacity to consent. The exception to this rule would be where there is the consent of an attorney (from a lasting power of attorney), a deputy or the Court of Protection. The Code notes at para. 24.5 that:

Hospital managers should keep a record of approved clinicians who are available to treat patients for whom they are responsible and should ensure that approved clinicians are in charge of treatment where the Act requires it.

Section 57

This deals with any surgical operation for destroying brain tissue or for destroying the functioning of brain tissue (generally known as neurosurgery), and the surgical implantation of hormones to reduce male sex drive. This section is unusual for Part 4 in that it covers informal as well as detained patients.

There are considerable safeguards under section 57. A SOAD and two other people who are appointed by the Mental Health Act Commission need to certify in writing that the patient is capable of understanding the nature, purpose and likely effects of the treatment in question and has consented to it. The SOAD then has to certify in writing that it is appropriate for the treatment to be given, having consulted two other persons who have been professionally concerned with the patient's medical treatment. One of these consultees needs to be a nurse and the other should be someone other than a nurse or a doctor. This could be an AMHP but neurosurgery under section 57 is very rare. There are usually only three or four cases per year in the whole of England and Wales.

Even less likely is a referral concerning the surgical implantation of hormones to reduce male sex drive as this has not been requested for 20 years.

Section 58

This section used to include ECT but this is now regulated by section 58A. Section 58 deals only with medication for mental disorder after three months of treatment under detention. This means it relates in practice to patients who are subject to section 3, section 37 or the equivalent. It does not cover medication if this is administered as part of ECT treatment as this is also covered by section 58A.

The safeguards provided by section 58 are that medication cannot be given unless:

- the patient has consented to the treatment and either the approved clinician in charge of it or a SOAD has certified in writing that the patient is capable of understanding its nature, purpose and likely effects and has consented to it; *or*

- a SOAD has certified in writing that the patient is not capable of understanding the nature, purpose and likely effects of that treatment, or is capable but has not consented to it, and that it is appropriate for the treatment to be given. The SOAD must have consulted two other persons who have been professionally concerned with the patient's medical treatment. One of these must be a nurse and the other shall be neither a nurse nor a registered medical practitioner; and neither can be the responsible clinician or the person in charge of the treatment in question.

If treatment is based on this procedure the Code recommends that there should be a record in the patient's notes of the relevant discussion where capacity was confirmed and full details of the specific treatment covered. The Code states at para. 24.17:

> *Certificates under this section must clearly set out the specific forms of treatment to which they apply. All the relevant drugs should be listed, including medication to be given 'as required' (prn), either by name or by the classes described in the British National Formulary (BNF). If drugs are specified by class, the certificate should state clearly the number of drugs authorised in each class, and whether any drugs within the class are excluded. The maximum dosage and route of administration should be clearly indicated for each drug or category of drugs proposed. This can exceed the dosages listed in the BNF, but particular care is required in these cases.*

The AMHP's Guide to Psychiatry and Medication (Brown, Adhead and Pollard 2009) provides some detail on treatments covered by this section.

Section 58A – ECT and related medication

This new section covers ECT and any medication administered as part of the ECT process. The rules apply to adult detained patients and to all patients under the age of 18, whether they are detained or not. No patient under 18 may be given ECT without the approval of a SOAD. There are some new safeguards and this is the first occasion where the Mental Health Act does not automatically take preference over the Mental Capacity Act. For example, a competent refusal or a valid and applicable advance decision will prevent treatment from being given under section 58A.

ECT may not be given to an adult unless:

- the patient has consented to that treatment and either the approved clinician in charge of it or a SOAD has certified in writing that the patient is capable of understanding its nature, purpose and likely effects and has consented to it; *or*

- a SOAD has certified in writing that the patient is not capable of understanding the nature, purpose and likely effects of the treatment, and that it is appropriate for the treatment to be given, and that this will not conflict with a valid and applicable advance decision or a decision made by a donee or a deputy or the Court of Protection. The SOAD must have consulted two other persons who have been professionally concerned with the patient's medical treatment. One of these must be a nurse and the other shall be neither a nurse nor a registered medical practitioner; and neither can be the responsible clinician or the person in charge of the treatment in question.

If the patient is under 18 a certificate from a SOAD is needed whether they have capacity or not. However, the certificate by itself is not sufficient authority to treat. The relevant clinician must also have the patient's own valid consent or some other legal authority at the time of giving the treatment.

Section 62

This deals with urgent treatment. It covers sections 57, 58 and 58A but in practice it will not be used in relation to section 57. It provides for emergency situations (e.g. where a patient withdraws consent during a course of treatment) and even then it allows treatment only:

(a) *which is immediately necessary to save the patient's life; or*
(b) *which (not being irreversible) is immediately necessary to prevent a serious deterioration of his condition; or*
(c) *which (not being irreversible or hazardous) is immediately necessary to alleviate serious suffering by the patient; or*
(d) *which (not being irreversible or hazardous) is immediately necessary and represents the minimum interference necessary to prevent the patient from behaving violently or being a danger to himself or to others.*

With ECT only (a) and (b) apply so the risk level needs to be very high before the normal requirements can be dispensed with. The grounds set out in (c) and (d) are no longer acceptable for ECT and this may be a significant change for practitioners. These grounds are still applicable for emergency treatment with medication.

The definition of 'irreversible' is where it has 'unfavourable irreversible physical or psychological consequences' and hazardous means 'significant physical hazard.'

There is no prescribed form for use when treating under section 62.

Section 63

This section covers treatment which does not require the consent of the patient. This is the source of much concern to many patients. The implications are that, apart from ECT and the section 57 treatments, any treatment can be given in the first three months of a patient's detention without their valid consent. After three months the safeguard of the SOAD's involvement applies but only in relation to medication. Many other treatments can continue to be given without the SOAD safeguard.

The Code contains a number of pointers on treatment, such as encouraging staff to seek the patient's consent wherever practicable and to record this, or the refusal as the case may be, in the notes. Paragraph 23.40 states:

- *compulsory administration of treatment which would otherwise require consent is invariably an infringement of Article 8 of the Convention (respect for family and private life). However, it may be justified where it is in accordance with law (in this case the procedures in the Mental Health Act) and where it is proportionate to a legitimate aim (in this case, the reduction of the risk posed by a person's mental disorder and the improvement of their health);*
- *compulsory treatment is capable of being inhuman treatment (or in extreme cases even torture) contrary to Article 3 of the Convention, if its effect on the person concerned reaches a sufficient level of severity. But the European Court of Human Rights has said that a measure which is convincingly shown to be of therapeutic necessity from the point of view of established principles of medicine cannot in principle be regarded as inhuman and degrading.*

Paragraph 23.41 goes on to state:

Scrupulous adherence to the requirements of the legislation and good clinical practice should ensure that there is no such incompatibility. But if clinicians have concerns about a potential breach of a person's human rights they should seek senior clinical and, if necessary, legal advice.

It is quite possible that there will be legal challenges to the forcible administration of medication, especially to competent adults where they do not pose a risk to others.

The flowchart in Figure 6.1 summarises consent to treatment under Part 4 of the Act.

Part 4A – Treatment of community patients not recalled to hospital

This sets out the law concerning treatment for patients who have been made subject to community treatment orders (CTOs). It is not always easy to follow and AMHPs may need to consider the implications for a few cases before it becomes easier to understand. This situation has arisen partly because the Bill was amended several times as it went through Parliament leaving the resulting Act a series of compromises between competing views.

Figure 6.1. Consent to treatment flowchart for Part 4 (adapted from Puri et al. (2005))

A patient on section 17 leave in the community is covered by Part 4 of the Act but a community patient (one subject to a CTO) is covered by the different rules contained in Part 4A. For a community patient to be made subject to Part 4 they need to be recalled to hospital. In effect recalls may therefore take place to make it easier to give compulsory treatment to a mentally capable refusing patient.

If a patient is subject to a CTO (and has not been recalled) they cannot be given treatment for mental disorder unless the requirements of Part 4A are met. These are:

- the person giving the treatment must have the authority to do so; and

- (in most cases) there must be a certificate.

Form CTO11 is needed for treatments which would require a certificate under section 58 or 58A if the patient were detained. In effect this means medication after the initial three-month period of detention and ECT and any related medication. However, a certificate is not required for medication during the first month following a patient's discharge from detention onto a CTO. This is the case even if the three-month period for section 58 has already expired or expires during this first month.

When they are giving Part 4A certificates, SOADs are not asked to certify whether a patient has capacity to consent to the treatments in question. The question is whether the treatment is appropriate. The SOAD may make it a condition of their approval that particular treatments are given only in certain circumstances. They could specify that a certain treatment only is to be given if the patient consents.

Paragraph 24.27 of the Code, elaborating on this point, states:

> *[The SOAD] might specify that a medication may be given up to a certain dosage if the patient lacks capacity to consent, but that a higher dosage may be given with the patient's consent.*

SOADs can also decide which treatments to approve should the patient be recalled to hospital and whether to impose any conditions on that approval. Unless it states otherwise, a certificate will authorise medication even if the patient has capacity to refuse it.

Before issuing a certificate the SOAD must consult two people who have been professionally concerned with the patient's medical treatment. Only one of these may be a doctor and neither of them can be the patient's responsible clinician or the approved clinician in charge of any of the treatments that are to be specified on the certificate.

Where a patient has capacity to consent to treatment this provides the authority to treat. In other cases there may be a donee of an LPA, or a deputy who has been appointed by the Court of Protection, who is able to consent on the patient's behalf.

If a community patient lacks capacity to consent to the treatment, the clinician wishing to have authority to treat must:

- take reasonable steps to establish that the patient lacks capacity to consent to the treatment; then, when giving the treatment, he must reasonably believe that the patient lacks capacity to consent to it;

- have no reason to believe that the patient objects to being given the treatment; or, if he does have reason to believe that the patient objects, it is not necessary to use force against the patient in order to give the treatment;

- be the person in charge of the treatment and an approved clinician; or the treatment must be given under the direction of that clinician;

- ensure that giving the treatment will not conflict with an advance decision which he is satisfied is valid and applicable, or with a decision made by a donee or deputy or the Court of Protection.

Emergency treatment

In an emergency, if treatment is to be given without a certificate, the treatment must fall into one of the categories set out in section 64G(5):

(a) *it is immediately necessary to save the patient's life; or*
(b) *it is immediately necessary to prevent a serious deterioration of the patient's condition and is not irreversible; or*
(c) *it is immediately necessary to alleviate serious suffering by the patient and is not irreversible or hazardous; or*
(d) *it is immediately necessary, represents the minimum interference necessary to prevent the patient from behaving violently or being a danger to himself or others and is not irreversible or hazardous.*

If it is necessary to use force against the patient in order to give the treatment this can only be to prevent harm to the patient. The use of such force must be proportionate to the likelihood of the patient's suffering harm, and to the seriousness of that harm.

Recalled patients

When a patient is recalled by the RC they revert to being covered by Part 4 and can be treated accordingly, except as noted in the Code at para. 24.28:

- *a certificate under section 58 is not needed for medication if less than one month has passed since the patient was discharged from hospital and became an SCT patient;*
- *a certificate is not needed under either section 58 or 58A if the treatment in question is already explicitly authorised for administration on recall on the patient's Part 4A certificate; and*
- *treatment that was already being given on the basis of a Part 4A certificate may be continued, even though it is not authorised for administration on recall, if the approved clinician in charge of the treatment considers that discontinuing it would cause the patient serious suffering. But it may only be continued pending compliance with section 58 or 58A (as applicable) – in other words while steps are taken to obtain a new certificate.*

The Mental Capacity Act 2005

The bulk of the Mental Capacity Act (MCA) came into effect in October 2007. The Act is having a significant impact on mental health care. The MCA definition of incapacity would apply to decisions under the MHA. Also, where the Mental Health Act does not provide authority for treating patients who are subject to compulsion the MCA may be relevant. This would include treatments that are not for mental disorder. Where patients have capacity they would be entitled to refuse such treatments but clinicians might be able to rely on the MCA in situations where patients lacks capacity.

The MCA provides a statutory framework for decision-making on behalf of people who lack the capacity to consent to their care or treatment. Before the Act came into effect incapacitated individuals were most commonly dealt with under the common law doctrine of necessity. This provided for the care or treatment of incapacitated adults in their best interests.

There is more detailed information on the MCA in *The Mental Capacity Act 2005: A Guide for Professionals* by Brown, Barber and Martin (2009).

The five principles

Section 1 of the MCA sets out five principles that should be applied by anyone relying on the Act for any purpose. The principles are intended to protect people who lack capacity, and to help them participate in decision-making as fully as possible. Section 1 of the Act states:

(1) *A person must be assumed to have capacity unless it is established that he lacks capacity.*

(2) *A person is not to be treated as unable to make a decision unless all practicable steps to help him to do so have been taken without success.*

(3) *A person is not to be treated as unable to make a decision merely because he makes an unwise decision.*

(4) *An act done, or decision made, under this Act for or on behalf of a person who lacks capacity must be done, or made, in his best interests.*

(5) *Before the act is done, or the decision is made, regard must be had to whether the purpose for which it is needed can be as effectively achieved in a way that is less restrictive of the person's rights and freedom of action.*

Definition of incapacity

The first principle requires any decision-maker to assume capacity unless it can be established that the person in question lacks capacity. The test for incapacity is set out in sections 2 and 3 of the Act. Section 2 states:

for the purpose of this Act, a person lacks capacity in relation to a matter if at the material time he is unable to make a decision for himself in relation to the matter because of an impairment of, or a disturbance in the functioning of, the mind or brain.

This requires two questions to be answered:

1 Is there a specific decision to be made now?
2 Is the person unable to make the decision because of an impairment of, or a disturbance in the functioning of the mind or brain, whether this be temporary or permanent?

If the potential decision-maker answers 'no' to either of these questions the MCA will not apply. However, if the answer is 'yes' to both questions the decision-maker must go on to establish whether the person is able to make their own decision. This must be done before the decision-maker is able to make decisions on behalf of the person. Section 3 of the MCA sets out the test for determining whether a person is incapable of making their own decisions:

a person is unable to make decisions for himself if he is unable –
(a) to understand the information relevant to the decision,
(b) to retain the information,
(c) to use or weigh that information as part of the process of making the decision, or
(d) to communicate his decision (whether by talking, using sign language or any other means).

Any decision-maker must decide what information about the decision is relevant and give that information in a way that the person can understand. If a person shows that they are able to use that information to weigh up the benefits and/or risks of the proposed action, and understand the consequences of inaction, retain the information for long enough to weigh the information up, and finally communicate a decision then they would be regarded as having capacity. So if the potential decision-maker is satisfied that the person is able to meet all four of the above requirements (a)–(d) they must regard the person as having the capacity to make the decision in question and would have no authority to make that decision on the person's behalf. If, however, they believe (on the balance of probability) that the person is unable to demonstrate one or more of the four requirements then the person would be deemed to lack the capacity to make the decision in question. The decision-maker would then be able to make the decision on the person's behalf as long as they were acting in the person's best interests.

Best interests

There is no definition of 'best interests' in section 4 of the Act. Rather there is a checklist of factors that any decision-maker must consider. The aim of the checklist is to ensure that any decisions made, or actions taken, are in the best interests of the incapacitated person. The factors to consider are broad, enabling them to be applied to all decisions and actions.

Table 6.1 provides a best interests checklist. It is based on the checklist from the statute as summarised at the beginning of Chapter 5 of the Code of Practice to the MCA.

Table 6.1. The best interests checklist

Encourage participation
- Do whatever is possible to permit and encourage the person to take part, or to improve their ability to take part, in making the decision.

Identify all relevant circumstances
- Try to identify all the things that the person who lacks capacity would take into account if they were making the decision or acting for themselves.

Find out the person's views
- Try to find out the views of the person who lacks capacity, including:
  - the person's past and present wishes and feelings – these may have been expressed verbally, in writing or through behaviour or habits;
  - any beliefs and values (e.g. religious, cultural, moral or political) that would be likely to influence the decision in question;
  - any other factors the person themselves would be likely to consider if they were making the decision or acting for themselves.

Avoid discrimination
- Do not make assumptions about someone's best interests simply on the basis of the person's age, appearance, condition or behaviour.

Assess whether the person might regain capacity
- Consider whether the person is likely to regain capacity (e.g. after receiving medical treatment). If so, can the decision wait until then?

If the decision concerns life-sustaining treatment
- Do not be motivated in any way by a desire to bring about the person's death. They should not make assumptions about the person's quality of life.

Consult others
- If it is practical and appropriate to do so, consult other people for their views about the person's best interests and to see if they have any information about the person's wishes and feelings, beliefs and values. In particular, try to consult:
  - anyone previously named by the person as someone to be consulted on either the decision in question or on similar issues;
  - anyone engaged in caring for the person;
  - close relatives, friends or others who take an interest in the person's welfare;
  - any attorney appointed under a lasting power of attorney or enduring power of attorney made by the person;
  - any deputy appointed by the Court of Protection to make decisions for the person.
- For decisions about major medical treatment or where the person should live and where there is no one who fits into any of the above categories, an independent mental capacity advocate (IMCA) must be consulted.
- When consulting, remember that the person who lacks capacity to make the decision or act for themselves still has a right to keep their affairs private – so it would not be right to share every piece of information with everyone.

Avoid restricting the person's rights
- See if there are other options that may be less restrictive of the person's rights.

Take all of this into account
- Weigh up all of these factors in order to work out what is in the person's best interests.

There are no statutory forms for the best interests checklist, or for the capacity test. However, decision-makers are well advised to record their decision-making process as this will provide authority for their actions and help protect them from liability.

'Section 5 acts'

This is the expression used when referring to acts made in connection with the care or treatment of people where section 5 is relied on to provide protection from liability. In effect, section 5 of the MCA allows decision-makers to carry out acts in connection with the care or treatment of people provided that they have followed the requirements of the Act. There are limitations in that certain actions are not permitted as section 5 acts.

Section 5 acts must not conflict with: a person's advance refusal of treatment, or the authority of an attorney appointed by the person, or the authority of a deputy appointed by the Court of Protection.

As long as none of these situations exists then someone can make decisions and carry out actions for or on behalf of an incapacitated person provided that:

- before doing the act the decision-maker takes reasonable steps to establish that the person lacks capacity in relation to the matter;

- when doing the act they believe the person lacks capacity in relation to the matter; and

- the act will be in the person's best interests (determined in accordance with section 4).

If these criteria are met the decision-maker would be protected from liability, assuming that they do not exceed the limitations detailed below or act negligently. Section 6 sets out a number of conditions which must be met if section 5 acts are to be regarded as lawful. If decision-makers have followed the correct procedures and do not exceed the limitations detailed below, their acts of care or treatment will fall within the scope of section 5.

Restraint can be used provided that the following criteria are met:

- the decision-maker believes that the restraint is necessary to do the act in order to prevent harm to the person; and

- the act is a proportionate response to:
  - the likelihood of the person suffering harm; and
  - the seriousness of that harm.

Where the person is causing harm to others the MCA cannot be relied on. In these circumstances decision-makers need to consider whether the Mental Health Act or the common law would provide a way of intervening to protect others. Restraint must also fall short of deprivation of liberty if someone is relying on the MCA.

Lawful responses to deprivation of liberty

If a decision-maker decides that the care or treatment being proposed amounts to a deprivation of liberty, then the following provisions are available, assuming that the criteria are met:

- detention under an appropriate section of the MHA 1983;

- a personal welfare order of the Court of Protection, under section 16 of the MCA 2005;

- Deprivation of Liberty Safeguards (DOLS, from April 2009);

- life-sustaining treatment, or treatment to prevent a deterioration, while awaiting a decision by the Court of Protection.

Detention under the Mental Health Act is covered in some detail in this book.

A personal welfare order can be made by the Court of Protection where a person lacks capacity. The order can include decisions about where the person lives, what contact they should have with others, consent to treatment issues, and determining who is responsible for the person's health care. The court can also make orders in relation to a person's property and affairs.

The Deprivation of Liberty Safeguards (DOLS) are an amendment to the Mental Capacity Act introduced in April 2009. They are intended to provide a procedure for the lawful deprivation of liberty of individuals living in care homes or in hospital settings. They apply to people aged 18 or over, who lack capacity and who have a mental disorder (see Chapter 11 for a detailed description).

The MCA 2005 allows life-sustaining treatment or treatment to prevent a deterioration in someone's condition if an application is being made to the Court of Protection for determination of lack of capacity and best interests.

Advance decisions

An advance decision can be made by a capacitated adult (18 or over). It need not be in writing unless it is for life-sustaining treatment. The advance decision would need to state what treatment cannot be given and under what circumstances. If the specific treatment is proposed and the person at that point lacks capacity in relation to the treatment decision then the advance decision may be valid and applicable. Advance decisions are limited to refusals of medical treatment (they cannot cover social care). They cannot be used to require a specific treatment to be given. With the exception of ECT an advance refusal of treatment for mental disorder can be overridden if a person is detained under a section of the Mental Health Act 1983 to which Part 4 applies. Additional safeguards for people who make advance refusals of ECT have been introduced, to ensure that their refusal is respected unless certain criteria are met.

Lasting Powers of Attorney

A Lasting Power of Attorney (LPA) can be made by capacitated adults (aged 18 and over) to cover either personal welfare decisions or property and affairs. It must be witnessed and registered. The information required depends on whether it is a personal welfare matter LPA or a financial one. LPAs provide for the appointment of someone (the donee) to make decisions on behalf of the donor once they lose the capacity to make their own decisions. Other statutory interventions can sometimes override the donee's decision-making powers (e.g. if the patient is detained under the Mental Health Act).

If a person loses capacity before they have made an LPA the Court of Protection could intervene either by making a one-off decision or by appointing a deputy to make certain decisions on behalf of the person.

ACTIVITY 6.1

Sample questions on consent to treatment and mental capacity.

1a What is an advance decision as defined in the Mental Capacity Act 2005 and how might this relate to psychiatric medication?

1b What issues may arise if someone makes an advance decision in relation to the use of a particular anti-psychotic drug and is later admitted to psychiatric hospital under section 3?

1c What difficulties might an AMHP face in these circumstances (before and after admission)?

2a A patient has been detained in hospital on section 3 for ten weeks and has consented to be on psychiatric medication for most of that period. The RC considers that a change in medication is now needed and is concerned that the patient may not agree. What are the legal options in terms of proceeding with the proposed treatment in this case?

2b Why might an AMHP who is working with the patient and their family become involved?

2c What dilemmas might an AMHP face in these circumstances?

Multiple choice questions
(Answers in Appendix 9)

1   Key principles of the Mental Capacity Act include:
(a) A presumption of capacity exists for all those aged 16 or over. ☐
(b) All practicable steps should be taken to help a person make a decision before they're considered incapable. ☐
(c) An unwise decision implies a lack of capacity. ☐
(d) Acts done on behalf of an incapacitated person must be in his/her best interests. ☐
(e) All decisions made on behalf of and for an incapacitated person must be registered with the Court of Protection. ☐

ACTIVITY 6.1 *continued*

    (f) Decisions should be the least expensive available in terms of cost to
        the person. ☐

    (g) Decisions should seek to be less restrictive in terms of the person's rights
        and freedom of action. ☐

2 A decision on a person's mental capacity needs to be made in relation to the
    particular matter at the time when the decision has to be made.
    (a) True ☐
    (b) False ☐

3 The test for capacity under the Mental Capacity Act is whether the person can:
    (a) understand the relevant information ☐
    (b) retain the relevant information ☐
    (c) believe the relevant information ☐
    (d) use or weigh the relevant information as part of the decision-making
        process ☐
    (e) communicate the decision ☐
    (f) read and sign a consent form ☐

Chapter 7
Mental Health Tribunals and Hospital Managers' Reviews

Summary of provisions concerning Mental Health Tribunals

See Tables 2.1 and 5.1 for summaries of when patients and their nearest relatives can apply to the Mental Health Tribunal and for information on when there will be an automatic hearing.

Introduction

Mental Health Review Tribunals were established with the radical provisions of the 1959 Mental Health Act. The main function of a tribunal is to review the justification for continued detention, a community treatment order or guardianship at the time of a hearing. In an important judgment in 2001 influenced by the Human Rights Act (*R (on the application of H) v MHRT North and East London Region* (2001)), the Court of Appeal ruled that a tribunal should express its decision in terms of a positive view (i.e. that the grounds for section 2 existed at the time of the hearing) rather than the traditional negative view (i.e. that the tribunal could not see that the grounds did not exist). Sections 72 and 73 were amended by a remedial order to reverse the burden of proof. It is no longer a case of the patient showing that the grounds for compulsion do not exist but rather on the detaining authority to show the tribunal that the grounds are still present. At a tribunal hearing, an AMHP is likely, therefore, to be asked if they would apply for or recommend detention if they were assessing on that day.

If a patient considers the original detention was unlawful, he can consider an application to the High Court for a writ of habeas corpus or an application for judicial review.

The main references to tribunals are to be found in Part 5 of the Mental Health Act 1983, in Schedule 2 to the Act and in the Tribunal Rules 2008 (SI 2699). These documents are all reprinted in Barber, Brown and Martin (2009). The Practice Directions, which are not in that text, form Appendix 7 of this book. These are a useful reference as they contain the headings for the various reports that are required by the Tribunal.

Key provisions

Section 65 provides for the establishment of one Mental Health Tribunal for England and one for Wales.

Schedule 2 states at para. 1:

> *Each of the Mental Health Review Tribunals shall consist of –*
> *(a) a number of persons (referred to in this Schedule as 'the legal members') appointed by the Lord Chancellor and having such legal experience as the Lord Chancellor considers suitable;*
> *(b) a number of persons (referred to in this Schedule as 'the medical members') being registered medical practitioners appointed by the Lord Chancellor after consultation with the Secretary of State; and*
> *(c) a number of persons appointed by the Lord Chancellor and having such experience in administration, such knowledge of social services or such other qualifications or experience as the Lord Chancellor considers suitable.*

Each tribunal hearing will have at least on legal member (who will preside), one medical member and one 'lay' member.

Section 66 sets out when a Part 2 patient (subject to civil detention, a CTO or guardianship) or their nearest relative may apply for a hearing (see Table 2.1).

Section 67 allows the Secretary of State to refer any Part 2 patient to the MHT (e.g. if the Secretary of State thinks there should be a hearing before a patient would next be eligible to apply).

Sections 67, 68 and 76 allow access for any doctor or approved clinician who is acting for a patient in connection with the MHT to

> *visit the patient and examine him in private and require the production of and inspect any records relating to the detention or treatment of the patient in any hospital or to any after-care services provided to the patient under section 117 below.*

Section 68 sets out when the hospital managers must refer the patient to the MHT.

Sections 69 and 70 state when Part 3 patients (those involved in court proceedings) and their nearest relatives have access to MHT hearings (see Table 5.1).

Section 71 allows, and sometimes requires, the Secretary of State (on this occasion this would be the Justice Secretary) to refer restricted patients to the MHT.

Section 72 gives details of MHT powers. In some circumstances, they must direct the patient's discharge, e.g. if they are not satisfied that the grounds for detention exist.

The MHT has the following powers:

- to decide that a patient should continue to be subject to compulsion;
- to direct that a patient should be discharged immediately;
- to direct that a patient should be discharged on a specified future date.

When dealing with a detained patient the MHT may recommend:

- leave of absence
- transfer to another hospital } with a view to future discharge
- transfer into guardianship
- or (for section 3) it may recommend the RC to consider making a CTO.

If any such recommendation is not complied with, the MHT can reconsider that case and make a further decision.

Section 77 limits applications to one per eligible person per period of detention and states that applications should be submitted in writing.

The procedure of MHTs is now regulated by the Tribunal Procedure (First-tier Tribunal) (Health Education and Social Care Chamber) Rules 2008. These rules introduce a new appeal process to the Upper Tribunal Administrative Appeals Chamber.

Applying for the detention of a patient discharged by a tribunal

This issue was considered in *R (von Brandenburg) v E. London and City Mental Health NHS Trust* (2003). The question raised in this case was in what circumstances can a patient who has been discharged by a tribunal be further detained without breach of Article 5(4) of the ECHR? The decision of the Law Lords was that a patient may not be re-sectioned following tribunal discharge unless the ASW (now AMHP) in good faith believes he has information not known to the tribunal which would have placed a significantly different complexion on the matter.

The Law Lords stressed the different roles of the ASW who made the decision whether to admit and the doctors who provided the recommendations upon which the ASW had a discretion whether to act.

The case is often misquoted as saying there needs to be a 'change of circumstances' before a fresh application can be made. The actual test is whether there is information not previously known to the tribunal.

If the tribunal has apparently erred in law it might be possible for the detaining authority to apply for a stay and then challenge the tribunal decision by judicial review. The details of the *von Brandenburg* case will be of some interest to AMHPs.

On 15 March 2000 the patient was lawfully admitted to St Clement's Hospital for assessment after an emergency application made under section 4 of the 1983 Act. The application was made by an ASW and was supported by the required medical recommendation. A second medical recommendation was obtained, and on the same day the patient's admission was converted, again lawfully, into an admission for assessment for a period not exceeding 28 days under section 2 of the Act. On 22 March the patient applied for a tribunal hearing. This hearing took place on 31 March. The patient's application for discharge was resisted by the responsible medical offier (RMO), who gave oral evidence to the tribunal, by a staff grade medical practitioner working with the RMO, and by the hospital. The tribunal ordered that the patient should be discharged with effect from 7 April, deferring the discharge for seven days to allow accommodation in the community to be found and a care plan to be made, including possible medication. On 6 April 2000 the patient, who had not left the hospital, was again detained, this time under section 3 of the Act. The application was made by the same ASW. The necessary medical recommendations were made by the RMO and the second doctor who had supported the earlier admission under section 2.

Extracts from the Lords' judgement:

> *It is plainly of importance that the ASW is subject to a statutory duty to apply for the admission of a patient where he is satisfied that such an application ought to be made and is of the opinion specified ... The problem at the heart of this case is to accommodate the statutory duty imposed on ASWs (by whom, in practice, most applications for admission are made) within the principles referred to ... above. The correct solution is ... that an ASW may not lawfully apply for the admission of a patient whose discharge has been ordered by the decision of a MHR tribunal of which the ASW is aware unless the ASW has formed the reasonable and bona fide opinion that he has information not known to the tribunal which puts a significantly different complexion on the case as compared with that which was before the tribunal. It is impossible and undesirable to attempt to describe in advance the information which might justify such an opinion.*

Lord Bingham gave three hypothetical examples for illustration only. The essential elements were:

1 new information on risk of self-harm;

2   the patient tells the tribunal that he will take medication but then refuses to do so after discharge; or

3   after the tribunal hearing the patient's mental condition significantly deteriorates.

Hospital Managers' Reviews

Section 23(2)(a) gives hospital managers the power to discharge some patients from compulsion. These are patients detained under Part 2 of the Act, unrestricted section 37 patients and patients who are subject to community treatment orders. This is not a function that can be exercised by employees or officers of the Trust. Those appointed to sit on panels are sometimes referred to as 'associate managers'. The managers' panel must consist of at least three authorised people. The Reference Guide has a useful table at 12.118 which sets out who can be authorised, depending on the type of hospital (see Table 7.1).

Table 7.1. Delegation of discharge decisions by hospital managers (Table 12.3 in the Reference Guide)

If the managers are	the discharge function may be performed on their behalf by	who are
an NHS trust	three or more: • authorised members of the trust board; or • members of an authorised committee or subcommittee of the trust	not employees of the trust.
an NHS foundation trust	three or more people authorised by the board of the trust	neither executive directors of the board of the trust, nor employees of the trust.
another NHS body (e.g. primary care trust, local health board)	three or more: • authorised members of the body; or • members of an authorised committee or subcommittee of the body	not officers of the body (within the meaning of the NHS Act 2006 or NHS (Wales) Act 2006).
another body of persons (e.g. company)	three or more: • authorised members of the body; or • members of an authorised committee or subcommittee of the body	–

In this table 'authorised' means that the person, committee or subcommittee (as the case may be) has been authorised by the managers (i.e. the body in question) specifically for this purpose. 'Members' of a body include its chairman.

The Reference Guide goes on to state at para. 12.120:

> *Patients can only be discharged when all three people acting on behalf of the managers agree that they should be discharged. A two to one majority decision is not sufficient (R. [on the application of Tagoe-Thompson] re the hospital managers of the Park Royal Centre [2003] EWCA Civ 330). If the decision is taken by more than three people, as well as a majority being in*

favour, the majority must consist of at least three people in favour of discharge before a decision to discharge can be made.

There is also some useful information in the Guide on the discharge of patients detained in independent hospitals. It notes that the Secretary of State may at any time discharge a Part 2 or Part 3 patient liable to be detained in an independent hospital, and then, at para. 12.122:

> *Where NHS patients are liable to be detained in an independent hospital, the relevant NHS body may discharge them in the same way as it could if they were detained in one of its own hospitals – and the same rules about delegating the decision apply. The relevant NHS body is the one which has contracted for the patient's care in the independent hospital in question.*

Hospital managers have discretion to undertake a review at any time but they must review a patient's detention if the RC submits a report under section 20 renewing detention. They must consider holding a review if they receive a request from a patient and also if the RC makes a report under section 25 opposing a nearest relative's application for a patient's discharge. The Code of Practice advises at para. 31.12 that, in deciding whether to conduct a review where they have a discretion, the managers are entitled to take into account whether there has been a recent tribunal hearing or whether one is due in the near future.

In exercising the power to discharge the managers must consider whether the criteria for detention under the relevant section continue to be met. In addition (if the review follows the RC's use of the barring order under section 25 to prevent discharge by the NR) they should consider whether the patient, if discharged, would be likely to act in a manner dangerous to other people or to themselves. Dangerousness, which is a more stringent test than the basic risk criteria which refer to health, safety or protection of others, might include psychological as well as physical harm.

The managers should be provided with CPA documentation and written reports from the RC and other appropriate professionals, and the patient should normally be given copies. There is no prescribed procedure for the conduct of managers' hearings but the Code of Practice states at para. 31.32:

- *the patient should be given a full opportunity, and any necessary help, to explain why they should be no longer be detained or on SCT;*
- *the patient should be allowed to be accompanied by a representative of their own choosing to help in putting their point of view to the panel;*
- *the patient should also be allowed to have a relative, friend or advocate attend to support them; and*
- *the responsible clinician and other professionals should be asked to give their views on whether the patient's continued detention or SCT is justified and to explain the grounds on which those views are based.*

Where there are disagreements between those giving evidence the Code gives the following guidance at para. 31.35:

Members of managers' panels will not normally be qualified to form clinical assessments of their own. They must give full weight to the views of all the professionals concerned in the patient's care. If there is a divergence of views among the professionals about whether the patient meets the clinical grounds for continued detention or SCT, managers' panels should consider adjourning to seek further medical or other professional advice.

AMHP reports for managers' hearings will usually follow the same headings that are used for tribunals.

Social circumstances reports

Introduction

The preparation of social circumstances reports is a familiar task for many mental health workers but the purpose of these, and the required content, varies considerably. Equally, expectations of social reports have changed significantly over the last thirty years. No longer do social workers, for example, expect to produce reports with a history of an individual's early childhood and a comprehensive list of psychological and social factors which may, or may not, have a crucial bearing on the matters currently under consideration. Instead, they expect reports to have a clear focus. There have been major changes in conventions on what is acceptable and appropriate to include. Increased rights of access to information have probably hastened these changes, as well as reinforcing the need to base conclusions and recommendations on a proper assessment of available facts, observed behaviour and expressed needs.

The question of making recommendations has always been a difficult one, and again practice has varied over time. Most mental health workers now make recommendations in tribunal reports whereas ten years ago they were often advised not to do this.

AMHPs may find that they are expected to contribute reports in the following areas:

- assessments for possible admission to hospital;
- cases where the nearest relative has made the application for detention (s14);
- general review reports on a patient's progress;
- assessments for possible admission to guardianship;
- assessments for access to resources;
- Mental Health Tribunals;
- Hospital Managers' Reviews;
- assessments for after-care arrangements under section 117;
- where an application for a community treatment order is considered.

Each of these is considered, in varying detail, on the following pages.

Assessments for possible admission to hospital

There are various reasons for completing a report at the time of making an assessment for a possible admission to hospital and many local authorities have an in-house form for such occasions. Information in such reports can be useful for a number of purposes, including:

- providing a record of the circumstances leading up to any decision reached and documenting the assessment of risk factors;

- for hospital staff in the case of an admission occurring (whether formal or informal);

- subsequent review of the person's needs;

- a Mental Health Tribunal (especially for section 2) or Hospital Managers' Review;

- in the case of a compulsory admission, to provide a much fuller account of the reasons for admission than would be apparent from the application form and recommendations.

The process of completing a social report form can have its own value, especially if this is done at the time of assessment. For example, the form might contain reminders of certain key issues: is an interpreter needed? Has the nearest relative been contacted and informed of their rights under section 23?

A typical form might cover the following:

- *Personal information* – name, address, date of birth, ethnic origin, relatives, GP;

- *Language* – and whether an interpreter is needed;

- *Origin of referral* – particularly note if it came from the nearest relative (s13(4));

- *Information at referral* – any particular concerns or risks;

- *Interview with patient* – their wishes and views;

- *Any known past wishes of the patient;*

- *Details of relatives and their views* – especially nearest relative's attitude;

- *Details of significant others;*

- *Medical opinions;*

- *Social, family and personal factors* (including visits by children – see below);

- *Alternatives to compulsory admission* (informal admission, guardianship, day care, GP, community psychiatric nurse (CPN), outpatient care, friends, relatives, etc.);

- *Outcome of assessment and the reasons for this;*

- **Accommodation;*

- *Employment/occupation/education;*
- *Financial position;*
- *Family history and relationships;*
- *Community support available on discharge* – if being admitted to hospital;
- *Summary and recommendations for future action.*

(*Starred items may be more or less relevant at the time of assessment but may be worth noting in case of a subsequent Mental Health Tribunal.)

Some local authorities produce such forms on self-duplicating pads to make it easier for AMHPs to complete handwritten reports at the time of the assessment and still be able to pass copies to others such as hospital staff and colleagues.

There are similarities between this list and the factors identified in the Code of Practice as key points to be taken into account when making an assessment (paras 4.5-4.16).

AMHP reports for applications under section 2, 3 or 4 (including advice on children)

Paragraph 4.94 of the Code states that:

> the AMHP should provide an outline report for the hospital at the time the patient is first admitted or detained, giving reasons for the application and details of any practical matters about the patient's circumstances which the hospital should know. Where possible, the report should include the name and telephone number of the AMHP or a care co-ordinator who can give further information. LSSAs should consider the use of a standard form on which AMHPs can make this outline report.

The Code, in an earlier passage, at para. 4.88, states that before making an application:

> AMHPs should ensure that appropriate arrangements are in place for the immediate care of any dependent children the patient may have and any adults who rely on the patient for care. Their needs should already have been considered as part of the assessment.

Circular LAC(99)32 contains more detailed advice and makes the following suggested approach at para. 9.1:

> In those instances where a compulsory admission is being considered, the needs of and arrangements for children involved with the patient should be considered by the AMHP as an integral element within the assessment. This information should be recorded by the AMHP and communicated to the hospital in the event of admission. The AMHP should alert their colleagues in children's services if they have any concerns about child care arrangements for dependent children of the patient. It would assist this process if

documents were designed to incorporate information from this element of the assessment.

Similarly, the AMHP should provide the hospital with information about the views of other person(s) with parental responsibility for the children of the patient, where it is appropriate to do so and if these can be ascertained. AMHPs should be sensitive to situations where the relationship between parents had broken down so that any decision about child visiting is not used inappropriately in residence or contact disputes . . .

In the vast majority of cases where no concerns are identified, arrangements should be made to support the patient and child and to facilitate contact.

Cases where the nearest relative has made the application for detention

Section 14 of the Mental Health Act 1983 requires the hospital managers to notify the local social services authority as soon as a patient is admitted on an application from the nearest relative on either a section 2 or 3. The local authority then, as soon as practicable, must arrange for an AMHP to interview the patient and provide the managers with a report on his social circumstances. It would be good practice for such a report to be provided in cases where the application was for a section 4, but this is not formally required.

Jones (2008, p103) considers that the social circumstances report

could include an account of the patient's family and social relationships (including the attitude of carers), history of mental disorder, previous contact with the local authority, access to community resources, his employment records, financial situation and his accommodation. The report should also contain an account of the circumstances of the admission. If the nearest relative's application was made after an AMHP had refused to make one, it is suggested that that AMHP should prepare the report which should include an account of the reasons for his or her decision.

It would be helpful for such a report to follow similar headings to those used in reports on assessments for admission. The reasons for the nearest relative being the applicant should be clearly stated. If the AMHP has doubts about the appropriateness of detention, these should be clearly stated.

General review reports on a patient's progress

These may be designed to be shared with members of a multi-disciplinary team and sometimes with the patient and their family. They may contain a summary of aims, facilities and services needed and a review of progress so far. See under after-care arrangements below for typical headings when used with patients who are covered by section 117, and the section on access to resources for some current views on reports.

Assessments for possible admission into guardianship

Sometimes, the same format might be used as for assessments for possible admission to hospital and, indeed, one could argue that every such assessment for hospital should include a view on the possibility of using guardianship. In many cases, however, where guardianship is being actively considered, there is time to produce a comprehensive care plan as recommended by the Code of Practice at para. 26.19. It suggests that the plan should identify the services which are needed by the patient and who will provide them. The plan should also indicate which of the guardianship powers are necessary to achieve the plan. At para. 26.21 it states that key elements of the plan are likely to be:

- *suitable accommodation to help meet the patient's needs;*
- *access to day care, education and training facilities, as appropriate;*
- *effective co-operation and communication between all those concerned in implementing the plan; and*
- *(if there is to be a private guardian) support from the LSSA for the guardian.*

Assessments for access to resources

There is often a specific in-house format for requests for resources administered by the local authority. These have frequently been revised over the last few years as assessment procedures have changed.

Mental Health Tribunals (and Hospital Managers' Reviews)

There are various advisory policy documents on social reports for tribunals but the simplest advice for AMHPs is to follow the headings which can be found in the Practice Directions (First-Tier Tribunal). These are reprinted at Appendix 7. The Directions set out what is expected in reports (other than for conditionally discharged patients):

a. *the patient's home and family circumstances;*
b. *insofar as it is practicable, and except in restricted cases, a summary of the views of the patient's nearest relative, unless (having consulted the patient) the person compiling the report thinks it would be inappropriate to consult the nearest relative;*
c. *insofar as it is practicable, the views of any person who plays a substantial part in the care of the patient but is not professionally concerned with it;*
d. *the views of the patient, including his concerns, hopes and beliefs in relation to the Tribunal proceedings and their outcome;*
e. *the opportunities for employment and the housing facilities available to the patient;*
f. *what (if any) community support is or will be made available to the patient and its effectiveness, if the patient is discharged from hospital;*

g.   the patient's financial circumstances (including his entitlement to benefits);

h.   an assessment of the patient's strengths and any other positive factors that the Tribunal should be aware of in coming to a view on whether he should be discharged; and

i.   an assessment of the extent to which the patient or other persons would be likely to be at risk if the patient is discharged by the Tribunal, and how any such risks could best be managed.

There is a very similar list for reports for CTOs which can be found at para. 26 of the Practice Directions.

Although it is the health authority which should ensure the provision of reports, it often falls to local authority mental health social workers (including AMHPs) to write them, although this is changing in some community teams who give the task to the care co-ordinator. The legal basis for the range of facilities which should be considered can be found in Chapter 9. Note that in the judicial review of *R v MHRT for West Midlands and North West ex parte H* (2000), it was held that restricted patients do not have a nearest relative and therefore one should not be named in any reports.

The Code of Practice asks hospital managers to ensure that they have relevant reports before they undertake a review. Social reports for reviews should probably be similar to those for Tribunals.

After-care arrangements under section 117

The Code of Practice to the Mental Health Act 1983 (para. 27.13) identifies some key issues when considering after-care which can be adapted into a sensible list of topics for anyone compiling a report:

- *continuing mental healthcare, whether in the community or on an out-patient basis;*
- *the psychological needs of the patient and, where appropriate, of their family and carers;*
- *physical healthcare;*
- *daytime activities or employment;*
- *appropriate accommodation;*
- *identified risks and safety issues;*
- *any specific needs arising from, for example, co-existing physical disability, sensory impairment, learning disability or autistic spectrum disorder;*
- *any specific needs arising from drug, alcohol or substance misuse (if relevant);*
- *any parenting or caring needs;*
- *social, cultural or spiritual needs;*
- *counselling and personal support;*
- *assistance in welfare rights and managing finances;*
- *the involvement of authorities and agencies in a different area, if the*

patient is not going to live locally;

- *the involvement of other agencies, for example the probation service or voluntary organisations;*
- *for a restricted patient, the conditions which the Secretary of State for Justice or the Tribunal has imposed or is likely to impose on their conditional discharge; and*
- *contingency plans (should the patient's mental health deteriorate) and crisis contact details.*

ACTIVITY **7.1**

Sample questions on Mental Health Tribunals.

1a When a patient is appealing against a section 3 detention, the Mental Health Tribunal has a number of powers at its disposal, as well as recommendations which it can make. These are conferred by section 72. What are the powers?

1b Identify any one of the recommendations which the MHT could make under section 72. In what circumstances might it be wise for the members of the tribunal to make this recommendation rather than use one of the powers at their disposal?

2a What powers does a Mental Health Tribunal have in terms of making decisions about a patient who is detained on section 2?

2b Why might a tribunal ask an AMHP attending a tribunal hearing whether they would be likely to apply for the patient's detention had that person been an informal patient and the AMHP were assessing them on the day of the tribunal?

2c Identify one dilemma an AMHP might face in these circumstances and how they might deal with this.

Multiple choice questions
(Answers in Appendix 9)

1 A Mental Health Tribunal can vary the conditions attached to a CTO.
   (a) True   ☐
   (b) False   ☐

2 A patient who is subject to a section 3 detention is first entitled to apply to the tribunal:
   (a) after six months   ☐
   (b) within six months   ☐
   (c) after one year   ☐

Chapter 8
The Mental Health Act Commission

Overview of the Commission

Mental Health Act Commission
Maid Marian House
56 Hounds Gate
Nottingham NG1 6BG
Tel: 0115 943 7100
Fax: 0115 943 7101
Chairman: Simon Armson
Acting Chief Executive: Gemma Pearce

As statutory mental health law has developed in England and Wales so there has been a number of independent bodies seeking to protect the rights of detained patients. In 1815–16 there was a Parliamentary Inquiry into Madhouses which was followed by the Lunacy Commission and then the Board of Control. Both of these bodies reported to parliament. The latest of these bodies, the Mental Health Act Commission, was established as a Special Health Authority in 1983.

Section 121 of the Mental Health Act 1983 establishes the Mental Health Act Commission and requires the Secretary of State and the Welsh Ministers to direct the Commission to appoint registered medical practitioners for the purposes of Part 4 of this Act. These are known as Second Opinion Appointed Doctors (SOADs). For Wales the Secretary of State's functions are performed by the National Assembly for Wales. In practice, as a result of delegated legislation, the Commission has been asked to take on a number of other functions which are listed below.

The Health and Social Care Act 2008 received Royal Assent in July 2008 and repeals section 121. The Act establishes the Care Quality Commission (CQC) so that the functions listed at the end of this chapter have been undertaken by the CQC in England from April 2009. In Wales the functions are expected to be performed by the Healthcare Inspectorate for Wales.

The Mental Health Act Commission has about 100 members including laypersons, lawyers, doctors, nurses, social workers, psychologists and other specialists. This group includes a chairman and a vice chairman. There is roughly an equal number of men and women. The percentage of current Commission members from black and minority ethnic groups is about 16 per cent. Commission members fall into three categories:

- There are four full-time Regional Commissioners.

- There is an Area Commissioner for each Welsh Region or English Strategic Health Authority (e.g. Dorset and Somerset, or Devon and Cornwall). Area Commission members undertake some visiting and, in addition, write reports to Trusts and co-ordinate Commission activities across a Strategic Health Authority area.

- The Area Commissioners are supported by one or more Local Commissioners. Local Commission members' primary duties include examining statutory documentation, meeting with detained patients and taking up immediate issues on their behalf.

The Commission also has a panel of about 120 consultant psychiatrists who operate as Second Opinion Appointed Doctors for consent to treatment purposes. This group is being expanded because of the demands of the new community treatment order provisions. There is a further group of three doctors and 20 other people who can be appointed to consider requests for neurosurgery for mental disorder. This procedure is rarely used.

At the time of writing the responsibility for the management of the Commission rests with the Mental Health Act Commission Board. Operational management is the responsibility of the chief executive. Members of the Commission, with the exception of the chairman and vice chairman, work within Regional Teams who undertake the Commission's visiting activity within a particular geographical area. They are managed by a Regional Director who is responsible for arranging and monitoring the teams' activities.

In April 2009 the Care Quality Commission brought together the work of the Mental Health Act Commission in England, the Commission for Social Care Inspection and the Healthcare Commission. In Wales the duties of the Mental Health Act Commission will be taken over by Healthcare Inspectorate Wales. In England there continues to be Mental Health Act Commissioners but the distinction between the roles of Area and

Local Commissioners disappeared. It remains to be seen what other changes will occur and how effective the new bodies in England and Wales bodies will be in protecting the rights of patients who are subject to compulsion. Some have argued that the CQC will have more powers of enforcement. Others have expressed concerns that there might be a loss of clear focus on the specific situation of patients who are subject to compulsory powers.

Currently the Commission has a staff of about 40 people who work under the operational direction of the Commission's chief executive. These members of staff are Department of Health civil servants who are seconded to the Commission. They are divided into teams which provide administrative support to the Commission Management Board, the Regional Visiting Teams, the Second Opinion Service and other Commission activities.

There is also a small unit which leads the Commission's development of policy. Finally, the Commission has a specialised team that directs the work involved with statutory complaints and all deaths of detained patients.

The Commission's functions

1. To keep under review the operation of the Mental Health Act 1983 in respect of patients liable to be detained under the Act.

2. To visit and interview, in private, patients detained under the Act in hospitals and mental nursing homes and those subject to community treatment orders.

3. To investigate complaints which fall within the Commission's remit.

4. To appoint medical practitioners and others to give second opinions in cases where this is required by the Act.

5. To review decisions to withhold mail of patients detained in high security hospitals.

6. To publish and lay before Parliament a report every two years.

7. To monitor the implementation of the Code of Practice and propose amendments to Ministers.

8. To offer advice to Ministers on matters falling within the Commission's remit.

The Commission's Biennial Reports (the most recent covers the period 2005–7) are available from The Stationery Office and are a useful source of material about the operation of the Mental Health Act in England and Wales. AMHPs will find them especially helpful as they provide a detailed analysis of issues arising from the operation of the Act in practice.

ACTIVITY 8.1

Sample questions on the Mental Health Act Commission.

1a Identify three of the main functions of the Mental Health Act Commission which might relate to consent to treatment issues.

1b In relation to any one of these, what would you see as the likely main strengths and weaknesses of the Commission from a detained patient's point of view?

2a Identify three of the main functions of the Mental Health Act Commission (other than those which relate to consent to treatment).

2b In relation to any one of these, what would you see as the likely main strengths and weaknesses of the Commission from a detained patient's point of view?

Multiple choice questions
(Answers in Appendix 9)

1 Which of the following functions might be performed by the Mental Health Act Commission?
   (a) Investigating complaints by detained patients ☐
   (b) Discharging patients from detention ☐
   (c) Appointing second opinion doctors for consent to treatment provisions ☐
   (d) Visiting and interviewing detained patients in private ☐
   (e) Recommending leave of absence with a view to discharge ☐

2 The Mental Health Act Commission does not have a remit to see patients subject to Community Treatment Orders.
   (a) True ☐
   (b) False ☐

Chapter 9
Other relevant legislation

AMHPs are bound by various duties under the Human Rights Act 1998, the Mental Capacity Act 2005, the Equality Act 2006 and other anti-discrimination legislation. This is because their role makes them individuals with functions of a public nature. A range of other legislation impacts on their work, e.g. the Children Act 1989, the National Assistance Act 1948, the Care Standards Act 2000, the Disability Discrimination Act 1995 and the Equal Opportunities Act 2006. This chapter looks at the broader legal framework within which AMHPs undertake their duties.

The following is a summary of law which may be relevant to mentally disordered people living in England and Wales. Welfare benefits law is not covered here: information about this should be sought from publications such as the Disability Alliance Guide. Acts covering 'community care services' as defined by section 46 of the NHS and Community Care Act 1990 are asterisked * below.

Summary of legislation
Disabled Persons (Employment) Acts 1944 and 1958

These Acts established registers, disablement resettlement officers (DROs), quotas, sheltered workshops, Remploy, etc. The definition of disability was updated by the Disability Discrimination Act 1995 (see below). Section 3 of the 1958 Act enables local authorities to provide facilities for disabled persons to be employed.

National Assistance Act 1948 (and National Assistance (Amendment) Act 1951)

This is also discussed in more detail later in the chapter. It replaced existing Poor Law.

*Part 3   Includes sections 21, 29. Part 4 includes sections 47, 48.

*Section 21   Provision of residential accommodation for persons 18 or over who by reason of age, illness or disability or other circumstances (including nursing or expectant mothers) are in need of care or attention which is not otherwise available to them. Need to have regard to welfare of all persons for whom accommodation is provided. Section 22 requires people to pay for the accommodation.

*Section 29   Promotes the provision of a variety of services to disabled people who are aged 18 or over. 'Disabled' here is defined as including people who are blind, deaf or dumb, those substantially or permanently handicapped by illness, injury or congenital deformity, and people suffering from any kind of mental disorder. These services may be charged for.

Section 47   Removal to hospital or other accommodation of persons who *(a) are suffering from grave chronic disease, or, being aged, infirm or physically incapacitated, are living in insanitary conditions, and (b) are unable to devote to themselves, and are not receiving from other persons, proper care and attention.* Removal must be necessary either in the person's own interests or for preventing injury to the health of, or serious nuisance to, other persons. It is used rarely, if at all; the quick procedure under the National Assistance (Amendment) Act 1951 is usually preferred. (See further detail below.)

Section 48   Protection of moveable property: a local authority responsibility when section 47 is used, when someone is admitted to hospital or to Part 3 accommodation, and where there appears to be a danger of loss of or damage to any moveable property and where no other suitable arrangements have been made. Allows right of access to do this and allows for recovery of expenses from the person concerned.

Health Services and Public Health Act 1968

*Section 45   Promotion by local authorities of the welfare of older people.

Section 64   Allows financial grants or loans from health authorities to voluntary organisations.

Section 65   Allows financial grants or loans from local authorities to voluntary organisations.

Chronically Sick and Disabled Persons Act 1970

Section 1   Local authorities must gather information on the number of people in their area covered by section 29 of the National Assistance Act 1948 and should inform themselves as to how they should meet these people's needs. LAs must also publish information about relevant services. (This provision was extended by the 1986 Act.)

Section 2   Provision of adaptations to the home and other services. See overlap with section 4 of 1986 Act.

Local Authority Social Services Act 1970

This Act, which resulted from the Seebohm Report, brought together separate departments and identified legislation which would be the responsibility of the new social services departments.

The Health and Safety at Work Act 1974

This Act stresses shared responsibility for safety. Everyone is to accept responsibility for the results of their actions and omissions. The Act sets out the following duties:

- The employer: *It shall be the duty of every employer, so far as it is reasonably practicable, to take care of the health, safety and welfare at work of all [their] employees.* They must provide *such information, instruction, training and supervision as is necessary to ensure, so far as it reasonably practicable, the safety at work of ... employees.*

- The employee: *It shall be the duty of every employee while at work (a) to take reasonable care for the health & safety of ... self and of other persons who may be affected by ... acts or omissions at work, and (b) to co-operate with the employer so far as is necessary to enable the employer to perform or comply with any statutory duty.* AMHPs are advised to seek out local policies on prevention and management of violence.

Sex Discrimination Act 1975

It is unlawful to discriminate on the grounds of sex.

Note: Sexuality is *not* covered by this Act.

Race Relations Act 1976 and 2000

Since April 2001, all public bodies have had a general duty to work towards the elimination of unlawful racial discrimination and to promote equality of opportunity and good relations between different racial groups (section 1 of 2000 Act).

Social services departments can lawfully discriminate on racial grounds if the need indicates, e.g. Vietnamese worker with disabled Vietnamese person. Similarly, discrimination is allowed by employers in training.

Note: Section 11 of Local Government Act 1966 provides funding for special provisions.

National Health Service Act 1977

*Section 21   Services for the prevention of illness, the care of people suffering
and Sched 8   from illness (including any form of mental disorder), and the after-
            care of people who have been suffering from illness.

Section 22   Duty for SSDs to co-operate with health authorities.

Health and Social Services and Social Security Adjudications Act 1983

Promotes joint planning and funding between health and local authorities. Also requires local authorities to charge for certain services.

Mental Health Act 1983

See separate chapters covering most provisions of this Act.

*Section 117   After-care services for those detained on long-term sections.

Public Health (Control of Disease) Act 1984

Section 46   Places a duty on local authorities to bury or cremate the body of a
            person if no other arrangements are being made and gives power to
            SSD to bury or cremate the body of a person who was accommo-
            dated in a Part III of the National Assistance Act home. A charge may
            be made for this.

Police and Criminal Evidence Act 1984

This sets out the rights of mentally disordered persons who are arrested and/or charged by the police. The most recent edition of the Codes of Practice, which govern procedures under this Act, was published in 2008. It includes details of the appropriate adult role.

Disabled Persons (Services, Consultation and Representation) Act 1986

Section 1   (This and other sections concerning authorised representatives are
            still not in force.) Representatives embodied the notion of advocacy

and would have negotiated for services and participated in assessments.

Section 4   Duty to consider disabled person's need for services when requested to do so by the person themselves or by their carer.

Section 5   Duty to consider disabled person's need for services when leaving special education.

Section 8   Carer's ability to continue providing care must be taken into account. 'Carer' is defined as someone providing substantial amount of care on a regular basis but who is not employed to do so by a statutory agency.

Health and Medicines Act 1988

Section 19   Abolishes the power of local authorities to charge health authorities for the services of their staff. This section consolidates arrangements which were agreed in 1974 but which were under threat by some local authorities who had declared their intention to charge for social workers' services.

Children Act 1989

(See also Chapter 36 in Code of Practice with regard to which legislation to use.)

Section 25   Secure accommodation order applies to children not detained under MH Act where risk exists of self-harm or of absconding followed by harm. No more than 72 hours detained per 28-day period without the authority of the court.

Section 31   Supervision order: LA may specify where child lives, have psychiatric examination, etc.

Section 31   Care order: LA then becomes 'nearest relative'.

Section 38   Interim care order or supervision order: maximum initial eight weeks with renewals of four weeks.

Section 43   Child assessment order: maximum seven days. May include psychiatric examination.

Section 44   Emergency protection order: maximum initial eight days with extension of seven days. May be removed to accommodation or kept in hospital.

Section 46   Police protection: maximum 72 hours where police believe risk of significant harm; may be removed to accommodation or kept in hospital.

Section 47   Local authority enquiries – to safeguard or promote child's welfare.

National Health Service and Community Care Act 1990

Part 3 of the Act is relevant to social services departments.

Section 42   Among other matters, this section allows SSDs to fulfil responsibilities in the provision of welfare services (e.g. under section 21 of the National Assistance Act 1948) by making arrangements with private concerns or voluntary organisations as their agents.

Section 46   Each social services authority must publish a strategic plan for the provision of community care services in their area.

Section 47   Requires LAs to assess individuals' needs if they appear to require community care.

Section 48   Inspection of premises used for provision of community care services.

Section 49   Makes arrangements for transfer of staff between health authorities and LAs.

Section 50   Makes amendments to the Local Authority Social Services Act 1970, e.g. the need to establish a complaints procedure.

General power to declare local authorities to be in default if they fail to carry out their functions under the above Acts of 1948, 1977 and 1983. Secretary of State can then direct local authorities to comply and can enforce this by an order of the High Court.

Carers (Recognition and Services) Act 1995

Requires local authorities to take proper account of carers' circumstances when carrying out an assessment of the need for community care services of the person being cared for.

Disability Discrimination Act 1995

This Act requires service providers to take reasonable steps to change practice, policies or procedures which make it impossible or unreasonably difficult for disabled people to use a service. 'Disability' is defined as *a physical or mental impairment which has a substantial and long-term adverse effect on ability to carry out normal day-to-day activities*. 'Long-term' is a year (or less if an illness is terminal). 'Mental impairment' here includes mental illness.

Housing Act 1996

Section 182   Requires housing authorities and social services authorities to have regard to guidance issued by the Secretary of State when dealing with homeless people.

Section 213   Requires housing authorities and social services authorities to co-operate with each other when dealing with homeless people.

Community Care (Direct Payments) Act 1996

Allows local authorities to deliver community care services via direct payments. It aims to give more control and choice to service users.

Human Rights Act 1998

(See Chapter 10 and Appendix 2 for further information.)

Commencement date 2 October 2000. Embodies European Convention on Human Rights within the British legal system. Individuals are able to pursue rights through British courts.

Health Act 1999

Part 3 of the Act is relevant to social services departments.

Section 28   Requires primary care trusts, NHS Trusts and local authorities to participate in the preparation and review of health authorities' health care plans.

Section 31   Provides for the Secretary of Health to issue regulations so that NHS bodies and local authorities can pool resources, delegate functions and transfer resources from one to another if this is likely to lead to improvement in the way functions are exercised. This can link to single provision of services (e.g. see Somerset Partnership). This does not, however, affect legal liability for such services.

These are permissive powers.

- No limit to size of partnerships or number of partners.

- Pooled funds are to achieve flexibility.

- Lead commissioning (HA, LA, PCT) is where one agency commissions services delegated to it by partner agencies.

- Delegation of functions could lead to secondment or transfer of staff.

- Integrated provision allows better co-ordination of services through one management structure.

Regulation 6 excluded appointment of ASWs from partnerships but this has changed with the implementation of the reforms to the Mental Health Act. AMHPs are accountable to local authorities but can be employed by other bodies.

Care Standards Act 2000

This establishes the framework for quality assurance of residential and care services.

Carers and Disabled Children Act 2000

This legislation allows local authorities to provide services and support directly to carers. This can include direct payments. A carer's own needs can now be directly assessed. The Act also introduced a short-term break voucher scheme designed to provide flexibility in the timing of carers' breaks. Any services to carers may be subject to charge.

Health and Social Care Act 2001

This establishes the boundaries between social care and health care. It prevents local authorities from providing nursing care as part of residential care. It also extended the direct payments scheme.

Community Care (Delayed Discharges) Act 2003

There is a duty to assess patients to see if they are ready for discharge from hospital. The local authority is penalised if it cannot then make arrangements for discharge within an identified time limit.

Compulsory removal under section 47 of the National Assistance Act 1948

People may be compulsorily admitted to hospital or to residential accommodation under section 47 of the National Assistance Act 1948 or under the emergency procedures set out in the 1951 Act. These controversial pieces of legislation have been the subject of some debate. Suggestions have been made for their repeal, amendment and even for their extension to wide use. Age Concern have estimated that about half of the people dealt with in this way are suffering from mental disorder. It is difficult to obtain statistics on their use but there are probably no more than about 200 instances per year.

The powers may be seen as a way of dealing with long-term neglect or of coping with a crisis. In considering the latter, and referring to section 135 of the Mental Health Act 1983 as well as to the National Assistance Act powers, the Law Commission's Consultation Paper No. 119 *Mentally Incapacitated Adults and Decision-Making: An Overview* (1991, p77) stated:

> These emergency powers are generally regarded as stigmatising and are rarely used. The National Assistance Acts are particularly unpopular and some local authorities have a policy of refusing to use them ... Because applications under section 135 are made by social workers, and those under section 47 by community physicians, responsibility for taking emergency action does not lie clearly in any one place.

The introduction of the Mental Capacity Act in 2005 would appear to have reduced still further the need for their use. Brayne and Carr (2005, p560) criticise aspects of section 47 in the following passage:

The person can be detained against his or her will only in the place mentioned in the court order; any variation requires a magistrates' court order. This is a sweeping power, made more so by the fact that there is often no funding for legal representation before the magistrates for the 'victim'. The Access to Justice Act 1999, shamefully, explicitly excludes this from the scope of Community Legal Service funding, though since liberty is at stake we would argue that this is incompatible with the right to a fair trial under Article 6. There is not even any requirement that the person be represented or receive legal advice before an order is made, which is surprising by the standards of 1948, let alone the standards of the Human Rights Act, given that the person whose future is being considered may lack the ability in many cases to be able to argue the case against removal in person.

When it is used, section 47 of the National Assistance Act 1948 provides for the district local authority to apply to the magistrates court for a removal order based on the certificate of the community physician. The subject of the order must fulfil the criteria of subsection (1) which are that they are:

(a) suffering from grave chronic disease or, being aged, infirm or physically incapacitated, are living in insanitary conditions; and

(b) are unable to devote to themselves, and are not receiving from other persons, proper care and attention.

Removal must be necessary either in the person's own interests or for preventing injury to the health of, or serious nuisance to, other persons.

Hoggett (1996, p93) states:

A nuisance in law is something which causes either physical damage to the neighbour's property or a substantial interference with its use and enjoyment. None of this, therefore, suggests that section 47 is simply a way of overcoming the reluctance of an old lady who might be safe or more comfortable in an old people's home.

Seven clear days' notice of the hearing must be given to:

- the person concerned (or to the person in charge of them); and

- the person in charge of the place to which it is proposed to remove the person.

The court must hear oral evidence of the allegations in the certificate.

If granted, the order allows for the person's removal by a named officer of the applying authority to a suitable hospital or other place so that the person can receive the necessary care and attention through his 'detention and maintenance therein' (s47(3)). The order may last for a maximum of three months in the first instance but may be renewed by the court for further periods of up to three months at a time.

National Assistance (Amendment) Act 1951

This provides a quicker procedure for use in emergencies and is probably used more frequently than the full procedure. Under section 1(1) the application must be necessary in the interests of the person and removal of the person must be seen as necessary without delay.

The process is simpler in a number of ways:

- The application may be made directly by the Community Physician supported by a second medical opinion.
- The application may be made to a single justice rather than to the full court.
- Periods of notice required by section 47 may be waived.
- An order can be made without notice (previously referred to as *ex parte*).

An order made under these emergency procedures lasts for up to three weeks. An application to the full court is necessary to extend this but it may well not be made once the initial removal has been made and where the person concerned shows no sign of attempting to return to their own home.

Neither of these powers carries with it the right to treat a person against their will. If psychiatric treatment is necessary, use of the Mental Health Act 1983 may be more appropriate. Where the person lacks capacity in relation to treatment issues, the Mental Capacity Act may be relevant for both psychiatric treatment and general physical treatment.

ACTIVITY 9.1

Sample questions on other relevant legislation

1a When does a local authority have a duty to protect a person's moveable property under section 48 of the National Assistance Act 1948?

1b Why might this aspect of law involve an AMHP who applies for someone's detention under section 2 of the Mental Health Act 1983?

1c What difficulties can arise with the operation of this piece of legislation?

2a What are the grounds for removing someone from their home under section 47 of the National Assistance Act 1948?

2b In what circumstances might this piece of law be proposed by someone as an alternative to reliance on the Mental Capacity Act or the Mental Health Act?

2c What criticisms might be made of the procedures involved with section 47?

Multiple choice questions

(Answers in Appendix 9)

1 Where a Care Order is made the local authority becomes the child's nearest relative.

(a) True ☐

(b) False ☐

ACTIVITY **9.1** *continued*

2 When a person is removed to a place of safety on section 47 of the
National Assistance Act under the emergency procedures they may be
kept there for what period in the first instance?
(a) 72 hours
(b) three days
(c) three weeks
(d) 28 days

3 The Mental Health Act provides an exemption from the Carers Act 1995
requirement that local authorities take proper account of carers'
circumstances when carrying out an assessment of the need for community
care services of a person being cared for.
(a) True
(b) False

Chapter 10
The Human Rights Act 1998

European Convention on Human Rights

The Act became operational on 2 October 2000. It does not incorporate the whole of the European Convention on Human Rights (EHR) but it does include the following Articles.

Article 2 *Right to life*
Everyone's right to life shall be protected by law.

Article 3 *Prohibition of torture*
No one to be subject to torture or inhuman or degrading treatment or punishment.

Article 5 *Right to liberty and security of person*
5.1 No one shall be deprived of their liberty except for specific cases and in accordance with procedure prescribed by law e.g. after conviction, lawful arrest on suspicion of having committed an offence, lawful detention of person of unsound mind, to prevent spread of infectious diseases.

5.4 Everyone deprived of liberty by arrest or detention shall be entitled to take proceedings by which the lawfulness of the detention shall be decided speedily by a court and release ordered if the detention is not lawful.

Note: In the *Bournewood* case (*HL* v *UK, 2004*) the European Court ruled there had been breaches of Article 5.1 and 5.4. For a detailed description of this case see Chapter 2.

Article 6	*Right to a fair trial*
	Everyone is entitled to a fair and public hearing within a reasonable time by an independent and impartial tribunal.
Article 8	*Right to respect for private and family life*
	Everyone has the right to respect for his private and family life, his home and his correspondence.
Article 9	*Freedom of thought, conscience and religion*
Article 11	*Freedom of assembly and association*
Article 12	*Right to marry*
	Men and women of marriageable age have the right to marry and to found a family.
Article 14	*Prohibition of discrimination*
	Enjoyment of the rights and freedoms set forth in this Convention shall be secured without discrimination on any ground such as sex, race, colour, language, religion, political or other opinion, national or social origin, association with a national minority, property, birth or other status.

The full text of the relevant articles of the European Convention on Human Rights is set out in Appendix 7.

Advice on implications of the Act

Section 3 of the Act states:

> So far as it is possible to do so, primary legislation and subordinate legislation must be read and given effect in a way which is compatible with the Convention rights.

This does not, however, affect the validity, continuing operation or enforcement of any incompatible primary legislation.

However, moving away from statute, where following the Mental Health Act Code of Practice would appear to be leading to a breach of a person's human rights this might provide cogent reasons for departing from the Code. (See discussion on Jones's view of DOLS in Chapter 11.)

Public authorities

Public authorities are required to act in a way which is compatible with ECHR rights unless they are prevented from doing so by statute. Advice from the Department of Health would suggest that the following would be defined as public authorities:

- courts;
- tribunals;
- NHS Trusts;
- private/voluntary contractors undertaking public functions under NHS contract;
- local authorities (including social services);
- primary care trusts;
- GPs, dentists, opticians and pharmacists when undertaking NHS work;
- bodies with public functions such as the General Medical Council.

The Sainsbury Centre states that the following would probably also be seen to be public authorities:

- Mental Health Act Commission;
- Commission for Health Improvement;
- National Institute for Clinical Excellence;
- Health Service Ombudsman.

Key terms

Absolute rights	These cannot be limited or qualified (e.g. Article 2).
Declarations of incompatibility	May be made by higher courts with the expectation that legislation will then be amended to make it compatible with the ECHR.
Limited rights	Specify limitations (e.g. the right to liberty allows for the detention of 'persons of unsound mind').
Living instrument	The European Court will interpret the ECHR in light of present-day conditions.
Margin of appreciation	Describes the measure of discretion given to the state in deciding on action under scrutiny (e.g. national security).
Positive obligations	Many articles expect positive action as well as non-interference with rights.
Proportionality	Interference with rights must be no more than necessary to achieve the intended objective.
Qualified rights	Set out when interference with such rights is permissible (where in accordance with the law, necessary in a democratic society, related to the tone of the aims in the relevant article).

Some examples of the impact of the Human Rights Act

The case of *Winterwerp* v *Netherlands* (1979) is important in that it established that a person must be reliably shown to be suffering from a true mental disorder based on objective medical expertise (except for emergencies). The mental disorder must be of a kind or degree justifying compulsory confinement and continued detention must be justified on the basis of the persistence of the disorder. There needs to be a true mental disorder and not just behaviour deviating from society's norms. This case may create dilemmas for AMHPs in at least two situations:

- if they are assessing someone with a paraphilia (such as paedophilia) and there is discussion as to whether the individual is presenting with a true mental disorder or just behaviour which deviates from society's norms;

- if they are put forward to train as an Approved Clinician, a role which is supposed to involve the ability to demonstrate objective medical expertise.

Another case of direct relevance to AMHPs was the case of *R (E)* v *Bristol City Council* (2005). In this case the judge decided that to interpret the words 'reasonably practicable' in relation to the obligation of the ASW under section 11(4) of the Act to consult with the nearest relative as meaning 'appropriate' rather than that the nearest relative was 'available' would avoid a potential infringement of the patient's rights under Article 8. This was in a situation where the patient did not wish that the nearest relative should be consulted. As we have seen, courts are required to interpret legislation if possible in a way which is compatible with Convention rights. This is what the judge did in the Bristol case and it has left the AMHP, in effect, with a decision to make as to when to consult the nearest relative in cases where this would cause a degree of distress to the patient.

The status of the Code of Practice was considered in *R (Munjaz)* v *Mersey Care NHS Trust* (2005). The key questions in this case were the legal status and effect of the Code of Practice and whether Ashworth Hospital's use of seclusion was lawful. This had departed from the guidance then contained in the Code of Practice.

The Law Lords decided that the Code does not have statutory force but that it is guidance which should be considered with great care. It is more than advice which a person under an obligation to have regard to it is free to follow or not. The decision was that the Code should be departed from only for 'cogent reasons'.

The Appeal Court had earlier decided that seclusion could constitute medical treatment for mental disorder under section 63 and the Lords did not depart from this view. Where a patient is subject to the compulsory powers of the MHA it is not seclusion which constitutes a deprivation of liberty but the fact that he has been detained under a relevant section. The importance of the ECHR was emphasised and it was noted that appropriate local policies and procedures in relation to seclusion could prevent a breach of the patient's rights under Articles 3 and 8, even if they allow for a departure from the Code's guidance.

For further information and examples of how the Human Rights Act impacts on the Mental Health Act see Chapter 17 of Barber, Brown and Martin (2009).

ACTIVITY **10.1**

Sample questions on the Human Rights Act

1a What were the key human rights issues in the HL v UK case decided in the European Court (the case formerly known as Bournewood)? (That is, identify the key Articles which were relevant to the case and why.)

1b Which Article(s) if any did the European Court decide had been breached and why?

1c What dilemmas does this judgment now pose for AMHPs in practice and how should they approach dealing with these dilemmas?

2a Who can apply to the County Court for the appointment of a Nearest Relative?

2b What aspects of this area of law have been amended to be compliant with the European Convention on Human Rights?

2c What arguments might be put for or against seeking a Nearest Relative for someone who does not seem to have one at the point of assessing for a section 3 admission?

Multiple choice questions
(Answers in Appendix 9)

1 Which rights are specifically enshrined in English law as a result of the Human Rights Act?
   (a) Freedom of thought, conscience and religion ☐
   (b) Freedom of expression ☐
   (c) Freedom to bear arms ☐
   (d) Freedom to give advance agreement to medical treatment ☐
   (e) The right to marry and found a family ☐
   (f) Freedom to travel without personal identification within Europe ☐
   (g) Prohibition of discrimination ☐

2 Under Article 3 (prohibition of torture) no one shall be subjected to:
   (a) inhuman or degrading treatment or punishment ☐
   (b) unwanted psychiatric treatment if detained but mentally capable ☐
   (c) seclusion for more than eight hours ☐
   (d) torture ☐

3 Everyone who is deprived of his liberty by arrest or detention shall be entitled to take proceedings by which the lawfulness of his detention shall be decided speedily by a court.
   (a) True ☐
   (b) False ☐

Chapter 11

The Deprivation of Liberty Safeguards

Introduction

The Mental Health Act 2007 made amendments to the Mental Capacity Act which are covered in summary in this chapter. Readers of the eleventh edition of Jones's Manual (2008, pv) may have seen his criticism of this new legislation as having created a procedure which is

> *hugely complex, voluminous, badly drafted, overly bureaucratic and difficult to understand, and yet provides mentally incapacitated people with minimum safeguards.*

This author would broadly agree with these sentiments but with two reservations.

Many people who have effectively been deprived of their liberty (especially in community settings) have never been properly assessed or given any safeguards whatsoever. At least the process of assessment, which these new measures will hopefully trigger, should provide some consideration of the need for safeguards during the assessment process itself. In some cases this may lead to the use of detention or guardianship under the Mental Health Act and we shall return to Jones's comments on the advantages of these measures later in the chapter.

The second point is that the complexity of the statute has been eased by an excellent Code of Practice which explains the provisions in a far more accessible way than the statute. This chapter will draw heavily on the Code as a way of conveying information on the new procedures. For a detailed analysis of the new Deprivation of Liberty Safeguards (DOLS) procedures and for access to the statute itself see Brown *et al.* (2009).

The full title of the Code is *The Deprivation of Liberty Safeguards (Code to supplement the main Mental Capacity Act 2005 Code of Practice)* and will be referred to as the DOLS Code for the rest of this chapter. The DOLS Code provides a useful summary of what amounts to a deprivation of liberty when it states at para. 2.5:

> *The ECtHR and UK courts have determined a number of cases about deprivation of liberty. Their judgments indicate that the following factors can be relevant to identifying whether steps taken involve more than restraint and amount to a deprivation of liberty. It is important to remember that this list is not exclusive; other factors may arise in future in particular cases.*
> - *Restraint is used, including sedation, to admit a person to an institution where that person is resisting admission.*
> - *Staff exercise complete and effective control over the care and movement of a person for a significant period.*
> - *Staff exercise control over assessments, treatment, contacts and residence.*
> - *A decision has been taken by the institution that the person will not be released into the care of others, or permitted to live elsewhere, unless the staff in the institution consider it appropriate.*
> - *A request by carers for a person to be discharged to their care is refused.*
> - *The person is unable to maintain social contacts because of restrictions placed on their access to other people.*
> - *The person loses autonomy because they are under continuous supervision and control.*

It continues by stating at para. 2.6:

> *In determining whether deprivation of liberty has occurred, or is likely to occur, decision-makers need to consider all the facts in a particular case. There is unlikely to be any simple definition that can be applied in every case, and it is probable that no single factor will, in itself, determine whether the overall set of steps being taken in relation to the relevant person amount to a deprivation of liberty. In general, the decision-maker should always consider the following:*
> - *All the circumstances of each and every case*
> - *What measures are being taken in relation to the individual? When are they required? For what period do they endure? What are the effects of any restraints or restrictions on the individual? Why are they necessary? What aim do they seek to meet?*

- *What are the views of the relevant person, their family or carers? Do any of them object to the measures?*
- *How are any restraints or restrictions implemented? Do any of the constraints on the individual's personal freedom go beyond 'restraint' or 'restriction' to the extent that they constitute a deprivation of liberty?*
- *Are there any less restrictive options for delivering care or treatment that avoid deprivation of liberty altogether?*
- *Does the cumulative effect of all the restrictions imposed on the person amount to a deprivation of liberty, even if individually they would not?*

In situations where an incapacitated adult is deprived of their liberty, or at risk of being deprived of their liberty, in a care home or hospital setting, the DOLS procedure should be set in motion. The managing authority has the responsibility of applying for an authorisation of deprivation of liberty. The managing authority is whoever is responsible for running the hospital or care home. They apply to the supervisory body which will, in England, be the Primary Care Trust (PCT) for hospitals, or the local authority for care homes.

The supervisory body then sets in motion six assessments which must be carried out by two or more qualified people. In practice the assessors will usually be a doctor and a Best Interests Assessor (referred to after this as a BIA). The assessments are: age, no refusals, mental capacity, mental health, eligibility and best interests. Each of these will be described below.

The six assessments

In contrast with detention or guardianship under the Mental Health Act, there are no forms prescribed by the Regulations for these assessments. However, standard forms are available and the use of these is strongly advised. The forms take people through the complex procedures in a way that asks all the relevant questions and leaves them to concentrate on their own professional judgment.

Age

(This will be carried out by a BIA.)

The person must be, or believed to be, 18 years of age or older. If there is no documentary evidence of age the assessor has to use their own judgment.

No refusals

(Again, this will be carried out by a BIA.)

The assessor needs to establish if a deprivation of liberty would conflict with any advance or substituted decision. This could be an advance decision made by the person refusing all or part of the proposed care and treatment, or it could be a refusal by either a donee/appointee (under an LPA), or it could be the objection of a deputy who has been appointed by the Court of Protection. If there is a conflict the DOLS procedures cannot be used.

Mental capacity

(This can be carried out by a BIA or by a doctor approved as a mental health assessor.)

The individual's capacity needs to be assessed in relation to the decision about residence in a residential care home or in a hospital for the purpose of providing care and treatment. The test for capacity is the one contained in the Mental Capacity Act. If the person has capacity then, again, the DOLS procedure cannot be used.

Mental health

(This needs to be carried out by a doctor approved under section 12 of the MHA, or a doctor with a minimum of three years' post-registration experience in the diagnosis or treatment of mental disorder. Both need to complete a DOLS course provided by the RCP.)

The doctor must establish if the relevant person has a mental disorder as defined by the Mental Health Act 1983, i.e. 'any disorder or disability of the mind'. This will exclude those solely with dependence upon alcohol or drugs, but will include those with a learning disability whether or not they exhibit 'abnormally aggressive or seriously irresponsible conduct'. Therefore the DOLS procedure may be used for people with a learning disability who would not be eligible for guardianship (s7) or detention for treatment (s3) of the MHA. The requirement to meet the definition of mental disorder could also, in rare cases, exclude someone who lacks capacity because of an impairment in the functioning of the brain which has not affected their mind.

Eligibility

(This needs to be carried out by a doctor approved as a mental health assessor or a BIA who is also an AMHP.)

This involves establishing if there are requirements placed upon the relevant person that would mean that they are not eligible for DOLS. A patient subject to most forms of detention under the MHA would not be eligible for DOLS. Similarly a deprivation of liberty could not be granted if it would be inconsistent with an obligation placed upon a patient subject to section 17 leave of absence or a patient who is subject to guardianship, a community treatment order or to conditional discharge.

Best interests

(This needs to be an AMHP, social worker, nurse, occupational therapist or psychologist who is two years post qualification and has completed approved BIA training.)

Best Interests Assessors must satisfy themselves that: the person is, or is going to be, a detained resident in a care home or hospital. This requires them to establish if the person's care and treatment is, or will amount to, a deprivation of liberty. In some cases the supervisory body may want this part of the assessment to be carried out at an early stage. If the BIA were to find that there was no deprivation of liberty the whole process could be called to a halt (which could save considerable work and expense).

If there is a deprivation of liberty the BIA needs to assess if it would be in the person's best interests to be a detained resident or patient; if it is necessary for the person to be a detained resident or patient to prevent harm to himself, and if a deprivation of liberty is a proportionate response to the likelihood of the person suffering harm and the seriousness of that harm.

During this process the BIA will also:

- identify a representative for the person;

- consider any conditions to be attached to the deprivation of liberty; and

- suggest the length of time for which a deprivation of liberty should be granted.

As part of the assessment the BIA needs to see if there are appropriate persons such as friends or family members who can be consulted as part of the process of deciding on the person's best interests. If they decide that there is no such person then an independent mental capacity advocate (IMCA) must be appointed.

The best interests checklist from section 4 of the MCA applies to BIA assessments. In addition they must consider the additional factors outlined at para. 4.61 of the DOLS Code:

- *whether any harm to the person could arise if the deprivation of liberty does not take place;*
- *what that harm would be;*
- *how likely that harm is to arise (i.e. is the level of risk sufficient to justify a step as serious as depriving a person of liberty?);*
- *what other care options there are which could avoid deprivation of liberty; and*
- *if deprivation of liberty is currently unavoidable, what action could be taken to avoid it in the future.*

If they are satisfied from the written evidence that all of the assessments are met, the supervisory body must give a standard authorisation. This could last for up to a year. If any of the six assessments results in a negative answer, then a standard authorisation cannot be given. In this case, if it is not seen possible to reduce the limitations on the person so that they fall short of deprivation of liberty, then consideration will need be given to alternative means of lawfully depriving a person of their liberty. This could be detention under the MHA or a personal welfare order from the Court of Protection under section 16 of the MCA.

Mental Health Act or DOLS procedure?

In many cases where there is an appropriate deprivation of liberty there will be the possibility of proceeding with either the use of the DOLS procedure under the Mental Capacity Act or detention via the Mental Health Act.

Jones gives a number of reasons for preferring the use of the MHA to the DOLS procedure if the patient is going to be detained in a hospital. Jones describes these reasons as 'cogent', almost certainly as a reference to the *R (Munjaz)* v Mersey Care NHS Trust (2005) case which we considered in Chapter 10. This is where the Law Lords said that a public authority could depart from the Code if it had 'cogent reasons' for so doing.

Both the Code to the Mental Health Act and the new DOLS Code tend towards a preference for using the DOLS procedures but Jones (2008, ppv–vi) lists the following reasons for using the Mental Health Act:

- *Parts IV and IVA of the MHA provide patients with significant protections relating to the provision of treatment for the patient's mental disorder. The provision of such treatment to patients subject to the MCA is unregulated.*
- *The MHA provides a patient's nearest relative with significant protective powers relating to the patient's detention. The nearest relative has no role to play under the MCA.*
- *A patient detained under the MHA has a right to make an application to a Mental Health Review Tribunal and his or her case will be referred to the tribunal if this right is not exercised. The MCA provides for no automatic judicial oversight of the patient's detention.*
- *A patient who is detained under the MHA can apply for a hearing before the hospital managers who have the power to order the patient's discharge. There is no similar power under the MCA.*
- *Unlike the MCA, the MHA contains explicit authority for the applicant to 'take and convey' the patient to the hospital named in the application (s.6(1)) and for the hospital authority to return the patient to the hospital in the event of the patient absconding (s.18(1)).*
- *Patients detained under the MHA and who are subject to s.117 receive after-care services provided under that section free of charge. MCA patients who are discharged from hospital will be subject to a mandatory charging regime if they are placed in a care home (National Assistance Act 1948, s.22) and a discretionary charging regime if they receive domiciliary care services (Health and Social Services and Social Security Adjudications Act 1983, s.17).*

It is difficult to find very powerful arguments to counter these points. Concerns about stigma and using the least restrictive approach do not really withstand any examination.

Indeed experience of discussion on AMHP refresher training has only added to the list of points made by Jones. Access to Mental Health Advocates, speed of access to tribunals, the cost and procedures involved in taking a case to the Court of Protection are just some of the points AMHPs have added. The conveyance point made by Jones has been an issue of concern for practitioners who have tried, unsuccessfully, to persuade ambulance or police colleagues to use restraint in some cases where this would be reliant on the MCA. The statutory forms and clear authority in the Act are of great importance in practice. One of the ironies of following Jones's line would be that DOLS would be reserved in hospital for the group initially considered in the *Bournewood* case, i.e. those with a learning disability. Apart from those who exhibited 'abnormally aggressive or seriously irresponsible conduct' the MHA could not be used to detain this group for more than 28 days. If one accepts that those covered by DOLS have fewer safeguards this could be seen as new kind of 'Bournewood gap'. Unless the safeguards are increased and demonstrated to be effective then criticism of the use of DOLS for hospital patients could mount.

The argument for use of the MHA for those in care homes in the community where the DOLS procedures are being considered is a more difficult area. Jones argues the case for using guardianship to authorise the deprivation of a person's liberty in these circumstances. He criticises para. 13.16 of the MCA Code of Practice which states that guardianship cannot be used to deprive someone of their liberty. Relying on the *JE* v *DE* and Surrey (2006) case, where Munby J held that not being 'free to leave' is crucial to the identification of deprivation of liberty, Jones argues that guardianship has the potential to be used in this way. It contains the power to take someone to where they do not wish to live, insist that they remain there and to return them if they abscond. It is a procedure prescribed by law and therefore meets the requirements of Article 5. If practitioners, their legal advisers and finally the courts accept this view it would certainly provide an alternative to DOLS. It doesn't have as many advantages as detention (no free after-care, no automatic tribunals and no protection under Part 4 of the MHA) but it retains some of them, and many would still prefer it to the new arrangements.

At the time of writing it seemed that the majority of those training as BIAs were not AMHPs and their views on these issues will be significant, as will the attitudes of those making referrals or receiving documents. Those AMHPs in training now are more likely to also be trained as BIAs and the history of guardianship suggests that the attitudes of staff are crucial as to whether it is used.

A test case may be slow in emerging as this is not an area of frequent legal challenge. However, a number of challenges are possible that might involve AMHPs. A reliance on DOLS rather than the MHA may be challenged by a family member in the following situation. An elderly patient, possibly with dementia, is admitted to hospital and then made subject to the DOLS procedure rather then being detained under the MHA. The plan is then to place them in the community and this will incur a charge on their estate. Their nearest relative is a son or daughter who can see that detention on section 3 would lead to free after-care services. They make a referral under section 13(4) and are not happy when the AMHP does not apply for detention.

Another challenge could occur if a patient were held in a residential care setting with the local authority relying on guardianship where the patient is, in effect, deprived of their liberty. The AMHP/BIA with their employer's backing decide that DOLS are unnecessary in these circumstances but a relative or the patient challenges the decision.

It would certainly be wise for an AMHP in any such situation to maintain clear communication with their local authority solicitors.

ACTIVITY 11.1

Multiple choice questions
(Answers in Appendix 9)

1 Which of the following assessments form part of the Deprivation of Liberty procedures?
   (a) Best interests ☐
   (b) No refusals (e.g. objection from LPA donee) ☐
   (c) Age ☐
   (d) Financial ☐
   (e) Eligibility ☐
   (f) Whether receiving MHA section 117 after-care ☐
   (g) Mental capacity ☐
   (h) Abnormally aggressive or seriously irresponsible conduct ☐
   (i) Mental disorder ☐

2 Under the new DOLS procedure one professional could carry out all of the required assessments.
   (a) True ☐
   (b) False ☐

3 Under the new DOLS procedure a representative will be appointed for the individual after deprivation of liberty has been authorised.
   (a) True ☐
   (b) False ☐

Appendix 1

Checklists for applications and forms

Applications for compulsory hospital admission or guardianship

YOU SHOULD BE ABLE TO ANSWER 'YES' TO ALL THE NUMBERED QUESTIONS OR BE ABLE TO FOLLOW THE INSTRUCTIONS. YOU MAY ALSO FIND HELPFUL THE GENERAL POINTS WHICH ARE PRINTED AT THE END OF SECTION 4 ADMISSIONS.

Important: All the forms were amended in 2008. Ensure you use current versions of the forms.

SECTION 2 – Admission for assessment (lasting for up to 28 days)

(1) Are you of the opinion 'having regard to any wishes expressed by relatives of the patient or any other relevant circumstances' that your making an application would be necessary or proper?

(2) Have you interviewed the patient 'in a suitable manner'?

(3) Are you satisfied that 'detention in a hospital is in all the circumstances of the case the most appropriate way of providing the care and medical treatment of which the patient stands in need'? Have you considered and decided against: informal admission, out-patient treatment, community psychiatric nursing support, crisis intervention centres, primary health care support, local authority social services or private provision, support from friends, relatives or voluntary organisations?

(4) Have you got two medical recommendations, which state that the patient is suffering from mental disorder 'of a nature or degree which warrants detention in hospital for assessment' and that he ought to be detained 'in the interests of his own health or safety or with a view to the protection of other persons'?

(5) Has one of the doctors had previous acquaintance with the patient? If not, every effort should be made to find one who has. If unsuccessful, you must give your reasons at the bottom of your application.

(6) Has one doctor been approved as having special experience in psychiatry? See your local list of section 12 approved doctors if you have any doubts.

(7) Have you seen the patient within the last 14 days?

(8) Have the doctors personally examined the patient together or within five days of each other? (This means five clear days so one on the first and the other on the seventh of the month is acceptable.)

(9) Can you confirm that there is no conflict of interests (see Appendix 8) unless this is an emergency?

(10) Have you checked the validity of the medical recommendations (e.g. that they have been signed and are from doctors entitled to make recommendations)? If not, and a serious mistake has been made, you could be notified and have to make a new application. Less important mistakes (e.g. spelling of names) can be corrected within 14 days of the admission. (See section 15 for more information if needed.)

(11) Have you informed the nearest relative that the application is to be made and of their rights of discharge under section 23(2)(a)? If not, you must do so after the admission if this is practicable. Inform the hospital when you have done this. (Remember the 'Bristol' definition of practicable.)

(12) Are the dates of the signatures of both medical recommendations on or before the date of your application?

(13) After signing an application you have 14 days to get the patient admitted into hospital beginning with the date when the patient was last examined for the purpose of making one of the medical recommendations. You have the authority to remove compulsorily the patient to hospital and/or to authorise anyone else to do this but should have the recommendations and application to hand to demonstrate this.

Forms required

Application on Form A2 (nearest relative would use Form A1 and an AMHP would subsequently prepare a report).

Recommendation on Form A3 (joint) or Form A4.

Note: If the request for an application to be considered came from the nearest relative and you have decided against it, you must give them your reasons in writing.

SECTION 3 – Admission for treatment (lasting up to six months and renewable)

(1) Are you of the opinion 'having regard to any wishes expressed by relatives of the patient or any other relevant circumstances' that your making an application would be necessary or proper?

(2)   Have you interviewed the patient 'in a suitable manner'?

(3)   Are you satisfied that 'detention in a hospital is in all the circumstances of the case the most appropriate way of providing the care and medical treatment of which the patient stands in need'? Have you decided against: informal admission, out-patient treatment, CPN support, crisis intervention centres, LA social services or private provision, support from primary health care, friends, relatives or voluntary organisations?

(4)   Have you got two medical recommendations, on one form or two, which state that the patient is suffering from a mental disorder 'of a nature or degree which makes it appropriate for him to receive medical treatment in a hospital' and 'it is necessary for the health or safety of the patient or for the protection of other persons that he should receive such treatment and it cannot be provided unless he is detained under section 3 of the Act'? and that 'appropriate medical treatment' is available at a specified hospital?

(5)   If the clinical description of the mental disorder indicates that the patient has a learning disability do the recommendations make it clear that there is also abnormally aggressive or seriously irresponsible conduct?

(6)   Have the doctors identified a hospital where appropriate treatment can be delivered? If a treatment plan is not clearly apparent from their forms you may need to ask them for more detail.

(7)   Has one doctor had previous acquaintance with patient? If not, every effort should be made to find one who has. If unsuccessful you must give reasons on Form A6.

(8)   Has one doctor been approved as having special experience in psychiatry? See your local list of section 12 approved doctors if you have any doubts.

(9)   Have you seen the patient within the last 14 days?

(10) Have the doctors personally examined the patient together or within five days of each other? (This means five clear days so one on the first and the other on the seventh is acceptable.)

(11) Can you confirm that there is no conflict of interests (see Appendix 8) unless this is an emergency (which would be very unusual circumstances for a section 3)?

(12) Have you checked the validity of the medical recommendations (e.g. they are signed and are from doctors entitled to make them)? If not, and a serious mistake is made, you could be notified and have to make a new application. Less serious errors (e.g. spelling of names) can be corrected within 14 days of admission. (See section 15 for more information.)

(13) Have you consulted the nearest relative and checked that they have no objection to an application? If you have not, would you say this was not reasonably practicable or would have involved unreasonable delay? (If unable to consult the nearest relative you should try to see them as soon as possible to let them

know their rights of discharge. Inform the hospital when you have done this.) Remember the 'Bristol' definition of practicable.

(14) Are the dates by both doctors' signatures on or before the date of your application?

(15) After signing an application you have 14 days to get the patient admitted into hospital beginning with the date when the patient was last examined for the purpose of making one of the medical recommendations. You have the authority to remove compulsorily the patient to hospital and/or to authorise anyone else to do this but should have the recommendations and application to hand to demonstrate this.

Forms required

Application on Form A6 (nearest relative would use Form A5 and an AMHP would subsequently prepare a report).

Recommendation on Form A7 (joint) or Form A8.

Note: If the request for an application to be considered came from the nearest relative and you have decided against it you must give them your reasons in writing.

SECTION 4 – Admission for assessment in cases of emergency (lasts up to 72 hours)

(1) Are you of the opinion 'having regard to any wishes expressed by relatives of the patient or another relevant circumstances' that your making an application would be necessary or proper?

(2) Have you interviewed the patient 'in a suitable manner'?

(3) Are you satisfied that 'detention in hospital is in all the circumstances of the case the most appropriate way of providing the care and medical treatment of which the patient stands in need'? Have you considered: informal admission, out-patient treatment, community nursing support, crisis intervention centres, primary health care support, local authority social services or private provision, support from friends, relatives or voluntary organisations?

(4) Is it of urgent necessity the patient be admitted and detained in hospital for assessment?

(5) Would obtaining a second recommendation to meet the needs of section 2 involve undesirable delay?

(6) Have you got a medical recommendation which states 'that this patient is suffering from mental disorder of a nature or degree which warrants the patient's detention in a hospital for assessment' and 'ought to be so detained' in the interests of the patient's own health or safety or with a view to the protection of other persons?

(7)   Has the doctor had previous acquaintance with the patient? If not, is it genuinely not practicable to find such a doctor? If unsuccessful you must give your reasons at the bottom of Form 6.

(8)   Do the details on the medical recommendation correspond with those on your application?

(9)   Have you and the doctor both seen the patient in the last 24 hours? *(For section 4 you can sign your form before or after the doctor signs a recommendation. Eldergill (1998) supports this view; Jones (2008) does not.)*

(10) After signing an application, you have 24 hours to get the patient admitted into hospital beginning with the time when the patient was examined for the purpose of making the medical recommendation or from when the application was made, whichever was the earlier. You have the authority to compulsorily remove the patient to hospital and/or to authorise anyone else to do this but should have the recommendation and application to hand to demonstrate this.

Forms required

Application on Form A10 (nearest relative would use Form A9 and if there were a conversion to section 2, through the provision of an additional medical recommendation, an AMHP would probably prepare a report).

Recommendation on Form A11.

Notes:

1   If the request for an application to be considered came from the nearest relative and you have decided against it, you must give them your reasons in writing.

2   The doctor providing the recommendation does not need to be section 12 approved and may not have previous acquaintance with the patient. This significantly reduces the safeguards for the patient and should be avoided if possible. It is important to remind the hospital to let the AMHP know if the section is converted to a section 2 so that the AMHP can inform the nearest relative as required by section 11(3).

General points for admissions to hospital from the community

If you have reached the point where you have signed an application form the following points are worth checking:

• Has a doctor organised a bed in the hospital and is the hospital expecting you?

• Have you arranged transport? It is your job to make sure that the patient gets to the hospital. The ambulance service should assist if needed. Check any local agreements.

- Have you made arrangements to protect any moveable property? Is there anyone to help with cancelling milk, etc.?

- You should leave a report at the hospital. This should include the patient's social circumstances and events leading up to the admission, including a note on alternatives that were not considered to be appropriate, plus any telephone numbers etc.

- Have you fully explained to the patient what is happening?

SECTION 7 – Application for guardianship (lasting up to six months and renewable)

(1) Are you of the opinion 'having regard to any wishes expressed by relatives of the patient or any other relevant circumstances' that your making an application would be necessary or proper?

(2) Is the patient at least 16 years old?

(3) If the clinical description of the mental disorder indicates that the patient has a learning disability do the recommendations make it clear that there is also abnormally aggressive or seriously irresponsible conduct?

(4) Have you got two medical recommendations which specify the mental disorder as above and state that this is 'of a nature or degree which warrants his reception into guardianship' and this is 'necessary in the interests of the welfare of the patient or for the protection of other persons'?

(5) Has one of the doctors had previous acquaintance with the patient? If not, every effort should be made to find one who has. If unsuccessful you must give your reasons near the bottom of Form 18.

(6) Has one doctor been approved as having special experience in psychiatry? See your local list of section 12 approved doctors.

(7) Have you seen the patient within the last 14 days and have the doctors personally examined the patient together or within five days of each other? (This means five clear days, i.e. one on the first and the other on the seventh is acceptable.)

(8) Have you consulted the nearest relative and checked that they have no objections to an application? If you have not, would you say that this was not reasonably practicable or would have involved unreasonable delay?

(9) Have you checked the validity of the medical recommendations (e.g. that they have been signed and that the disorder described is appropriate for this section)? If not, and a mistake has been made, you could be notified and have to make a new application.

(10) Has the person you are naming as guardian (if not the local authority) given you a statement in writing that she/he is willing to act as guardian? Use Part 2 of Form G2.

(11) Are the dates of the signatures of both medical recommendations on or before the date of your application?

(12) You must now seek the approval of the social services department for the guardianship. You have 14 days from the date when the patient was last examined for one of the recommendations to forward the application to the responsible person in the social services department. There is no formal time limit on when the social services department then has to make a decision but any significant delay could lead to a complaint. You will almost certainly be asked to provide a detailed report on the patient and, where necessary, on the proposed guardian to help whoever has to make these decisions. Note that the person approving the guardian and agreeing to the guardianship would not have to be an Approved Mental Health Professional.

Forms required

Application on Form G2 (nearest relative would use Form G1). The social services department would then make its assessment of the appropriateness of guardianship, usually involving an approved mental health professional in this process.

Recommendations on Form G3 (joint) or Form G4.

Note: It is also possible for someone to be transferred into guardianship from detention in hospital using Form G6. Transfers from guardianship to detention under section 3 are also possible but require two medical recommendations and a fresh application from an AMHP.

Form A2 *Regulation 4(1)(a)(ii)* Mental Health Act 1983

Section 2 – application by an approved mental health professional for admission for assessment

To the managers of (*name and address of hospital*)

I (*PRINT your full name and address*)

apply for the admission of (*PRINT full name and address of patient*)

for assessment in accordance with Part 2 of the Mental Health Act 1983.

I am acting on behalf of (*PRINT name of local social services authority*)

and am approved to act as an approved mental health professional for the purposes of the Act by (*delete as appropriate*)

that authority

(*name of local social services authority that approved you, if different*)

Complete the following if you know who the nearest relative is.

Complete (a) or (b) as applicable and delete the other.

continue overleaf

(a) To the best of my knowledge and belief (*PRINT full name and address*)

is the patient's nearest relative within the meaning of the Act.

(b) I understand that (*PRINT full name and address*)

has been authorised by a county court/the patient's nearest relative* to exercise the functions under the Act of the patient's nearest relative. (*Delete the phrase which does not apply*)

I have/have not yet* informed that person that this application is to be made and of the nearest relative's power to order the discharge of the patient. (*Delete the phrase which does not apply*)

Complete the following if you do not know who the nearest relative is. Delete (a) or (b).

(a) I have been unable to ascertain who is the patient's nearest relative within the meaning of the Act.

(b) To the best of my knowledge and belief this patient has no nearest relative within the meaning of the Act.

The remainder of the form must be completed in all cases.

I last saw the patient on

 [date],

which was within the period of 14 days ending on the day this application is completed.

I have interviewed the patient and I am satisfied that detention in a hospital is in all the circumstances of the case the most appropriate way of providing the care and medical treatment of which the patient stands in need.

This application is founded on two medical recommendations in the prescribed form.

If neither of the medical practitioners had previous acquaintance with the patient before making their recommendations, please explain why you could not get a recommendation from a medical practitioner who did have previous acquaintance with the patient –

continue overleaf

(If you need to continue on a separate sheet please indicate here ( ) and attach that sheet to this form)

Signed   Date

/   /

Form A4 *Regulation 4(1)(b)(ii)* Mental Health Act 1983

Section 2 – Medical recommendation for admission for assessment

I (*PRINT full name and address of practitioner*)

a registered medical practitioner, recommend that

(*PRINT full name and address of patient*)

be admitted to a hospital for assessment in accordance with Part 2 of the Mental Health Act 1983.

I last examined this patient on

 [date],

* I had previous acquaintance with the patient before I conducted that examination.

* I am approved under section 12 of the Act as having special experience in the diagnosis or treatment of mental disorder.

(* *Delete if not applicable*)

In my opinion,

(a) this patient is suffering from mental disorder of a nature or degree which warrants the detention of the patient in hospital for assessment (or for assessment followed by medical treatment) for at least a limited period,

AND

(b) ought to be so detained
  (i) in the interests of the patient's own health

  (ii) in the interests of the patient's own safety

  (iii) with a view to the protection of other persons.

  (*Delete the indents not applicable*)

My reasons for these opinions are:

continue overleaf

(Your reasons should cover both (a) and (b) above. As part of them: describe the patient's symptoms and behaviour and explain how those symptoms and behaviour lead you to your opinion; explain why the patient ought to be admitted to hospital and why informal admission is not appropriate.)

(If you need to continue on a separate sheet please indicate here ( ) and attach that sheet to this form)

Signed   Date

	/	/

Form A6 *Regulation 4(1)(c)(ii)* Mental Health Act 1983

Section 3 – Application by an approved mental health professional for admission for treatment

To the managers of (*name and address of hospital*)

I (*PRINT your full name and address*)

apply for the admission of (*PRINT full name and address of patient*)

for treatment in accordance with Part 2 of the Mental Health Act 1983.

I am acting on behalf of (*name of local social services authority*)

and am approved to act as an approved mental health professional for the purposes of the Act by (*delete as appropriate*)

that authority

(*name of local social services authority that approved you, if different*)

Complete the following where consultation with the nearest relative has taken place.

Complete (a) or (b) and delete the other.

(a)   I have consulted (*PRINT full name and address*)

continue overleaf

who to the best of my knowledge and belief is the patient's nearest relative within the meaning of the Act.

(b)   I have consulted *(PRINT full name and address)*

```
┌──────────────────────────────────────────────────────────────┐
│                                                                │
│                                                                │
│                                                                │
└──────────────────────────────────────────────────────────────┘
```

who I understand has been authorised by a county court/the patient's nearest relative* to exercise the functions under the Act of the patient's nearest relative. (*Delete the phrase which does not apply)

That person has not notified me or the local social services authority on whose behalf I am acting that he or she objects to this application being made.

Complete the following where the nearest relative has not been consulted.

Delete whichever two of (a), (b) and (c) do not apply.

(a)   I have been unable to ascertain who is this patient's nearest relative within the meaning of the Act.

(b)   To the best of my knowledge and belief this patient has no nearest relative within the meaning of the Act.

(c)   I understand that *(PRINT full name and address)*

```
┌──────────────────────────────────────────────────────────────┐
│                                                                │
│                                                                │
│                                                                │
└──────────────────────────────────────────────────────────────┘
```

is

(i)   this patient's nearest relative within the meaning of the Act,

(ii) authorised to exercise the functions of this patient's nearest relative under the Act,

(Delete either (i) or (ii))

but in my opinion it is not reasonably practicable/would involve unreasonable delay *(delete as appropriate)* to consult that person before making this application, because –

```
┌──────────────────────────────────────────────────────────────┐
│                                                                │
│                                                                │
│                                                                │
│                                                                │
│                                                                │
│                                                                │
│ (If you need to continue on a separate sheet please indicate   │
│ here ( ) and attach                                            │
│ that sheet to this form)                                       │
└──────────────────────────────────────────────────────────────┘
```

continue overleaf

The remainder of this form must be completed in all cases.

I saw the patient on

| / | / | [date], |

which was within the period of 14 days ending on the day this application is completed.

I have interviewed the patient and I am satisfied that detention in a hospital is in all the circumstances of the case the most appropriate way of providing the care and medical treatment of which the patient stands in need.

This application is founded on two medical recommendations in the prescribed form.

If neither of the medical practitioners had previous acquaintance with the patient before making their recommendations, please explain why you could not get a recommendation from a medical practitioner who did have previous acquaintance with the patient –

(If you need to continue on a separate sheet please indicate here ( ) and attach that sheet to this form)

Signed   Date

/   /

Form A8 *Regulation 4(1)(d)(ii)* Mental Health Act 1983

Section 3 – medical recommendation for admission for treatment

I (*PRINT full name and address of practitioner*)

a registered medical practitioner, recommend that

(*PRINT full name and address of patient*)

be admitted to a hospital for treatment in accordance with Part 2 of the Mental Health Act 1983.

I last examined this patient on

 [date],

* I had previous acquaintance with the patient before I conducted that examination.

* I am approved under section 12 of the Act as having special experience in the diagnosis or treatment of mental disorder.

(* *Delete if not applicable*)

In my opinion,

(a)   this patient is suffering from mental disorder of a nature or degree which makes it appropriate for the patient to receive medical treatment in a hospital,

AND

(b)   it is necessary

    (i)   for the patient's own health

    (ii)   for the patient's own safety

    (iii) for the protection of other persons

    (*Delete the indents not applicable*)

that this patient should receive treatment in hospital,

AND

continue overleaf

(c)   such treatment cannot be provided unless the patient is detained under section 3 of the Act,

because –

(Your reasons should cover (a), (b) and (c) above. As part of them: describe the patient's symptoms and behaviour and explain how those symptoms and behaviour lead you to your opinion; say whether other methods of treatment or care (e.g. out-patient treatment or social services) are available and, if so, why they are not appropriate; indicate why informal admission is not appropriate.)

(If you need to continue on a separate sheet please indicate here ( ) and attach that sheet to this form)

I am also of the opinion that, taking into account the nature and degree of the mental disorder from which the patient is suffering and all the other circumstances of the case, appropriate medical treatment is available to the patient at the following hospital (or one of the following hospitals) –

(Enter name of hospital(s). If appropriate treatment is available only in a particular part of the hospital, say which part.)

Signed   Date

/   /

Appendix 2

The Human Rights Act 1998

Some key sections of the Human Rights Act given below are followed by the Articles of the European Convention of Human Rights that are enshrined in English law and relevant to mental health law.

Section 1 identifies which of the Convention rights are covered by the Human Rights Act. These are:

(a) Articles 2 to 12 and 14 of the Convention
(b) Articles 1 to 3 of the First Protocol, and
(c) Articles 1 and 2 of the Sixth Protocol
as read with Articles 16 to 18 of the Convention.

Section 2 requires courts or tribunals determining questions which have arisen in connection with a Convention right to take into account the decisions of Strasbourg (the European Court and Commission of Human Rights and the Committee of Ministers) so far as is relevant.

Section 3 requires legislation to be interpreted as far as possible in a way which is compatible with the Convention rights.

Section 4 gives the higher courts a power to make a 'declaration of incompatibility' where they find that primary legislation is incompatible with a Convention right. This does not strike down the existing legislation but relies on the government making a remedial order or introducing new law.

Section 6 makes it unlawful for a public authority to act in a way which is incompatible with a Convention right unless it is required to do so by primary legislation. A public authority would include a court or tribunal or any person certain of whose functions are of a public nature.

Section 7 states that victims may rely on the Convention rights in legal proceedings in UK courts and tribunals or may institute separate proceedings. Separate proceedings must usually be brought within one year of the date on which the act complained of took place.

Section 10 allows the relevant Minister to amend infringing legislation by order following a declaration of incompatibility or a finding of the European Court of Human Rights if he is satisfied that there is a compelling reason to do so.

Section 11 states that the Act does not restrict any existing rights that an individual might have under UK law or his right to bring proceedings under existing law.

Section 13 obliges courts to have particular regard to the importance of the right to freedom of thought, conscience and religion.

Section 19 requires that when legislation is introduced into either House for a second reading, the Minister responsible must make a written statement that he considers the Bill is compatible with the Convention rights or that he is unable to make such a statement but wishes Parliament to proceed with the Bill anyway.

The text of the European Convention of Human Rights

(This includes those articles which are enshrined in English law as a result of the Human Rights Act.)

Article 2: Right to Life

1. Everyone's right to life shall be protected by law. No one shall be deprived of his life intentionally save in the execution of a sentence of a court following his conviction of a crime for which this penalty is provided by law.
2. Deprivation of life shall not be regarded as inflicted in contravention of this Article when it results from the use of force which is no more than absolutely necessary:
   (a) in defence of any person from unlawful violence;
   (b) in order to effect a lawful arrest or to prevent the escape of a person lawfully detained;
   (c) in action lawfully taken for the purpose of quelling a riot or insurrection.

Article 3: Prohibition of Torture

No one shall be subjected to torture or to inhuman or degrading treatment or punishment.

Article 4: Prohibition of Slavery and Forced Labour

1. No one shall be held in slavery or servitude.
2. No one shall be required to perform forced or compulsory labour.
3. For the purpose of this Article the term 'forced or compulsory labour' shall not include:

(a) any work required to be done in the ordinary course of detention imposed according to the provisions of Article 5 of this Convention or during conditional release from such detention;
(b) any service of a military character or, in case of conscientious objectors in countries where they are recognised, service exacted instead of compulsory military service;
(c) any service exacted in case of an emergency or calamity threatening the life or well-being of the community;
(d) any work or service which forms part of normal civic obligations.

Article 5: Right to Liberty and Security

1. Everyone has the right to liberty and security of person. No one shall be deprived of his liberty save in the following cases and in accordance with a procedure pre-scribed by law:
   (a) the lawful detention of a person after conviction by a competent court;
   (b) the lawful arrest or detention of a person for non-compliance with the lawful order of a court or in order to secure the fulfilment of any obligation prescribed by law;
   (c) the lawful arrest or detention of a person effected for the purpose of bringing him before the competent legal authority on reasonable suspicion of having committed an offence or when it is reasonably considered necessary to prevent his committing an offence or fleeing after having done so;
   (d) the detention of a minor by lawful order for the purpose of educational super-vision or his lawful detention for the purpose of bringing him before the competent legal authority;
   (e) the lawful detention of persons for the prevention of the spreading of infec-tious diseases, of persons of unsound mind, alcoholics or drug addicts or vagrants;
   (f) the lawful arrest or detention of a person to prevent his effecting an unauthorised entry into the country or of a person against whom action is being taken with a view to deportation or extradition.
2. Everyone who is arrested shall be informed promptly, in a language which he understands, of the reasons for his arrest and of any charge against him.
3. Everyone arrested or detained in accordance with the provisions of paragraph 1(c) of this Article shall be brought promptly before a judge or other officer authorised by law to exercise judicial power and shall be entitled to trial within a reasonable time or to release pending trial. Release may be conditioned by guarantees to appear for trial.
4. Everyone who is deprived of his liberty by arrest or detention shall be entitled to take proceedings by which the lawfulness of his detention shall be decided spee-dily by a court and his release ordered if the detention is not lawful.
5. Everyone who has been the victim of arrest or detention in contravention of the provisions of this Article shall have an enforceable right to compensation.

Article 6: Right to a Fair Trial

1. In the determination of his civil rights and obligations or of any criminal charge against him, everyone is entitled to a fair and public hearing within a reasonable time by an independent and impartial tribunal established by law. Judgement shall be pronounced publicly but the press and public may be excluded from all or part of the trial in the interest of morals, public order or national security in a democratic society, where the interest of juveniles or the protection of the private life of the parties so require, or to the extent strictly necessary in the opinion of the court in special circumstances where publicity would prejudice the interests of justice.
2. Everyone charged with a criminal offence shall be presumed innocent until proved guilty according to law.
3. Everyone charged with a criminal offence has the following minimum rights:
   (a) to be informed promptly, in a language which he understands and in detail, of the nature and cause of the accusation against him;
   (b) to have adequate time and facilities for the preparation of his defence;
   (c) to defend himself in person or through legal assistance of his own choosing or, if he has not sufficient means to pay for legal assistance, to be given it free when the interests of justice so require;
   (d) to examine or have examined witnesses against him and to obtain the attendance and examination of witnesses on his behalf under the same conditions as witnesses against him;
   (e) to have the free assistance of an interpreter if he cannot understand or speak the language used in court.

Article 7: No Punishment without Law

1. No one shall be held guilty of any criminal offence on account of any act or omission which did not constitute a criminal offence under national or international law at the time when it was committed. Nor shall a heavier penalty be imposed than the one that was applicable at the time the criminal offence was committed.
2. This Article shall not prejudice the trial and punishment of any person for any act or omission which, at the time when it was committed, was criminal according to the general principles of law recognised by civilised nations.

Article 8: Right to Respect for Private and Family Life

1. Everyone has the right to respect for his private and family life, his home and his correspondence.
2. There shall be no interference by a public authority with the exercise of this right except such as is in accordance with the law and is necessary in a democratic society in the interests of national security, public safety or the economic well-being of the country, for the prevention of disorder or crime, for the protection of health or morals, or for the protection of the rights and freedoms of others.

Article 9: Freedom of Thought, Conscience and Religion

1. Everyone has the right to freedom of thought, conscience and religion; this right includes freedom to change his religion or belief and freedom, either alone or in community with others and in public or private, to manifest his religion or belief, in worship, teaching, practice and observance.
2. Freedom to manifest one's religion or beliefs shall be subject only to such limitations as are prescribed by law and are necessary in a democratic society in the interests of public safety, for the protection of public order, health or morals, or for the protection of the rights and freedoms of others.

Article 10: Freedom of Expression

1. Everyone has the right to freedom of expression. This right shall include freedom to hold opinions and to receive and impart information and ideas without interference by public authority and regardless of frontiers. This Article shall not prevent States from requiring the licensing of broadcasting, television or cinema enterprises.
2. The exercise of these freedoms, since it carries with it duties and responsibilities, may be subject to such formalities, conditions, restrictions or penalties as are prescribed by law and are necessary in a democratic society, in the interests of national security, territorial integrity or public safety, for the prevention of disorder or crime, for the protection of health or morals, for the protection of the reputation or rights of others, for preventing the disclosure of information received in confidence, or for maintaining the authority and impartiality of the judiciary.

Article 11: Freedom of Assembly and Association

1. Everyone has the right to freedom of peaceful assembly and to freedom of association with others, including the right to form and to join trade unions for the protection of his interests.
2. No restrictions shall be placed on the exercise of these rights other than such as are prescribed by law and are necessary in a democratic society in the interests of national security or public safety, for the prevention of disorder or crime, for the protection of health or morals or for the protection of the rights and freedoms of others. This Article shall not prevent the imposition of lawful restrictions on the exercise of these rights by members of the armed forces, of the police or of the administration of the State.

Article 12: Right to Marry

Men and women of marriageable age have the right to marry and to found a family, according to the national laws governing the exercise of this right.

Article 14: Prohibition of Discrimination

The enjoyment of the rights and freedoms set forth in this Convention shall be secured without discrimination on any ground such as sex, race, colour, language, religion, political or other opinion, national or social origin, association with a national minority, property, birth or other status.

Article 16: Restrictions on Political Activity of Aliens

Nothing in Articles 10, 11 and 14 shall be regarded as preventing the High Contracting Parties from imposing restrictions on the political activity of aliens.

Article 17: Prohibition of Abuse of Rights

Nothing in this Convention may be interpreted as implying for any State, group or person any right to engage in any activity or perform any act aimed at the destruction of any of the rights and freedoms set forth herein or at their limitation to a greater extent than is provided for in the Convention.

Article 18: Limitation on use of Restrictions on Rights

The restrictions permitted under this Convention to the said rights and freedoms shall not be applied for any purpose other than those for which they have been prescribed.

Part 2: The First Protocol

Article 1: Protection of property

Every natural or legal person is entitled to the peaceful enjoyment of his possessions. No one shall be deprived of his possessions except in the public interest and subject to the conditions provided for by law and by the general principles of international law.

The preceding provisions shall not, however, in any way impair the right of a State to enforce such laws as it deems necessary to control the use of property in accordance with the general interest or to secure the payment of taxes or other contributions or penalties.

Article 2: Right to education

No person shall be denied the right to education. In the exercise of any functions which it assumes in relation to education and to teaching, the State shall respect the right of parents to ensure such education and teaching in conformity with their own religious and philosophical convictions.

Article 3: Right to free elections

The High Contracting Parties undertake to hold free elections at reasonable intervals by secret ballot, under conditions which will ensure the free expression of the opinion of the people in the choice of the legislature.

Part 3: The Sixth Protocol

Article 1: Abolition of the death penalty

The death penalty shall be abolished. No one shall be condemned to such penalty or executed.

Article 2: Death penalty in time of war

A State may make provision in its law for the death penalty in respect of acts committed in time of war or of imminent threat of war; such penalty shall be applied only in the instances laid down in the law and in accordance with its provisions. The State shall communicate to the Secretary General of the Council of Europe the relevant provisions of that law.

Appendix 3

The Mental Health Act 1983: arrangement of sections

s72   powers of tribunals
6   **Removal and return of patients within UK etc.**
7   **(Repealed – used to be Court of Protection)**
8   **Miscellaneous functions of local authorities and Secretary of State**
s114 appointment of Approved Mental Health Professionals
s115 powers of entry and inspection
s117 after-care
9   **Offences**
s129 obstruction
s130 prosecutions by local authorities
10   **Miscellaneous and supplementary**
s131 informal admission of patients
s135 warrant to search for and remove patients
s136 mentally disordered persons found in public places
s137 provisions as to custody, conveyance and detention
s139 protection for acts done in pursuance of this Act
s145 interpretation (includes definition of AMHP)

Note: See also various regulations, rules, circulars and the Code of Practice.

Appendix 4A

The AMHP Regulations for England

The Mental Health (Approved Mental Health Professionals) (Approval) (England) Regulations 2008 Statutory Instrument No. 1206 2008 (England)

The Secretary of State, in exercise of the powers conferred by section 114 of the Mental Health Act 1983,[1] makes the following Regulations:

Citation, commencement and application

1. (1) These Regulations may be cited as the Mental Health (Approved Mental Health Professionals) (Approval) (England) Regulations 2008 and shall come into force on 3rd November 2008.
   (2) These Regulations apply to England only.

Interpretation

2. In these Regulations –
   'the Act' means the Mental Health Act 1983;
   'AMHP' means an approved mental health professional;
   'approve' and 'approval' include 're-approve' and 're-approval';
   'approving LSSA' means the local social services authority in England that has approved the person to act as an AMHP;
   'Care Council for Wales' has the meaning given by section 54(1) of the Care Standards Act 2000;[2]
   'General Social Care Council' has the meaning given by section 54(1) of the Care Standards Act 2000;
   'LSSA' means a local social services authority in England;
   'professional requirements' means the requirements set out in Schedule 1.

Granting approval

3. (1) An LSSA may only approve a person to act as an AMHP if it is satisfied that the person has appropriate competence in dealing with persons who are suffering from mental disorder.

(2) In determining whether it is satisfied a person has appropriate competence, the LSSA must take into account the following factors –
(a) that the person fulfils at least one of the professional requirements, and
(b) the matters set out in Schedule 2.

(3) Before an LSSA may approve a person to act as an AMHP who has not been approved, or been treated as approved, before in England and Wales, the person must have completed within the last five years a course approved by the General Social Care Council or the Care Council for Wales.

Period of approval

4. An LSSA may approve a person to act as an AMHP for a period of five years.

Conditions

5. When any approval is granted under these Regulations, it shall be subject to the following conditions –

(a) in each year that the AMHP is approved, the AMHP shall complete at least 18 hours of training agreed with the approving LSSA as being relevant to their role as an AMHP;

(b) the AMHP shall undertake to notify the approving LSSA in writing as soon as reasonably practicable if they agree to act as an AMHP on behalf of another LSSA, and when such agreement ends;

(c) the AMHP shall undertake to cease to act as an AMHP and to notify the approving LSSA immediately if they are suspended from any of the registers or listings referred to in the professional competencies, or if any such suspension ends; and

(d) the AMHP shall undertake to cease to act as an AMHP and to notify the approving LSSA immediately if they no longer meet at least one of the professional requirements.

Suspension of approval

6. (1) If at any time after being approved, the registration or listing required by the professional requirements of a person approved to act as an AMHP is suspended, the approving LSSA shall suspend that AMHP's approval for as long as the AMHP's registration or listing is suspended.

(2) Where an AMHP's approval is suspended, that person may not act as an AMHP unless and until the suspension of approval is ended by the approving LSSA in accordance with subsection (3).

(3) Where the approving LSSA is notified that the suspension of the AMHP's registration or listing has ended, the approving LSSA shall, unless it is not satisfied the AMHP has appropriate competence in dealing with persons suffering from mental disorder, end the suspension of approval.

(4) Where the suspension of approval has ended, the approval shall continue to run for any unexpired period of approval, unless the approving LSSA ends it earlier in accordance with regulation 7.

End of approval

7. (1) Except where paragraph (2) applies, a person shall cease to be approved to act as an AMHP at the end of the day on which their period of approval expires.

(2) Except where regulation 6 applies, the approving LSSA shall end the approval of a person it has approved to act as an AMHP before their period of approval expires –
   (a) in accordance with a request in writing to do so from that AMHP;
   (b) if it is no longer satisfied that the AMHP has appropriate competence taking into account the matters set out in Schedule 2;
   (c) immediately upon becoming aware that the AMHP –
      (i) is no longer a person who meets at least one of the professional requirements;
      (ii) is in breach of any of the conditions set out in regulation 5; or
      (iii) has been approved to act as an AMHP by another LSSA.

(3) When an approval ends, the approving LSSA shall notify the AMHP immediately that the approval has ended and give reasons for ending the approval.

(4) When an approval ends, the approving LSSA shall notify that fact to any other LSSA for whom it knows the AMHP has agreed to act as an AMHP.

(5) If an LSSA approves a person as an AMHP knowing that that AMHP is already approved by another LSSA, it shall notify the previous approving LSSA.

Records

8. (1) The approving LSSA shall keep a record of each AMHP it approves which shall include –
   (a) the name of the AMHP;
   (b) the AMHP's profession;
   (c) the AMHP's date of approval;
   (d) details of any period of suspension under regulation 6;
   (e) details of the completion of training to comply with regulation 5(a);
   (f) details of any previous approvals as an AMHP within the previous five years;
   (g) the names of other LSSAs for whom the AMHP has agreed to act as an AMHP; and
   (h) the date of and reason for the end of approval, if applicable.

(2) The record referred to in paragraph (1) shall be retained by the approving LSSA for a period of five years commencing with the day on which the AMHP's approval ended.

Signed by authority of the Secretary of State for Health.

Ivan Lewis

Parliamentary Under-Secretary of State, Department of Health, 28th April 2008

SCHEDULE 1   Regulation 2

Professional requirements

The professional requirements are as follows –

(a) a social worker registered with the General Social Care Council;
(b) a first level nurse, registered in Sub-Part 1 of the Nurses' Part of the Register maintained under article 5 of the Nursing and Midwifery Order 2001,[3] with the inclusion of an entry indicating their field of practice is mental health or learning disabilities nursing;
(c) an occupational therapist registered in Part 6 of the Register maintained under article 5 of the Health Professions Order 2001;[4] or
(d) a chartered psychologist who is listed in the British Psychological Society's Register of Chartered Psychologists and who holds a relevant practising certificate issued by that Society.[5]

SCHEDULE 2   Regulation 3(2)

Matters to be taken into account to determine competence

1. **Key Competence Area 1: Application of Values to the AMHP Role**
   Whether the applicant has –
   (a) the ability to identify, challenge and, where possible, redress discrimination and inequality in all its forms in relation to AMHP practice;
   (b) an understanding of and respect for individuals' qualities, abilities and diverse backgrounds, and is able to identify and counter any decision which may be based on unlawful discrimination;
   (c) the ability to promote the rights, dignity and self-determination of patients consistent with their own needs and wishes, to enable them to contribute to the decisions made affecting their quality of life and liberty; and
   (d) a sensitivity to individuals' needs for personal respect, confidentiality, choice, dignity and privacy while exercising the AMHP role.

2. Key Competence Area 2: Application of Knowledge: The Legal and Policy Framework

(1) Whether the applicant has –
   (a) appropriate knowledge of and ability to apply in practice –
      (i) mental health legislation, related codes of practice and national and local policy guidance, and
      (ii) relevant parts of other legislation, codes of practice, national and local policy guidance, in particular the Children Act 1989,[6] the Children Act 2004,[7] the Human Rights Act 1998[8] and the Mental Capacity Act 2005;[9]
   (b) a knowledge and understanding of the particular needs of children and young people and their families, and an ability to apply AMHP practice in the context of those particular needs;
   (c) an understanding of, and sensitivity to, race and culture in the application of knowledge of mental health legislation;
   (d) an explicit awareness of the legal position and accountability of AMHPs in relation to the Act, any employing organisation and the authority on whose behalf they are acting;
   (e) the ability to –
      (i) evaluate critically local and national policy to inform AMHP practice, and
      (ii) base AMHP practice on a critical evaluation of a range of research relevant to evidence-based practice, including that on the impact on persons who experience discrimination because of mental health.
(2) In paragraph (1), 'relevant' means relevant to the decisions that an AMHP is likely to take when acting as an AMHP.

3. Key Competence Area 3: Application of Knowledge: Mental Disorder

Whether the applicant has a critical understanding of, and is able to apply in practice -

(a) a range of models of mental disorder, including the contribution of social, physical and development factors;
(b) the social perspective on mental disorder and mental health needs, in working with patients, their relatives, carers and other professionals;
(c) the implications of mental disorder for patients, their relatives and carers; and
(d) the implications of a range of treatments and interventions for patients, their relatives and carers.

4. Key Competence Area 4: Application of Skills: Working in Partnership

Whether the applicant has the ability to –
(a) articulate, and demonstrate in practice, the social perspective on mental disorder and mental health needs;

(b) communicate appropriately with and establish effective relationships with patients, relatives and carers in undertaking the AMHP role;

(c) articulate the role of the AMHP in the course of contributing to effective inter-agency and inter-professional working;

(d) use networks and community groups to influence collaborative working with a range of individuals, agencies and advocates;

(e) consider the feasibility of and contribute effectively to planning and implementing options for care such as alternatives to compulsory admission, discharge and after-care;

(f) recognise, assess and manage risk effectively in the context of the AMHP role;

(g) effectively manage difficult situations of anxiety, risk and conflict, and an understanding of how this affects the AMHP and other people concerned with the patient's care;

(h) discharge the AMHP role in such a way as to empower the patient as much as practicable;

(i) plan, negotiate and manage compulsory admission to hospital or arrangements for supervised community treatment;

(j) manage and co-ordinate effectively the relevant legal and practical processes including the involvement of other professionals as well as patients, relatives and carers; and

(k) balance and manage the competing requirements of confidentiality and effective information-sharing to the benefit of the patient and other persons concerned with the patient's care.

5. Key Competence Area 5: Application of Skills: Making and Communicating Informed Decisions

Whether the applicant has the ability to –

(a) assert a social perspective and to make properly informed independent decisions;

(b) obtain, analyse and share appropriate information having due regard to confidentiality in order to manage the decision-making process including decisions about supervised community treatment;

(c) compile and complete statutory documentation, including an application for admission;

(d) provide reasoned and clear verbal and written reports to promote effective, accountable and independent AMHP decision-making;

(e) present a case at a legal hearing;

(f) exercise the appropriate use of independence, authority and autonomy and use it to inform their future practice as an AMHP, together with consultation and supervision;

(g) evaluate the outcomes of interventions with patients, carers and others, including the identification of where a need has not been met;

(h) make and communicate decisions that are sensitive to the needs of the individual patient; and

(i) keep appropriate records with an awareness of legal requirements with respect to record keeping and the use and transfer of information.

Notes

1 1983 c.20. Section 114 was substituted by section 18 of the Mental Health Act 2007 (c.12). The Welsh Ministers are making separate Regulations in relation to Wales.
2 2000 c.14.
3 SI 2002/253. The Register is divided into parts in accordance with the Nurses and Midwives (Parts of and Entries in the Register) Order of Council 2004 (SI 2004/ 1765).
4 SI. 2002/254.
5 The British Psychological Society is a Royal Charter body, registered as a charity in England and Wales No. 229642 and is at St Andrews House, 48 Princess Road East, Leicester, LE1 7DR.
6 1989 c.41.
7 2004 c.31.
8 1998 c.42.
9 2005 c.9.

Appendix 4B

The AMHP Regulations for Wales

The Mental Health (Approval of Persons to be Approved Mental Health Professionals) (Wales) Regulations 2008 Statutory Instrument No. 2436 (W.209) 2008 (Wales)

The Welsh Ministers, in exercise of the powers conferred upon them by section 114 of the Mental Health Act 1983,[1] hereby make the following Regulations:

Title, commencement and application

1. (1) The title of these Regulations is the Mental Health (Approval of Persons to be Approved Mental Health Professionals) (Wales) Regulations 2008 and they come into force on 3 November 2008.
   (2) These Regulations apply in relation to Wales.

Interpretation

2. In these Regulations –
   'the Act' ('*y Ddeddf*') means the Mental Health Act 1983;
   'AMHP' ('*GPIMC*') means an approved mental health professional;
   except in the context of regulation 3, 'approve' ('*cymeradwyo*') and 'approval' ('*cymeradwyaeth*') include 're-approve' ('*ail gymeradwyo*') and 're-approval' ('*ail gymeradwyaeth*');
   'approving LSSA' ('*AGCLI sy'n cymeradwyo*') means the LSSA that has approved the person to be an AMHP;
   'Care Council for Wales' ('*Cyngor Gofal Cymru*') has the meaning given by section 54(1) of the Care Standards Act 2000;[2]
   'LSSA' ('*AGCLI*') means a local social services authority in Wales;
   'professional requirements' ('*gofynion proffesiynol*') means the requirements set out in Schedule 1;
   'relevant competencies' ('*cymwyseddau perthnasol*') means the skills set out in Schedule 2.

Granting approval

3. (1) Subject to paragraph (2), an LSSA may only grant approval to a person to be
an AMHP, where that person is not already approved as an AMHP under these
Regulations, or has not been so approved within the previous five years, if that
person –
   (a) fulfils the professional requirements;
   (b) is able to demonstrate that he or she possesses the relevant competencies;
   and
   (c) has completed within the last two years a course for the initial training of
   AMHPs approved by the Care Council for Wales.

   (2) An LSSA may only approve a person to be an AMHP, where the person is not
   already approved as an AMHP under these Regulations, but is approved to act
   in relation to England, or has been so approved within the previous five years
   if that person –
   (a) fulfils the professional requirements; and
   (b) is able to demonstrate that he or she possesses the relevant competencies
   such as will enable that person to act within Wales, or if not, completes
   such course as the approving LSSA deems necessary to enable him or her
   to do so.

   (3) In determining whether a person seeking approval as an AMHP possesses the
   relevant competencies as required under paragraphs (1)(b) or (2)(b) above, the
   LSSA must have regard to the references of that person.

Period of approval

4. Subject to regulation 5, an LSSA may approve a person to be an AMHP for a period
of up to five years.

End of approval

5. (1) Subject to paragraph (2) below, the approval of an AMHP will cease as soon as
the period of the approval has expired.

   (2) The approval of a person as an AMHP will cease before the period of approval
   has expired in the following circumstances –
   (a) if that person ceases to carry out functions as an AMHP on behalf of the
   approving LSSA;
   (b) if that person fails to meet any of the conditions attached to his or her
   approval in accordance with regulation 7;
   (c) if, in the opinion of the approving LSSA, that person no longer possesses
   the relevant competencies;
   (d) if that person no longer fulfils the professional requirements;
   (e) if that person becomes approved as an AMHP by another LSSA;
   (f) if that person makes a written request for cessation of approval.

   (3) Following the end of an approval, the approving LSSA must notify that fact to
   any other LSSA for whom it knows that person has agreed to act as an AMHP.

(4) If the approval of a person as an AMHP ends in the circumstance provided in paragraph (2)(e) above, the new approving LSSA must notify that fact to the previous approving LSSA.

(5) Where an approving LSSA ends the approval of an AMHP under paragraph (2), that LSSA must immediately notify that person in writing of the date of the ending of and the reasons for ending that approval.

Suspension of or conditions attaching to registration

6. (1) If at any time after being approved, an AMHP's registration or listing in accordance with fulfilment of the professional requirements as required under regulation 3(1) is suspended, the approving LSSA must suspend that person's approval for the duration of the suspension of his or her registration or listing.

(2) In the event of conditions being attached to an AMHP's registration or listing, as the case may be, the LSSA may attach such conditions to the approval as it may deem necessary, or it may suspend the approval.

(3) Where the suspension of approval has ended, the approval will continue to run for any unexpired period of approval, unless the approving LSSA ends it earlier in accordance with regulation 5.

Conditions of approval

7. Any approval is subject to the following conditions –

(a) the AMHP must complete whilst he or she remains approved such training as required by the approving LSSA, at such intervals as determined by the LSSA as being necessary;

(b) the AMHP must provide evidence to the reasonable satisfaction of the approving LSSA, at no less than annual intervals of the date of his or her approval, that he or she continues to have appropriate competence to carry out functions as an AMHP;

(c) the AMHP must notify the approving LSSA in writing as soon as reasonably practicable if he or she agrees to carry out duties as an AMHP on behalf of another LSSA, and when such agreement ends;

(d) the AMHP must notify the approving LSSA, in writing as soon as reasonably practicable, if the AMHP is approved by a different LSSA;

(e) the AMHP must notify the approving LSSA immediately if he or she no longer meets any of the requirements set out in regulation 3 or regulation 8 as the case may be;

(f) the AMHP must notify the approving LSSA immediately in the event of him or her being suspended from registration or listing, as the case may be, or having conditions attached to the same.

Reapproval

8. (1) An LSSA may grant approval of a person who has previously been approved within Wales, such approval having been in force within the previous five years prior to the proposed date of reapproval, in accordance with these Regulations where that person –
(a) fulfils the professional requirements; and
(b) is able to demonstrate that he or she possesses the relevant competencies.

(2) In determining whether the person seeking approval as an AMHP possesses the relevant competencies as required under paragraph (1)(b) above, the LSSA must have regard to the references of that person.

Monitoring and records

9. (1) The approving LSSA must keep a record of all persons that it approves as AMHPs, including –
(a) their names;
(b) their professions;
(c) the dates of approval;
(d) the periods for which approval is given;
(e) details of completion of any training referred to in regulation 7(a);
(f) evidence provided to it by the AMHPs under regulation 7(b);
(g) names of other LSSAs for whom such persons act as an AMHPs;
(h) any details of the ending or suspension of approval, or conditions attached to the same.

(2) The approving LSSA must keep the records referred to in paragraph 1 above relating to persons approved by it as AMHPs for three years following the ending of such persons' approval.

Edwina Hart, Minister for Health and Social Services, one of the Welsh Ministers, 15 September 2008

SCHEDULE 1   Regulations 2 and 3

Professional requirements

1. In order to fulfil the professional requirements, a person must be one of the following –
(a) a social worker registered with the Care Council for Wales;
(b) a first level nurse, registered in Sub-Part 1 of the Register maintained under article 5 of the Nurses and Midwifery Order 2001,[3] with the inclusion of an entry indicating that his or her field of practice is mental health or learning disabilities nursing;
(c) an occupational therapist registered in Part 6 of the Register maintained under article 5 of the Health Professions Order 2001;[4]

(d)   a chartered psychologist listed in the British Psychological Society's Register of Chartered Psychologists and who holds a relevant practising certificate issued by that Society.[5]

SCHEDULE 2 Regulation 3(4) and (5)

Factors to be taken into account to determine competence

Key Competence Area 1: Values-based Practice

1.1   The ability to identify what constitutes least restrictive health and social care for those dealt with or who may be dealt with under the Act;

1.2   The ability to identify, challenge and, where practicable, redress discrimination and inequality in all its forms in relation to AMHP practice;

1.3   Understanding and respect for diversity and the ability to identify and counter any decision which may be based upon oppressive practice;

1.4   Understanding and respect for individuals' qualities, abilities and diverse backgrounds;

1.5   Race and culturally-sensitive understanding in the application of knowledge of mental health legislation;

1.6   Consideration of the needs of individuals for whom Welsh is their language of choice;

1.7   The ability to promote the rights, dignity and self-determination of patients consistent with their own needs and wishes, to enable them to contribute to the decisions made affecting their quality of life and liberty.

Key Competence Area 2: Application of Knowledge: Legislation and Policy

2.1   Appropriate knowledge of and ability to apply in practice –
(a) mental health legislation, related codes of practice and national and local policy guidance, and
(b) relevant parts of other legislation, codes of practice, national and local policy guidance, in particular the Children Act 1989,[6] the Children Act 2004,[7] the Human Rights Act 1998[8] and the Mental Capacity Act 2005;[9]

2.2   Application of knowledge of Welsh language legislation and policy;

2.3   An explicit awareness of the legal position and accountability of AMHPs in relation to the Act, any employing organisation and the authority on whose behalf they are acting;

2.4   The ability to evaluate critically local and national policy and relevant case law to inform AMHP practice;

2.5   The ability to base AMHP practice on a critical evaluation of a range of research relevant to evidence based practice, including that on the impact of the experience of discrimination on mental health.

Key Competence Area 3: Application of Knowledge: Mental Disorder

3.1 Critical and applied understanding of a range of models of mental health and mental disorder, including the contribution of social, physical and development factors;

3.2 Critical and applied understanding of the social perspective on mental disorder and mental health needs in working with patients, relatives, carers and other professionals;

3.3 Critical and applied understanding of the implications of mental disorder for patients, children, families and carers;

3.4 Critical and applied understanding of the implications of a range of relevant treatments and interventions for patients, children, families and carers;

3.5 Critical understanding of the resources that might be available to provide an alternative to admission to hospital.

Key Competence Area 4: Application of Skills: Effective Partnership Working

4.1 The ability to articulate, and demonstrate in practice, the social perspective on mental disorder and mental health needs;

4.2 The ability to communicate appropriately with, and to establish effective relationships with, patients, relatives and carers;

4.3 The ability to articulate the role of the AMHP in the course of contributing to effective inter-agency and inter-professional working;

4.4 The ability to use networks and community groups to influence collaborative working with a range of individuals, agencies and advocates;

4.5 The ability to contribute effectively to planning and implementing options for care, such as alternatives to compulsory admission, discharge and aftercare;

4.6 The ability to recognise, assess and manage effectively risk in the context of the AMHP role;

4.7 The ability to manage effectively difficult situations of anxiety, risk and conflict, reflecting on the potential impact of such situations on patients and others;

4.8 The ability to balance the inherent power in the AMHP role with the objectives of empowering patients;

4.9 The ability to plan, negotiate and, manage, compulsory admission to hospital, reception into guardianship or arrangements for supervised community treatment;

4.10 The ability to manage and co-ordinate effectively the relevant legal and practical processes including the involvement of other professionals as well as patients, relatives and carers;

4.11 The ability to balance and manage the competing requirements of confidentiality and effective information sharing to the benefit of patients and other stakeholders.

Key Competence Area 5: Application of Skills: Professional Decision-Making

5.1 The ability to assert a social perspective in decision-making and to make properly informed, independent decisions;

5.2 The ability to obtain, analyse and share appropriate information from individuals and other resources in order to manage the decision-making process;

5.3 The ability to provide reasoned and clear oral and written reports to promote effective, accountable and independent AMHP decision-making;

5.4 The ability to present a case at a legal hearing;

5.5 The ability to exercise their functions as an AMHP independently, and with authority and autonomy;

5.6 The ability to evaluate the outcomes of interventions with patients, carers and others, including the identification of any unmet need.

Notes

1 1983 c.20. Section 114 was substituted by section 18 of the Mental Health Act 2007 (c.12). The Secretary of State has issued separate regulations in relation to England.

2 2000 c.14.

3 SI 2002/253

4 SI 2002/254.

5 The British Psychological Society is a Royal Charter body, registered as a charity in England and Wales No. 229642 and is at St Andrews House, 48 Princess Road East, Leicester, LE1 7DR.

6 1989 c.41.

7 2004 c.31.

8 1998 c.42.

9 2005 c.9.

Appendix 5

Forms used in England and Wales

This appendix shows the statutory forms in England and Wales. Not all of the forms in England share the same title as those in Wales, and there are some differences in the content of the forms. Welsh forms are in the left-hand column with English equivalents on the right. To fill in some gaps in the sequence of the right-hand column the English forms are inserted but in italics. Generally these forms then appear again when their place in the Welsh sequence arrives.

Wales	Title of form	England
HO1	Section 2 – application by NR for admission for assessment	A1
HO2	Section 2 – application by an AMHP for admission for assessment	A2
HO3	Section 2 – joint medical recommendation for admission for assessment	A3
HO4	Section 2 – medical recommendation for admission for assessment	A4
HO5	Section 3 – application by NR for admission for treatment	A5
HO6	Section 3 – application by an AMHP for admission for treatment	A6
HO7	Section 3 – joint medical recommendation for admission for treatment	A7
HO8	Section 3 – medical recommendation for admission for treatment	A8
HO9	Section 4 – emergency application by NR for admission for assessment	A9
HO10	Section 4 – emergency application by AMHP for admission for assessment	A10
HO11	Section 4 – medical recommendation for emergency admission for assessment	A11
HO12	Section 5(2) – report on hospital in-patient	H1
HO13	Section 5(4) – record of hospital in-patient	H2
HO14	Sections 2, 3 and 4 – record of detention in hospital	H3
TC1	*Authority for transfer from one hospital to another under different managers*	*(H4)*

Wales	Title of form	England
HO15	Section 20 – renewal of authority for detention	H5
HO16	Section 21B – authority for detention after AWOL for more than 28 days	H6
HO17	Section 23 – discharge by the responsible clinician or the hospital managers	No form
GU1	Section 7 – guardianship application by NR	G1
GU2	Section 7 – guardianship application by an AMHP	G2
GU3	Section 7 – joint medical recommendation for reception into guardianship	G3
GU4	Section 7 – medical recommendation for reception into guardianship	G4
GU5	Section 7 – record of acceptance of guardianship application	G5
TC2	*Section 19 – authority for transfer from hospital to guardianship*	G6
TC3	*Section 19 – authority for transfer of a patient from the guardianship of one guardian to another*	G7
TC4	*Section 19 – authority for transfer from guardianship to hospital*	G8
GU6	Section 20 – renewal of authority for guardianship	G9
GU7	Section 21B – authority for guardianship after AWOL more than 28 days	G10
GU8	Section 23 – discharge by the RC or the responsible LSSA	No form
CP1	Section 17A – CTO	CTO1
CP2	Section 17B – variation of conditions on a CTO	CTO2
CP3	Section 20A – report extending the community treatment period	CTO7
CP4	Section 21B – authority for community treatment after AWOL for more than 28 days	CTO8
CP5	Section 17E – notice of recall to hospital	CTO3
CP6	Section 17E – record of patient's detention in hospital after recall	CTO4
CP7	Section 17F – revocation of CTO	CTO5
TC6	*Section 17F(2) – authority for transfer of recalled community patient to a hospital under different managers*	CTO6
TC8	*Part 6 – transfer of patient subject to compulsion in the community*	CTO9
TC5	*Section 19A – authority for assignment of responsibility for a community patient from one hospital to another under different managers*	CTO10
CP8	Section 23 – discharge by the RC or the hospital managers	No form
TC1	Section 19 – authority for transfer from one hospital to another under different managers	H4
TC2	Section 19 – authority for transfer from hospital to guardianship	G6
TC3	Section 19 – authority for transfer of a patient from the guardianship of one guardian to another	G7
TC4	Section 19 – authority for transfer from guardianship to hospital	G8

Wales	Title of form	England
TC5	Section 19A – authority for assignment of responsibility for a community patient from one hospital to another under different managers	CTO10
TC6	Section 17F(2) – authority for transfer of recalled community patient to a hospital under different managers	CTO6
TC7	Part 6 – date of reception of a patient to hospital or into guardianship in Wales	M1
TC8	Part 6 – transfer of patient subject to compulsion in the community	CTO9
NR1	Section 25 – report barring discharge by NR	M2
CO1	Section 57 – certificate of consent to treatment and second opinion	T1
CO2	Section 58(3)(a) – certificate of consent to treatment	T2
CO3	Section 58(3)(b) – certificate of second opinion	T3
CO4	Section 58A(3)(c) – certificate of consent to treatment (patients at least 18 years of age)	T4
CO5	Section 58A(4)(c) – certificate of consent to treatment and second opinion (patients under 18 years of age)	T5
CO6	Section 58A(5) – certificate of second opinion (patients not capable of understanding nature, purpose and likely effects of the treatment)	T6
CO7	Part 4A – certificate of appropriateness of treatment to be given to a community patient (Part 4A Certificate)	CTO11

Appendix 6

Tasks for an AMHP involved in an MHA assessment (answers)

No.	AMHP task – identify words within quotation marks	Source (Act, Code or Guide)
1	To interview the patient in a 'suitable manner'.	MHA s13(2)
2	To have 'regard to any wishes expressed by relatives'.	MHA s13(1A)(b)
3	Consider all the circumstances of the case including: 'the past history of the patient's mental disorder, the patient's present condition and the social, familial and personal factors bearing on it, as well as the other options available for supporting the patient, the wishes of the patient and the patient's relatives and carers, and the opinion of other professionals involved in caring for the patient'.	Guide 2.32
4	'Because a proper assessment cannot be carried out without considering alternative means of providing care and treatment, AMHPs and doctors should, as far as possible in the circumstances, identify and liaise with services which may potentially be able to provide alternatives to admission to hospital. That could include crisis and home treatment teams.'	Code 4.32
5	Decide whether 'detention in a hospital is in all the circumstances of the case the most appropriate way of providing the care and medical treatment of which the patient stands in need'.	MHA s13(2)
6	Ensure that it is 'necessary or proper for the application to be made by' the AMHP.	MHA s13(1A)(b)
7	'Take such steps as are practicable' to inform the nearest relative that an application for section 2 has been or is about to be made and inform them of their powers of discharge under section 23.	MHA s11(3)
8	If considering section 3 consult NR to ensure that they do not object to the application being made unless 'such consultation is not reasonably practicable or would involve unreasonable delay'.	MHA s11(4)(b)
9	'Take the patient and convey him to hospital' if an application is made by the AMHP.	MHA s6(1)
10	'If they do not consult or inform the nearest relative, AMHPs should record their reasons. Consultation must not be avoided purely because it is thought that the nearest relative might object to the application.'	Code 4.63

11	If the patient is admitted, the AMHP should make sure that any 'moveable property' of the patient is protected.	National Assistance Act 1948 (s48)
12	If the nearest relative applies for section 2 or 3, an AMHP must 'interview the patient and provide the [hospital] managers with a report on his social circumstances'.	MHA s14
13	If required to do so by the nearest relative, the SSD must direct an AMHP 'to consider the case with a view to making an application for his admission to hospital'. If AMHP does not apply he must give his reasons in writing to NR.	MHA s13(4)
14	'Provide an outline report for the hospital at the time the patient is first admitted or detained, giving reasons for the application and details of any practical matters about the patient's circumstances which the hospital should know.'	Code 4.94

Appendix 7

Practice Direction (First-tier Tribunal) (Health, Education and Social Care Chamber) Mental Health Cases

1. This Practice Direction applies to a 'mental health case' as defined in Rule 1(3) the Tribunal Procedure (First-Tier Tribunal) (Health, Education and Social Care Chamber) Rules 2008 ('the 2008 Rules').

2. For the purposes of this Practice Direction, a patient is an 'in-patient' if at the time of the application or referral he is receiving in-patient treatment for mental disorder, even if it is being given informally or under an application, order or direction other than that to which the Tribunal application or reference relates.

Contents of Statements from the Responsible Authority and Secretary of State

3. The responsible authority must send a statement to the Tribunal and, in the case of a restricted patient other than a conditionally discharged patient, to the Secretary of State, so that it is received by the Tribunal as soon as is practicable and in any event within three weeks after the responsible authority received a copy of the application or reference.

4. If the patient is a conditionally discharged patient, the Secretary of State must send or deliver a statement to the Tribunal so that it is received by the Tribunal as soon as practicable, and in any event within six weeks after the Secretary of State received a copy of the application or a request from the Tribunal.

5. If the patient is neither a conditionally discharged patient, nor a community patient subject to supervised community treatment, nor a patient subject (or to be subject) to after-care under supervision, the statement to the Tribunal must contain the information, documents and reports specified in paragraphs 8(a) to (e) below.

6. If the patient is a conditionally discharged patient, the statement to the Tribunal must, where possible, contain the reports specified in paragraphs 8(c) and (d) below.

7. If the patient is a community patient subject to supervised community treatment the statement to the Tribunal must contain the reports specified in paragraph 8(f) below.

8. The information, documents and reports referred to above are:
   (a) the information about the patient set out at Section B below;

(b) the documents concerning the patient set out at Section C below;

(c) the clinician's report set out at Section D below;

(d) the social circumstances report set out at Section E below;

(e) if the patient is an in-patient, the nursing report set out at Section F below;

(f) the reports set out in Section H below.

9. Where the patient is a restricted patient, the Secretary of State must send to the Tribunal as soon as practicable and in any event within three weeks after the Secretary of State received the responsible authority's statement (within two weeks in proceedings under section 75(1) of the Mental Health Act 1983), a statement containing the information set out at Section G below.

10. If the patient is subject (or to be subject) to after-care under supervision, the statement must include the information, documents and reports specified in the Annex to this Practice Direction.

Section B. Information About the Patient

11. The statement provided to the Tribunal must, in so far as it is within the knowledge of the responsible authority, include the following information:

(a) the patient's full name (and any alternative names used in his patient records);

(b) the patient's date of birth, age and usual place of residence;

(c) the patient's first language and, if it is not English, whether an interpreter is required, and if so in which language;

(d) if the patient is deaf whether the patient will require the services of a British Sign Language interpreter, or a Relay Interpreter;

(e) the date of admission or transfer of the patient to the hospital in which the patient is detained or liable to be detained, or of the reception of the patient into guardianship, together with details of the application, order or direction that constitutes the original authority for the detention or guardianship of the patient, including the Act of Parliament and the section of that Act by reference to which detention was authorised and details of any subsequent renewal of or change in the authority for detention;

(f) details as applicable of the hospital at which the patient is detained or liable to be detained, or the place where the patient is living if received into guardianship;

(g) details of any transfers under section 19 or section 123 of the Mental Health Act 1983 since the application, order or direction was made;

(h) where the patient is detained or liable to be detained in an independent hospital, details of any NHS body that funds or will fund the placement;

(i) where relevant, the name and address of the local social services authority and NHS body having the duty under section 117 of the Mental Health Act 1983 to provide after-care services for the patient (or which would have it were the patient to leave hospital);

(j) the name of the patient's responsible clinician and the period which the patient has spent under the care of that clinician;

(k) the name of any care co-ordinator appointed for the patient;

193

(l) except in the case of a restricted patient, the name and address of the patient's nearest relative or of the person exercising that function, and whether the patient has requested that this person is not consulted or kept informed about their care or treatment;

(m) the name and address of any person who plays a significant part in the care of the patient but who is not professionally concerned with it;

(n) where the patient is subject to the guardianship of a private guardian, the name and address of that guardian;

(o) the name and address of any deputy or attorney appointed under the Mental Capacity Act 2005;

(p) details of any registered lasting power of attorney made by the patient that confers authority to make decisions about his personal welfare, and the donee(s) appointed by him;

(q) details of any registered lasting or enduring power of attorney made by the patient that confers authority to make decisions about his property and affairs, and the donee(s) appointed by him; and

(r) details of any existing advance decisions to refuse treatment for mental disorder made by the patient.

Section C. Documents Concerning the Patient

12 If the Tribunal so directs, copies of the following documents must be included in the statement provided to the Tribunal if they are within the possession of the responsible authority (otherwise they must be made available to the Tribunal if requested at any other time by the Tribunal):

(a) the application, order or direction that constitutes the original authority for the patient's detention or guardianship under the Mental Health Act 1983, together with all supporting recommendations, reports and records made in relation to it under the Mental Health (Hospital, Guardianship and Treatment) Regulations 2008;

(b) a copy of every Tribunal decision, and the reasons given, since the application, order or direction being reviewed was made or accepted; and

(c) where the patient is liable to be detained for treatment under section 3 of the Mental Health Act 1983, a copy of any application for admission for assessment that was in force immediately prior to the making of the section 3 application.

Section D. Clinician's Report

13. The statement provided to the Tribunal must include an up-to-date clinical report prepared for the Tribunal.

14. Unless it is not reasonably practicable, the report must be written or counter-signed by the patient's responsible clinician.

15. This report must describe the patient's relevant medical history, to include:

(a) full details of the patient's mental state, behaviour and treatment for mental disorder;

(b) insofar as it is within the knowledge of the person writing the report a statement as to whether the patient has ever neglected or harmed himself, or has ever harmed other persons or threatened them with harm, at a time when he was mentally disordered, together with details of any neglect, harm or threats of harm;

(c) an assessment of the extent to which the patient or other persons would be likely to be at risk if the patient is discharged by the Tribunal, and how any such risks could best be managed;

(d) an assessment of the patient's strengths and any other positive factors that the Tribunal should be aware of in coming to a view on whether he should be discharged; and

(e) if appropriate, the reasons why the patient might be treated in the community without continued detention in hospital, but should remain subject to recall on supervised community treatment.

Section E. Social Circumstances Report

16. The statement provided to the Tribunal must, include an up-to-date social circumstances report prepared for the Tribunal.

17. This report must include the following information:

(a) the patient's home and family circumstances;

(b) insofar as it is practicable, and except in restricted cases, a summary of the views of the patient's nearest relative, unless (having consulted the patient) the person compiling the report thinks it would be inappropriate to consult the nearest relative;

(c) insofar as it is practicable, the views of any person who plays a substantial part in the care of the patient but is not professionally concerned with it;

(d) the views of the patient, including his concerns, hopes and beliefs in relation to the Tribunal proceedings and their outcome;

(e) the opportunities for employment and the housing facilities available to the patient;

(f) what (if any) community support is or will be made available to the patient and its effectiveness, if the patient is discharged from hospital;

(g) the patient's financial circumstances (including his entitlement to benefits);

(h) an assessment of the patient's strengths and any other positive factors that the Tribunal should be aware of in coming to a view on whether he should be discharged; and

(i) an assessment of the extent to which the patient or other persons would be likely to be at risk if the patient is discharged by the Tribunal, and how any such risks could best be managed.

Section F. In-Patient Nursing Report

18. This report must include in relation to the patient's current in-patient episode, full details of the following:
    (a) the patient's understanding of and willingness to accept the current treatment for mental disorder provided or offered;
    (b) the level of observation to which the patient is subject;
    (c) any occasions on which the patient has been secluded or restrained, including the reasons why seclusion or restraint was considered to be necessary;
    (d) any occasions on which the patient has been absent without leave whilst liable to be detained, or occasions when he has failed to return when required, after being granted leave of absence; and
    (e) any incidents where the patient has harmed himself or others, or has threatened other persons with violence.
19. A copy of the patient's current nursing plan must be appended to the report.

Section G. The Secretary of State's Statement (Restricted Patients Only)

20. In cases involving a restricted patient, the Secretary of State must provide a statement to the Tribunal containing any written comments he wishes to make upon the statement he has received from the responsible authority, together with any further information relevant to the application as may be available to him.
21. In addition, the Secretary of State must provide to the Tribunal the following further information:
    (a) a summary of the offence or alleged offence that resulted in the patient being detained in hospital subject to a restriction order or, in the case of a patient subject to a restriction or limitation direction, that resulted in him being remanded in custody, kept in custody or sentenced to imprisonment;
    (b) a record of any other criminal convictions or findings recorded against the patient;
    (c) full details of the history of the patient's liability to detention under the Mental Health Act 1983 since the restrictions were imposed.

Section H. Patients Receiving Supervised Community Treatment (SCT)

Clinical Reports

22. The statement provided to the Tribunal must include an up-to-date clinical report prepared for the Tribunal.
23. Unless it is not reasonably practicable to do so, the report must be written or countersigned by the patient's responsible clinician.
24. This report must include:
    (a) details of the original authority for the patient's supervised community treatment under the Mental Health Act 1983;

(b) the name of the patient's responsible clinician and the length of time the patient has been under their care;

(c) full details of the patient's mental state, behaviour and treatment for mental disorder, and relevant medical history;

(d) insofar as it is within the knowledge of the person writing the report, a statement as to whether the patient has ever neglected or harmed himself, or has ever harmed other persons or threatened them with harm, at a time when he was mentally disordered, together with details of any neglect, harm or threats of harm;

(e) an assessment of the extent to which the patient or other persons would be likely to be at risk if the patient is discharged by the Tribunal, and how any such risks could best be managed;

(f) an assessment of the patient's strengths and any other positive factors that the Tribunal should be aware of in coming to a view on whether he should be discharged;

(g) the reasons why the patient can be treated as a community patient without continued detention in hospital, and why it is necessary that the responsible clinician should be able to exercise the power under section 17E(1) of the Mental Health Act 1983 to recall the patient to hospital; and

(h) details of any specific conditions in force regarding the patient under section 17B of the Mental Health Act 1983.

Social Circumstances Report

25. The statement provided to the Tribunal must include an up-to-date social circumstances report prepared for the Tribunal.

26. This report must include the following information:

(a) the patient's home and family circumstances;

(b) insofar as it is practicable a summary of the views of the patient's nearest relative, unless (having consulted the patient) the person compiling the report thinks it would be inappropriate to consult the nearest relative;

(c) the views of any person who plays a significant part in the care of the patient but is not professionally concerned with it;

(d) the views of the patient, including his concerns, hopes and beliefs in relation to the Tribunal;

(e) the opportunities for employment, or for occupation and the housing facilities available to the patient;

(f) the effectiveness of the community support available to the patient; or the likely effectiveness of the community support which would be available to the patient if discharged from supervised community treatment;

(g) details of the patient's financial circumstances (including his entitlement to benefits);

(h) an assessment of the patient's strengths and any other positive factors that the Tribunal should be aware of in coming to a view on whether he should be discharged;

(i) an account of the patient's progress while a community patient, and any conditions or requirements to which he is subject under the community treatment order, and details of any behaviour that has put him or others at risk of harm; and

(j) an assessment of the extent to which the patient or other persons would be likely to be at risk if the patient remains a community patient.

ANNEX

Patients who are, or will be, Subject to After-Care Under Supervision

27. The statement provided to the Tribunal must include:
    (a) the details of the after-care services being (or to be) provided under section 117 of the Mental Health Act 1983;
    (b) details of any requirements imposed (or to be imposed) on the patient under section 25D of the Mental Health Act 1983;
    (c) the information about the patient specified in Section I below;
    (d) the documents concerning the patient specified in Section J below;
    (e) the reports specified in Section K below.

Section I. Information About the Patient

28. The statement provided to the Tribunal must include, insofar as it is within the knowledge of the responsible authority, the following information:
    (a) the patient's full name, date of birth, age and address;
    (b) the date of the acceptance of the supervision application in respect of the patient;
    (c) any reclassification of the form of mental disorder from which the patient is recorded as suffering in the supervision application reported in accordance with section 25F(1) of the Mental Health Act 1983;
    (d) the name and address of the person who is (or is to be) the patient's responsible clinician and the period (if any) during which he has been in charge of the patient's medical treatment;
    (e) the name and address of the person who is (or is to be) the patient's supervisor;
    (f) where a registered medical practitioner other than the patient's responsible clinician is or has recently been largely concerned in the treatment of the patient, details of the name and address of that practitioner and the period which the patient has spent under his care;
    (g) the name and address of any place where the patient (if he has been discharged) is receiving medical treatment;
    (h) the name and address of the hospital where the patient was detained or liable to be detained when the supervision application was made;
    (i) the dates of any previous tribunal hearings in relation to the patient since he became subject to after-care under supervision, the decisions reached at such hearings and the reasons given;

(j) details of any proceedings in the Court of Protection and of any receivership order made in respect of the patient;

(k) the name and address of the patient's nearest relative or of any other person who is exercising that function;

(l) the name and address of any other person who takes a close interest in the patient.

Section J. Documents Concerning the Patient

29. Copies of the following documents must be made available to the Tribunal if they are within the possession of the responsible authority:

(a) the original supervision application;

(b) any report furnished under section 25G(3)(b) of the Mental Health Act 1983 in relation to renewal of the supervision application;

(c) any record of modification of the after-care services provided.

Section K. Reports

Clinical report

30. The statement provided to the Tribunal must include an up-to-date clinical report prepared for the Tribunal.

31. Unless it is not reasonably practicable, the report must be written or counter-signed by the patient's responsible clinician.

32. This report must describe the patient's relevant medical history and contain a full report on the patient's mental condition.

Supervisor's report

33. Where the patient is subject to after-care under supervision the statement provided to the Tribunal must include an up-to-date report prepared for the Tribunal by the patient's supervisor.

34. This report must include the following information:

(a) the patient's home and family circumstances, including the attitude of the patient's nearest relative or the person so acting and the attitude of any person who plays a substantial part in the care of the patient but is not professionally concerned with any of the after-care services provided to the patient;

(b) his progress in the community whilst subject to after-care under supervision including an assessment of the effectiveness of that supervision.

Social circumstances report

35. Where the patient has not yet left hospital the statement provided to the Tribunal must include an up-to-date social circumstances report prepared for the Tribunal.

36. This report must include the following information:

 (a) the patient's home and family circumstances, including the attitude of the patient's nearest relative or the person so acting;

 (b) the opportunities for employment or occupation and the housing facilities which would be available to the patient upon his discharge from hospital;

 (c) the availability of community support and relevant medical facilities;

 (d) the financial circumstances of the patient.

37. This Practice Direction is made by the Senior President of tribunals with the agreement of the Lord Chancellor. It is made in the exercise of powers conferred by the Tribunals, Courts and Enforcement Act 2007.

30 October 2008

Appendix 8

The Mental Health (Conflicts of Interest) (England) Regulations 2008 Statutory Instrument No. 1205/2008 (England)

The Secretary of State, in exercise of the powers conferred by section 12A of the Mental Health Act 1983, makes the following Regulations:

Citation, commencement and application

1. (1) These Regulations may be cited as the Mental Health (Conflicts of Interest) (England) Regulations 2008 and shall come into force on 3rd November 2008.
   (2) These Regulations apply in relation to England only.

Interpretation

2. In these Regulations –
   'the Act' means the Mental Health Act 1983;
   'AMHP' means an approved mental health professional;
   'application' means an application mentioned in section 11(1) of the Act;
   'assessor' means – (a) an AMHP, or (b) a registered medical practitioner.

General

3. Regulations 4 to 7 set out the circumstances in which there would be a potential conflict of interest within the meaning of section 12A(1) of the Act such that an AMHP shall not make an application or a registered medical practitioner shall not give a medical recommendation.

Potential conflict for financial reasons

4. (1) An assessor shall have a potential conflict of interest for financial reasons if the assessor has a financial interest in the outcome of a decision whether or not to make an application or give a medical recommendation.
   (2) Where an application for the admission of the patient to a hospital which is a registered establishment is being considered, a registered medical practitioner

who is on the staff of that hospital shall have a potential conflict of interest for financial reasons where the other medical recommendation is given by a registered medical practitioner who is also on the staff of that hospital.

Potential conflict of interest for business reasons

5. (1) When considering making an application or considering giving a medical recommendation in respect of a patient, an assessor shall have a potential conflict of interest for business reasons if both the assessor and the patient or another assessor are closely involved in the same business venture, including being a partner, director, other office holder or major shareholder of that venture.

(2) Where the patient's nearest relative is making an application, a registered medical practitioner who is considering giving a medical recommendation in respect of that patient shall have a potential conflict of interest for business reasons if that registered medical practitioner and the nearest relative are both closely involved in the same business venture, including being a partner, director, other office holder or major shareholder of that venture.

Potential conflict of interest for professional reasons

6. (1) When considering making an application or considering giving a medical recommendation in respect of a patient, an assessor shall have a potential conflict of interest for professional reasons if the assessor –

(a) directs the work of, or employs, the patient or one of the other assessors making that consideration;

(b) except where paragraph (3) applies, is a member of a team organised to work together for clinical purposes on a routine basis and –

(i) the patient is a member of the same team, or

(ii) the other two assessors are members of the same team.

(2) Where the patient's nearest relative is making an application, a registered medical practitioner who is considering giving a medical recommendation in respect of that patient shall have a potential conflict of interest for professional reasons if that registered medical practitioner –

(a) directs the work of, or employs, the nearest relative, or

(b) works under the direction of, or is employed by, the patient's nearest relative.

(3) Paragraph (1)(b) shall not prevent a registered medical practitioner giving a medical recommendation or an AMHP making an application if, in their opinion, it is of urgent necessity for an application to be made and a delay would involve serious risk to the health or safety of the patient or others.

Potential conflict of interest on the basis of a personal relationship

7. (1) An assessor who is considering making an application or considering giving a medical recommendation in respect of a patient, shall have a potential conflict of interest on the basis of a personal relationship if that assessor is –
   (a) related to a relevant person in the first degree;
   (b) related to a relevant person in the second degree;
   (c) related to a relevant person as a half-sister or half-brother;
   (d) the spouse, ex-spouse, civil partner or ex-civil partner of a relevant person; or
   (e) living with a relevant person as if they were a spouse or a civil partner.
   (2) For the purposes of this regulation –
   (a) 'relevant person' means another assessor, the patient, or, if the nearest relative is making the application, the nearest relative;
   (b) 'related in the first degree' means as a parent, sister, brother, son or daughter and includes step relationships;
   (c) 'related in the second degree' means as an uncle, aunt, grandparent, grandchild, first cousin, nephew, niece, parent-in-law, grandparent-in-law, grandchild-in-law, sister-in-law, brother-in-law, son-in-law or daughter-in-law and includes step relationships;
   (d) references to step relationships and in-laws in sub-paragraphs (b) and (c) are to be read in accordance with section 246 of the Civil Partnership Act 2004.

Appendix 9
Multiple choice answers

This appendix gives the answers to the questions that appear at the end of some chapters. The first number gives the chapter number, so 2.1 is the first question at the end of Chapter 2. If the reasons for the answers are not clear, return to the body of the chapter for an explanation.

1.1 For the purposes of an admission under section 3 which of the following could, by themselves, be considered as a form of 'mental disorder'?
   (a) Learning disability ☐
   (b) Dependence on alcohol ☐
   (c) Disorder of mind ☑
   (d) Dependence on drugs ☐
   (e) Disability of mind ☑
   (f) Learning disability associated with abnormally aggressive or seriously irresponsible conduct ☑

1.2 Psychopathic disorder does not appear in the Mental Health Act 1983 as amended.
   (a) True ☑
   (b) False ☐

1.3 Learning disability is defined in the Act as 'a state of arrested or incomplete development of mind which includes significant impairment of intelligence and social functioning'.
   (a) True ☑
   (b) False ☐

2.1 Which of the following criteria are necessary before a doctor can recommend compulsory admission on section 3?
   (a) The patient is suffering from a mental disorder of a nature or degree which makes it appropriate for him to receive medical treatment in a hospital. ☑
   (b) The patient is a danger to himself or others. ☐
   (c) Appropriate medical treatment is available to him. ☑

(d) Treatment is likely to alleviate or prevent a deterioration of his condition. ☐

(e) Treatment cannot be provided unless the patient is detained. ☑

(f) Admission is necessary for the health or safety of the patient or for the protection of other persons. ☑

2.2. Sections 135 and 136 allow people to be moved from one place of safety to another.

(a) True ☑

(b) False ☐

2.3 A duly completed application form combined with the necessary medical recommendations provides sufficient authority for the applicant to force their way into the patient's home.

(a) True ☐

(b) False ☑

3.1 Which of the following can make a written order to discharge a patient detained in hospital under Part 2 of the Act?

(a) The hospital managers ☑

(b) The nearest relative ☑

(c) Any relative ☐

(d) An approved mental health professional ☐

(e) The responsible clinician ☑

3.2 Which of these may apply to the County Court for the appointment of someone to act as nearest relative?

(a) Any relative of the patient ☑

(b) The hospital managers ☐

(c) Any other person with whom the patient is residing ☑

(d) The patient ☑

(e) An approved clinician ☐

(f) An approved mental health professional ☑

(e) The responsible clinician ☐

4.1. Which of the following may apply to admit a patient to hospital in an emergency under section 4?

(a) Any relative ☐

(b) The nearest relative ☑

(c) An approved mental health professional ☑

4.2 An applicant who conveys a patient to hospital has all the powers that police officers have when they take someone into custody.

(a) True ☑

(b) False ☐

5.1   A patient remanded to a hospital on an interim hospital order under
      section 38 may be detained after renewals for a maximum of:
      (a) 28 days   ☐
      (b) 12 weeks   ☐
      (c) six months   ☐
      (d) a year   ☑

5.2   A patient who is subject to a hospital order made by the court under
      section 37 is first entitled to apply to the Mental Health Review Tribunal:
      (a) after six months   ☑
      (b) within six months   ☐
      (c) after one year   ☐

6.1 Key principles of the Mental Capacity Act include:
     (a) A presumption of capacity exists for all those aged 16 or over.   ☑
     (b) All practicable steps should be taken to help a person make a decision
         before they're considered incapable.   ☑
     (c) An unwise decision implies a lack of capacity.   ☐
     (d) Acts done on behalf of an incapacitated person must be in his/her
         best interests.   ☑
     (e) All decisions made on behalf of an incapacitated person must be
         registered with the Court of Protection.   ☐
     (f) Decisions should be the least expensive available in terms of cost
         to the person.   ☐
     (g) Decisions should seek to be less restrictive in terms of the person's
         rights and freedom of action.   ☑

6.2   A decision on a person's mental capacity needs to be made in relation
      to the particular matter at the time when the decision has to be made.
      (a) True   ☑
      (b) False   ☐

6.3   The test for capacity under the Mental Capacity Act is whether the
      person can:
      (a) understand the relevant information   ☑
      (b) retain the relevant information   ☑
      (c) believe the relevant information   ☐
      (d) use or weigh the relevant information as part of the decision-making
          process   ☑
      (e) communicate the decision   ☑
      (f) read and sign a consent form   ☐

7.1   A Mental Health Tribunal can vary the conditions attached to a CTO.
      (a) True   ☐
      (b) False   ☑

7.2 A patient who is subject to a section 3 detention is first entitled to apply to the Tribunal:
(a) after six months ☐
(b) within six months ☑
(c) after one year ☐

8.1 Which of the following functions might be performed by the Mental Health Act Commission?
(a) Investigating complaints by detained patients ☑
(b) Discharging patients from detention ☐
(c) Appointing second opinion doctors for consent to treatment provisions ☑
(d) Visiting and interviewing detained patients in private ☑
(e) Recommending leave of absence with a view to discharge ☐

8.2 The Mental Health Act Commission does not have a remit to see patients subject to Community Treatment Orders.
(a) True ☐
(b) False ☑

9.1 Where a care order is made the local authority becomes the child's nearest relative.
(a) True ☑
(b) False ☐

9.2 When a person is removed to a place of safety on section 47 of the National Assistance Act under the emergency procedures they may be kept there for what period in the first instance?
(a) 72 hours ☐
(b) three days ☐
(c) three weeks ☑
(d) 28 days ☐

9.3 The Mental Health Act provides an exemption from the Carers Act 1995 requirement that local authorities take proper account of carers' circumstances when carrying out an assessment of the need for community care services of a person being cared for.
(a) True ☐
(b) False ☑

10.1 Which rights are *specifically* enshrined in English law as a result of the Human Rights Act?
(a) Freedom of thought, conscience and religion ☑
(b) Freedom of expression ☑
(c) Freedom to bear arms ☐
(d) Freedom to give advance agreement to medical treatment ☐

(e) The right to marry and found a family ☑

(f) Freedom to travel without personal identification within Europe ☐

(g) Prohibition of discrimination ☑

10.2 Under Article 3 (prohibition of torture) no one shall be subjected to:

(a) inhuman or degrading treatment or punishment ☑

(b) unwanted psychiatric treatment if detained but mentally capable ☐

(c) seclusion for more than eight hours ☐

(d) torture ☑

10.3 Everyone who is deprived of his liberty by arrest or detention shall be entitled to take proceedings by which the lawfulness of his detention shall be decided speedily by a court.

(a) True ☑

(b) False ☐

11.1 Which of the following assessments form part of the Deprivation of Liberty procedures?

(a) Best interests ☑

(b) No refusals (e.g. objection from LPA donee) ☑

(c) Age ☑

(d) Financial ☐

(e) Eligibility ☑

(f) Whether receiving MHA section 117 after-care ☐

(g) Mental capacity ☑

(h) Abnormally aggressive or seriously irresponsible conduct ☐

(i) Mental disorder ☑

11.2 Under the new DOLS procedure one professional could carry out all of the required assessments.

(a) True ☐

(b) False ☑

11.3 Under the new DOLS procedure a representative will be appointed for the individual after deprivation of liberty has been authorised.

(a) True

(b) False ☐

References

Barber, P., Brown, R. and **Martin, D.** (2009) *Mental Health Law in England and Wales*, Learning Matters.

Barnes, M., Bowl, R. and Fisher, M. (1990) *Sectioned: Social Services and 1983 Mental Health Act*, Routledge.

Bartlett, P. and **Sandland, R.** (2007) *Mental Health Law* (third edition), Oxford University Press.

Brayne, H. and **Carr, H.** (2005) *Law for Social Workers* (sixth edition), Blackstone Press.

Brown, R., Adshead, G. and **Pollard, A.** (2009) *The Approved Mental Health Professional's Guide to Psychiatry and Medication,* Learning Matters.

Brown, R., Barber, P. and **Martin, D.** (2009) *The Mental Capacity Act 2005: A Guide for Professionals*, Learning Matters.

Department of Health (1997) *Who Decides? Making Decisions on Behalf of Mentally Incapacitated Adults*, TSO.

Department of Health (1999) *Reform of the Mental Health Act 1983*, TSO.

Department of Health (2008) *Mental Health Act 1983: Code of Practice*, TSO.

Department of Health/Home Office (1992) *Review of Health and Social Services for Mentally Disordered Offenders and Others Requiring Similar Services. Final Summary Report*, Cmnd 2088, HMSO.

DHSS (1975a) *Better Services for the Mentally Ill*, Cmnd 6233, HMSO.

DHSS (1975b) *Report of Committee on Mentally Abnormal Offenders*, Cmnd 6244 (Butler Report), TSO.

DHSS (1978) *Review of the Mental Health Act 1959*, Cmnd 7230, HMSO.

DHSS (1981) *Reforming Mental Health Legislation*, Cmnd 8405, HMSO.

Eldergill, A. (1998) *Mental Health Review Tribunals*, Sweet & Maxwell.

Fennell, P. (2007) *Mental Health: The New Law*, Jordans.

Fernando, S. (ed.) (1995) *Mental Health in a Multi-Ethnic Society*, Routledge.

Goldberg, D. and **Huxley, P.** (1992) *Common Mental Disorders: A Bio-social Model*, Tavistock/Routledge.

Gostin, L. (1975) *A Human Condition*, Vol.1, MIND.

Gostin, L. (1977) *A Human Condition*, Vol. 2, MIND.

Gostin, L. and **Fennell, P.** (1992) *Mental Health: Tribunal Procedure,* Longman.

Hansard (1995) House of Commons, vol 258.

Harbour, A. and **Ayotte, W.** (1995) *Mental Health Handbook: A Guide to the Law Affecting Children and Young People* (second edition), Children's Legal Centre.

Heller, T., Shackman, J. and Reynolds, J. (eds) (1996) *Mental Health Matters, A Reader*, Palgrave Macmillan.

Hoggett, B. (1996) *Mental Health Law* (fourth edition), Sweet & Maxwell.

Home Office (2003) *Police and Criminal Evidence Act 1984: Codes of Practice*, HMSO.

House of Commons and **House of Lords** (2005) *Report of the Joint Scrutiny Committee on the Mental Health Bill*, HL Paper 79, HC Paper 95.

Jones, R. (ed.) (2008) *Mental Health Act Manual* (eleventh edition), Sweet & Maxwell.

Law Commission (1991) *Mentally Incapacitated Adults and Decision-Making. An Overview*, Consultation Paper No. 119, HMSO.

Law Commission (1995) *Mental Incapacity*, LAW COM No. 231.

Leff, J. and **Vaughn, C.** (1985) *Expressed Emotion in Families*, Guilford.

Martin, E. and **Law, J.** (eds) (2006) *Oxford Dictionary of Law* (sixth edition), Oxford University Press.

Montgomery, J. (2002) *Health Care Law*, Oxford University Press.

National Institute for Mental Health in England (2008) *Mental Health Act 2007: New Roles*, NIMHE.

Peay, J. (1989) *Tribunals on Trial: Study of Decision Making Under the MH Act 1983*, Oxford University Press.

Peay, J. (2003) *Decision and Dilemmas: Working with Mental Health Law*. Hart

Pilgrim, D. (2002) The biopsychosocial model in Anglo-American psychiatry: past, present and future? *Journal of Mental Health*, 11 (6), 585–94.

Puri, B., Brown, R., McKee, H. and **Treasaden, I.** (2005) *Mental Health Law*, Hodder Arnold.

Wadham, J. and **Mountfield, H.** (1999) *Human Rights Act 1998*, Blackstone.

Welsh Assembly (2001) *Adult Mental Health Services for Wales*, Welsh Assembly.

Yeates, V. (2005) Death of the nearest relative? Carers' and families' rights to challenge compulsion under current and proposed mental health legislation. *Journal of Mental Health Law*, November, pp123–37.

Cases

B v Barking, Havering and Brentwood Community Healthcare NHS Trust (1999) 1 FLR 106

Bibby v Chief Constable of Essex Police (Court of Appeal 2000) *The Times*, 24 April 2000

HL v UK (2004) 40 EHHR 761

JE v DE and Surrey CC (2006) EWHC 3459 (Fam)

JT v UK (2000) 30 EHRR CD 77

R (CS) v MHRT (2004) MHLR 355

R (on the application of DR) v Mersey Care NHS Trust (2002) MHLR 386

R (on the application of E) v Bristol City Council (2005) EWHC 74 (Admin)

R (H) v MHRT for NE London (2001) EWCA Civ 415

R (Munjaz) v Mersey Care NHS Trust (2005) UKHL 58

R (on the application of Tagoe-Thompson) re the hospital managers of the Park Royal Centre (2003) EWCA Civ 330
R (von Brandenburg) v E London and City Mental Health NHS Trust (2003) UKHL 58
R v Bournewood Community and Mental Health Trust ex p. L (1990) 3 WLR 107
R v Gloucestershire CC ex p. Barry (1997) 2 All ER 1
R v Manchester City Council, ex p. Stennett (2002) UKHL 34
R v MHRT for West Midlands and North West ex parte H (2000) 1 WLR 1323
R v Wilson ex p. Williamson (1996) COD 42 QBD
Re D (Mental patient: Habeas corpus) (2000) 2 FLR
Re F (Mental Health Act Guardianship) (2000) 1 FLR 192
Re F a child (Care order: Sexual abuse) (1999) 2 CCL Rep 445
Re Whitbread (Times Law Reports) 14 July 1997
Reed (Trainer) v Bronglais Hospital (2001) EWHC 792 (Admin)
Storck v Germany (2005) 43 EHRR 96
Ward v Commissioner of Police (2005) MHLR 128
Winterwerp v Netherlands (1979) 2 EHRR 387

Some useful websites

*Dave Sheppard: **www.davesheppard.co.uk**
*Institute of Mental Health Practitioners (IMHAP): **www.imhap.org.uk**
Department of Health: **www.dh.gov.uk**
Mental Health Act Commission: **www.mhac.org.uk**
Welsh Assembly: **www.wales.gov.uk**
*These websites require membership.

Index

Added to the page number 'f' denotes a figure and 't' denotes a table.

already in hospital 16, 26–30
discharged by Mental Health
Tribunals 70, 107–8
and the DOLS procedure 141
right of the nearest relative to
object 53
see also civil admissions
risk and 3
short-term 23
and supervised after-care 33
diminished responsibility 81
Director of Public Prosecutions 68
disability, definition 122, 123, 127
Disability Discrimination Act (1995) 127
disabled children 60–1
disabled persons 61
Disabled Persons (Employment) Acts (1944
and 1958) 122–3
Disabled Persons (Services, Consultation
and Representation) Act (1986) 61,
125–6
discharge 129
and after-care *see* after-care
of CTOs 40, 53
notice of 56
from independent hospitals 109–10
and hospital managers *see* hospital
managers, and discharge
and Mental Health Tribunals 70, 107–8
of patients concerned in criminal
proceedings 79–80
right of the nearest relative to 16, 17,
19, 20, 40, 52, 53–4
see also conditional discharge
discrimination 65, 83, 100t, 122, 124–5,
134
see also European Convention on
Human Rights, Article 14
diversion 84–5
doctors
and admission for assessment 17–18,
51, 55
in emergencies 23
and admission for treatment 20, 51
assessment 11, 65
and the DOLS procedure 140
guardianship applications 30
holding power 16, 26
and learning disability 12
and medical treatment 13

and Mental Health Tribunals 106
and patients concerned in criminal
proceedings 78, 79, 80, 81, 82, 84
previous acquaintance with patients
17–18, 20, 23
special experience 17, 20, 23
see also SOADS (second–opinion
appointed doctors)
DOLS 3, 30, 32, 38, 42, 102, 138–45
six assessments 140–2
age 140
best interests 141–2
eligibility 141
mental capacity 141
mental health 141
no refusals 140–1
use of the Mental Health Act (1983) or
143–5
DOLS Code 139–40, 142, 143
Draft Mental Health Bill (2004) 5
drug dependency 9–10

ECT treatment 2, 92–3, 102
emergencies
civil admissions 131
admission for assessment 15, 23–4,
149–51
and consent to treatment 93, 97
emotional factors, in models of mental
disorder 6
employment, of disabled people 122
entry, powers of 16, 24–6, 36, 39, 71, 85
environmental factors, in models of
mental disorder 6
equality 124–5, 134
ethnic minority individuals, black and 83
European Convention on Human Rights
65, 69, 133–5, 136, 165–70
Article 2 133, 165
Article 3 94, 133, 136, 165
Article 4 165–6
Article 5 29, 107, 133–4, 144, 166
Article 6 130, 134, 167
Article 7 167
Article 8 21, 47, 48, 94, 134, 136, 167
Article 9 134, 168
Article 10 168
Article 11 134, 168
Article 12 134, 168
Article 14 134, 169